THE DYNAMITE WAR

K. R. M. SHORT

THE
DYNAMITE
WAR

Irish-American Bombers in Victorian Britain

HUMANITIES PRESS, INC.
Atlantic Highlands, New Jersey

First published in the U.S.A. 1979 by
Humanities Press Inc
Atlantic Highlands
New Jersey 07716

Library of Congress Cataloging in Publication Data

Short, Kenneth
    The dynamite war.

    Bibliography: p.271
    Includes index.
    1. Irish question. 2. Irish Americans—Great
Britain—History. 3. Terrorism—England—London—
History. 4. Terrorism—English—Liverpool—History.
5. Terrorism—Scotland—Glasgow—History. 6. Great
Britain. Metropolitan Police Office. Criminal Investi-
gation Dept.—History. I. Title.
DA957.9.S53   364.1'31   78-31113
ISBN 0-391-00964-8

Printed in Great Britain by Bristol Typesetting Co. Ltd,
Barton Manor, St Philips, Bristol

Contents

To my Parents

Acknowledgments

I should like to thank many people for their help during the research and preparation of this book, particularly the staff of the Public Record Office; H. G. Pearson, G. D. A. Riley, P. Bradshaw of the Home Office; Mrs E. J. Browning and Mr M. G. Down, MBE of the Metropolitan Police; P. J. Herbert of the Greater London Council, the London Library, the staffs of the Reading Room, Department of Manuscripts, and Newspaper Library at the British Reference Division, the staff of Duke Humphrey's Library, Bodleian Library Oxford, Mr Frank Corr and his staff at the State Paper Office, Dublin Castle and the National Library Dublin, Lord Crowther Hunt, and finally John Warmington of the Westminster College library. I am especially indebted to Richard Hawkins for his valued reading of the manuscript and his considerable widening of my own knowledge on this period of Irish history. A special word of thanks is due to Mr Roy Jenkins who, during his tenure as Home Secretary, provided me with access to Home Office and Scotland Yard documents which were not due to be opened for public use until the 1980s. Lord Harcourt has given his kind permission to quote from the papers of William Vernon Harcourt. Julie Hounslow not only converted much of the first draft from my appalling handwriting into a workable typescript but also prepared the index. Lastly I thank my wife Mary Jane for encouraging me to track down my 'bombers' while she stayed at home and carefully read the text. The illustration on page 42 is reproduced by kind permission of the Submarine Force Library and Museum, New London, Groton, Connecticut. That on page 111 is by kind permission of the Home Office, London, and those on pages 107, 120 and 185 are reproduced from the Harcourt Papers.

Kenneth Short
Kidlington, Oxford, September 1978.

REAL NAMES AND ALIASES OF SOME BOMBERS AND SUSPECTS MENTIONED IN THE TEXT

Group	Real Name	Alias
The Glasgow/ Liverpool Team	Edmund O'Brien Kennedy	Timothy Featherstone
	John O'Connor	Henry Dalton
	Denis Deasy	—
	Patrick (Patsy) Flanagan	—
	Daniel O'Herlihy	—
	Timothy Carmody	—
	Henry Morgan	—
The Gallagher Team	Dr Thomas Gallagher	Fletcher
	John J. Murphy	Alfred George Whitehead
	William Lynch	E. R. Norman
	Thomas Clarke	Henry Hammond Wilson
	John Kent	John Curtin
The London Bombers	James Moorhead	Thomas J. Mooney

Introduction

BETWEEN 1880 and 1887 three of Britain's major cities came
under attack from teams of bombers whose leadership, finance,
and most of whose personnel came from two Irish-American
organisations based in the United States of America, Jeremiah
O'Donovan Rossa's Skirmishers and Clan na Gael. Although
Liverpool and Glasgow were to suffer in the initial phases of
this struggle against English 'imperialism', it was London which
for almost five years daily faced the threat of gunpowder and
dynamite explosions occurring in the City of London, the
streets of Westminster, the Tower of London, the House of
Commons, under London Bridge, in its railway stations' left
luggage rooms, and the tunnels of the underground. The goal of
the dynamiters was to force Westminster to withdraw from
Ireland and allow the development of a free and independent
nation. London was to be held to ransom.

The weapons chosen by the Irish-American terrorists (a term
which they never applied to themselves) were bombs manufactured either with gunpowder or the recently invented dynamite. Dynamite had been discovered and named by the Swedish
chemist Alfred Bernhard Nobel (1833–1896). He had been
involved in experiments with the manufacture of nitroglycerine,
a liquid explosive, with his father. Accidents in the production
and transportation of this highly unstable but powerful modern
explosive were common. Faced with the tremendous dangers of
transporting an explosive which was so sensitive to shock and to
temperature extremes, Nobel stumbled upon the process by
which the nitroglycerine could be absorbed in diatomaceous
earth (kieselguhr found in vast amounts near Hamburg) making
it safe to transport without impairing its ability to be detonated
with the same type of blasting cap as used with gunpowder.

Nobel's commercial interests continued to grow and he built what was to become Europe's largest dynamite works at Ardeer in the west of Scotland in 1871. The next step was gelatinising nitroglycerine by adding 7 per cent nitrocellulous (guncotton). Experiments in 1875 proved that this form of the explosive, named 'blasting gelatin' or gelignite, could be detonated under water as well as increasing the explosive force of the nitroglycerine by 46 per cent. Although nitroglycerine had been discovered by the Italian chemist Ascanio Sobrero in 1847 and the Nobels had been introduced to its potential by the great Russian chemist Professor Nikolai Nikolayevich Zinin it was Alfred Nobel who finally developed it. Nobel's expectations for the use of the newly developed explosive forms of nitroglycerine included military applications but more directly the blasting of railways through the mountains of North America and Europe; he did not anticipate its use in a new form of warfare—terrorism.[1]

Terrorism developed in the late 1870s as a method by which an organised group sought to achieve its objectives through the systematic use of violence. This definition, as it is commonly accepted, excluded government terror, mob violence and mass insurrection. Caution has to be exercised in comparing the two most active terrorist groups of the 1880s, the Irish-American Clan na Gael and Skirmishers, and the Russian People's Will (*Narodnaya Volya*). These organisations were all committed to the use of dynamite terrorism (Skirmishers used gunpowder) but their philosophy of application was markedly different over their respective targets. The People's Will was committed to a programme of assassination, with the Czar as their primary target, and they sought to use his death to provoke or stimulate a revolutionary uprising against the Romanov despotism. The group consistently rejected the use of pistols or rifles because only the use of dynamite would adequately highlight the fact that this was no ordinary murder but a crucial stage in the developing revolutionary struggle; it was a 'modern revolutionary alchemy'. Johanne Most, a German anarchist who sheltered in London for a time editing *Freiheit*, saw it within the range of dynamite to destroy the capitalist regimes even as feudalism had been destroyed by the rifle and gunpowder. The People's Will made several attempts on the Czar's life by planting dynamite under railway lines, bridges, streets, as well as under the dining room of St Petersburg's Winter Palace. Alexander II was finally assassinated by the second of two bombs thrown at his carriage on Sunday, 13 March 1881. Six years later the remnants of the People's Will made an unsuccessful attempt on Alexander III. Five of its members were executed including the presumed ringleader, Lenin's older brother, Alexander Ulyanov.[2]

Whereas the Russian revolutionary or the London anarchist like Johanne Most might direct their attacks against the leaders of the repressive systems which they were pledged to destroy, no such option was realistically open to the Irish-American revolutionaries. Clan na Gael did not expect their explosions to produce a spontaneous uprising in Ireland for dynamite was only part of an overall strategy which included arming the Irish Republican Brotherhood for the eventual revolution. Nor, most significantly, were they willing to emulate the Russian penchant for assassination. The circumstances differed enormously for while the People's Will members incriminated only themselves, Clan na Gael or Rossa's Skirmishers incriminated the Irish Catholic population of Ireland and Britain by association. The Irish-American plotters took seriously the possible reprisals which the government in Dublin Castle might take against Ireland's population which traditionally suffered under the Coercion legislation which deprived them of their normal rights as British citizens. Even more frightening was the prospect of a public 'mob' backlash generated against the Catholic Irish masses huddled in the great urban ghettoes of Manchester, Birmingham, Glasgow, London and Liverpool. The Irish-American targets, for the most part, had to be limited to public buildings, underground train tunnels and late-night explosions in railway luggage rooms. Only in the case of John Daly, arrested in 1884, was there any claim that Clan na Gael had embarked on the path of assassination. There was no way for the British government to be sure that the Irish-American dynamiters would not launch a campaign of assassination : the exploits of the People's Will were constantly before the horrified reading public. Queen Victoria lived in constant fear of her life, especially when travelling by train to London or Balmoral. The leading members of her government were closely guarded by Scotland Yard although the assumption of the security chiefs was that assassination was not in the Irish-American revolutionary strategy, much

less in that of the Irish Republican Brotherhood which strongly
rejected the use of dynamite altogether.

What one is able to learn concerning these Irish-American
secret societies has been reconstructed from the surviving files
of two organisations founded to deal with their threat, the Secret
Service and the Special Irish Branch of Scotland Yard. In addition to these sources a great deal of information surfaced during
the trials of those bombers who, despite the high odds in their
favour, had been caught. Although the security forces, particularly the Secret Service, received information from spies and
informers, the implication of the surviving material leads one to
believe that the government, despite the increasing sophistication
of the methods of investigation and organisation, operated very
much in the dark during the 1880s. The technical limitations
faced by the police were almost insurmountable. Photography
was just beginning to come into practical use and the passport
with photograph, that most important tool of alien-watching
and control, had not as yet become necessary for international
travel, despite the recognition by some men of its potential
usefulness; nor had that essential tool of the modern police
force, the fingerprint, been sufficiently developed to be of much
help.

During these Irish-American troubles the British government
did not have a permanent Secret Service to rely upon in con-
trast to most, if not all, of the continental governments and
apparently even the United States. There had been a temporary
Secret Service operation established in 1867 as part of the
response to an Irish Revolutionary Brotherhood attempt to
rescue one of its leading gun-runners, an Irish-American, from
Clerkenwell House of Detention. The IRB blew down a wall of
the exercise yard, demolished the adjoining street, and killed or
seriously injured almost one hundred and fifty people. When it
became apparent that this was not the first of a series of blasts
intended to systematically level London with gunpowder, the
Secret Service group was discontinued. Robert Anderson, who
first came to secret service work during this crisis, continued in
it until the 1880s on a part-time basis through his contacts with
Major Henri Le Caron in the United States. Between 1868
and 1882 there does not appear to be any organisation within
the British government worthy of being called a Secret Service,

although money continued to be allocated in the annual estimates for the Home Secretary, who had to justify expenditure in the account to the Treasury; whether this money was spent or how is unknown.

However, in May of 1882, as the result of the Phoenix Park murders, Gladstone's Liberal government was forced to take radical action and establish a Secret Service operation for Ireland. One of the extraordinary aspects of this situation was the publicity given to the appointment of the 'spymaster', an assistant under secretary for crime, based at Dublin Castle. No need was seen for a duplication of this organisation in England until the Local Government offices in Whitehall were bombed on the night of 15 March 1883 and then the solution was to form the Special Irish Branch of the Criminal Investigation Division at Scotland Yard. Eventually the head of the Irish operation, Edward George Jenkinson, was transferred to London where he controlled the Secret Service work on both sides of the Irish Sea. Jenkinson faced the almost impossible task of penetrating the plans, or forecasting the targets of the bombers coming from the United States, not to mention identifying them before they set off their explosives within sound of Bow Bells. Furthermore the government never provided Jenkinson or Le Caron with what they considered adequate funds for the work, and there was constant bickering between the Irish government and the Home Office as to which of the departments was to pay for what and how much, neither wanting to pay the bills for protecting the nation from the destructive horrors of dynamite attacks. At points one would imagine that the civil servants were paying for the Secret Service out of their own pockets, rather than from the nation's purse. The fact that both the Home Office and the Irish Office felt that they got poor value for their money may explain the prevailing attitude. When the attacks finally tapered off and then by the end of 1885 ceased, either because of the work of the Secret Service and the Special Irish Branch or, more likely, because of a change of Irish-American tactics which rejected the continued use of dynamite terrorism, Salisbury's Home Secretary, R. A. Cross, moved quickly to cut back the size of the operation, but not, as in the case of 1867, to abolish it. H. C. E. Childers and Henry Matthews, who succeeded to the Home Office in quick succession, found no reason to countermand Cross's directives on the matter. The Secret Service, in reduced circumstances, carried on into the 1890s and its activities drifted into the protection of the Home Office's hundred-year ruling on documents where the continuation of the story safely resides.

This then is the story of what might be called the first phase of the dynamite war against the British government, which encompassed the attacks and attempts between 1880 and 1887. It is the record of those Irish-American bombers that served an unborn nation and the men of the Special Irish Branch and the Secret Service who sought to prevent dynamite's use as a coercive force in the separation of Ireland from the United Kingdom.

I

Fenianism:
an Irish Root and American Branches

Never was the tremendous power of gunpowder more clearly
shown . . . a barrel wheeled on a truck and simply placed on
the pavement beside the prison wall has sufficed to crush and
shatter everything that was exposed to the force of its explosion.
The Times, 17 December 1867

ON the night of 20 November 1867 Detective Inspector James
J. Thomson of Scotland Yard, accompanied by a Fenian informer, headed towards Clarendon Street, St Pancras, in north
London. The informer, John Devany, was to see if he could
identify either of two Irish-Americans whom Thomson had under
surveillance, men who only came out at night quite obviously to
frustrate such identification. The men were spotted; Devany
identified one of them as he passed under a gas street light as
'Colonel' Ricard O'Sullivan Burke, the Irish Republican Brotherhood's key arms agent in Britain. Thomson and Devany trailed
the two men in the direction of Tavistock Square where the
detective was joined by a police constable whose duty took him
through the square.

Thomson stopped the two men in Woburn Square, the older
about thirty-five and the younger man in his early twenties. The
older man was tapped on the shoulder by the detective and was
told that he had a warrant for the arrest of Ricard Burke and
that he was under arrest. The man denied that his name was
Burke saying that he was George Bowery, a medical student just
arrived from Hamburg. Furthermore he was not prepared to go
anywhere until the non-existent warrant was produced. When
he was seized by the two policemen his younger friend, Joseph T.
Casey, immediately came to his aid. 'Bowery' broke away from
the policemen and began to run while Casey struck Thomson
several times. Thomson forced his way past with revolver drawn
shouting, 'By God, Burke, if you don't stop I will fire at you'.

Burke stopped and replied, 'Don't do anything desperate'. Casey unsuccessfully appealed for help from the crowd which had gathered as Burke was forced into a nearby cab and driven to Bow Street police station.

The informer had disappeared when the policemen made their arrest but Devany reappeared at Bow Street where he positively identified the man claiming to be Bowery as Ricard Burke, a man of 'great physical strength, and of prepossessing appearance and manners'. Amazingly, Casey then proceeded to show up at Bow Street police station where he was promptly arrested! Three days later the two men were charged at Bow Street police court with Casey being held for obstructing the police and Burke for treason felony. They were remanded to the Middlesex House of Detention at Clerkenwell. Devany's identification was confirmed by the most famous Fenian informer of the time, J. J. Corydon, who had served in the same regiment with Burke during the American Civil War.

Thomson's capture of Burke was a crippling blow to the IRB, for he had been a leading figure in the March 1867 Rising in Ireland. Burke was most famous for having planned and supervised the rescue of 'Colonel' Thomas J. Kelly and 'Captain' T. Deasy from prison in Manchester on 18 September of that year. The two men had been dramatically rescued in an attack on the van in which they were being taken to prison. When the lock was blown off one of the police-guards was accidentally shot dead. Five Fenians were subsequently arrested for their part in the rescue and three were to be executed, and immortalised in later years as the 'Manchester Martyrs'.

Burke, like Kelly, was part of that group of some one hundred and fifty Irish-American Civil War veterans who had committed themselves to the Irish revolution. Born at Keneagh, near Dunmanway, Co. Cork in 1838, Burke had served in the Cork Militia and after his regiment was disbanded in 1856 went to sea. He joined the Federal Army under the alias of Edward C. Winslow, serving with distinction, rising through the ranks of the 15th New York Engineers until he was made a colonel at the close of the war. Having joined the Fenian Brotherhood soon after his enlistment, he returned to Ireland in 1865. There he joined Kelly who placed him in charge of procuring arms, for which he proved to have a great flair, usually convincing the unwary seller that they were destined for South American filibustering.

Inspector Thomson knew from Corydon and Devany of Burke's part in the Manchester escape and he recommended to the Commissioner of the Metropolitan Police, Sir Richard Mayne, that the two informers, with a party of plainclothes police, attempt to locate Kelly in London. Thomson was convinced that Kelly would try to 'return the favour' by seeking to free Burke. Mayne agreed but discontinued the plan after a few nights partly because the informers complained of being overworked from having to patrol from 7 p.m. to 1 a.m. The group must have been particularly obvious, despite the plain clothes, since Mayne's detectives continued to wear the distinctive police pattern boots. Thomson however continued to watch the Clerkenwell House of Detention as best he could in the normal course of his duties in hopes that he might identify Burke's would-be rescuers.[1]

Another Irish-American, 'Captain' Murphy, arrived in London shortly after the arrest to organise Burke's escape. Although the original plan had been to carry out the rescue while Burke and Casey were being taken to Bow Street court in a police van, it was soon rejected when it became evident that the large police escort armed with cutlasses and revolvers would be too strong to overcome. The would-be rescuers managed to set up communications with Burke despite the vigilance of the prison staff and it was he that suggested that a hole be blasted in the north-west wall of the prison facing St James's Passage and the Bell public house on Corporation Lane. There was a spot in the wall which had been used by contractors to gain access to the prison and only recently bricked up. Burke, as a former engineer officer, and certainly present at the explosion of the 8,000 pound mine under the Confederate lines at Petersburg on 30 July 1864, knew exactly what to expect.

A group of some fifteen or sixteen local IRB members assisted Murphy and Michael Barrett, a Glasgow Fenian, in making the preparations which included the purchase on Burke's instructions of two hundred pounds of gunpowder from the firm of Curtis and Harvey in the City. The gunpowder was collected on 6 December and transferred to a used kerosene barrel. The escape was set for Thursday 12 December. The prisoners were exercised in the yard bounded by the north-west wall every afternoon between 3 and 4.30 p.m. Burke was to be warned of the impending explosion by a white rubber ball to be thrown over the twenty-five foot wall immediately before lighting the fuse. At about 3.45 p.m. on the twelfth a truck carrying the barrel was wheeled to the bricked-up section in the wall and the barrel was rolled off the truck onto the pavement, fuse inserted, and the ball thrown over the wall. Burke promptly fell out and pretended to remove a stone from his shoe in a protected corner of the yard. The fuse was lit but failed. Burke, realising that the plan had mis-fired, returned to the line of prisoners, a warder unsuspectingly pocketed the ball for his children, and the bomb was trundled away for a second attempt the next day.

Four hours earlier, an urgent message had been received by the Home Office permanent under secretary Adolphus Liddell, who then transmitted it to Sir Richard Mayne. Sent by Daniel Ryan, Superintendent of the Dublin Metropolitan Police's 'G' (Detective) Division, dated 11 December, it read:

> I have to report that I have just received information from a reliable source to the effect that the rescue of Richard [sic] Burke from prison in London, is contemplated. The plan is to blow up the exercise walls by means of gunpowder, the hour between 3 & 4 pm and the signal for all right, a white ball thrown up outside when he is at exercise.[2]

The governor of the House of Detention was immediately notified and prison guards were armed that afternoon. Security was increased on the night of the twelfth and the governor had the prisoners exercised the next morning while Burke was moved to another cell which was double locked. Sir Richard Mayne, increased police surveillance of the prison, but did not institute systematic patrolling of the walls.

At about 3.45 p.m. on Friday the thirteenth the drama was re-enacted with the barrel, under a tarpaulin, placed up against the wall in the same position. Another white ball was thrown over the wall into the now deserted exercise yard, the fuse lit and moments later the gunpowder exploded with a tremendous report. A sixty-foot section of the wall was demolished as were the houses on the opposite side of the street. Chief Inspector Adolphus Williamson of the Detective Branch described the houses deprived of their front walls as 'so many dolls' houses with the kettles still singing on the hobs'.[3] The destruction of life and property in this working-class neighbourhood was unprecedented. Six people were killed outright; six died from the effects of the explosion according to later inquests; five died indirectly; one young woman was judged insane; forty women gave birth prematurely and it was claimed that twenty babies died from the effects of the explosion on their mothers. According to contemporary reports, other babies were 'dwarfed and unhealthy'. At least 120 people were seriously injured of whom fifteen suffered permanent disabilities.

Immediate relief was offered by the government to the devastated area and the Queen offered her condolences. Over the next weeks a relief committee headed by the local vicar raised close to £10,000 as the result of an appeal through *The Times*. Three people had been immediately arrested by the Detective Division in the vicinity, but one turned out to be a police informer and was not charged. The trial of the six accused of murder (including a young woman) opened in April 1868 and faced the jury with the almost hopeless task of determining guilt and innocence on the basis of the confused and contradictory evidence given by witnesses of the blast. In addition there was great difficulty in assessing the value of the Queen's evidence given by two members of the conspiracy. In the end five of the accused were exonerated of the murder charges, but held on other charges. Only Michael Barrett, for whom the defence provided several witnesses who swore that he was in Glasgow throughout the entire proceedings, was to die for the Fenian outrage in Clerkenwell. He died on 26 May 1868, the last person to be publicly hanged in England. A month before Ricard O'Sullivan Burke had been sentenced to fifteen years in prison for his illegal arms purchasing, along with one of his associates, Harry Shaw Mulleda, who received seven years penal servitude. Casey was discharged.

The effect of the Clerkenwell explosion upon the nation had been one of panic and hysteria. Fifty thousand or more Special Constables had been sworn in to defend the gas works and public buildings. Sewer workers were sworn in as Special Constables as they joined four teams of police in searching the sewers under government offices. Scotland Yard detectives travelled to Paris in search of clues. The army and police stood ready to defend the nation from a Fenian onslaught of explosives, 'Fenian fire' (a highly inflammable liquid), assassination and terrorism. The explosion had unleashed the hysterical fear of the Irish Roman Catholics which was England's historical heritage, the almost inevitable gift of the vanquished to the victor. The Englishman in his castle 'knew' he had much to fear from the Irishman at his gate but much more so from the Irishman *within* the gate; at least so he thought as he counted the hordes crossing the Irish Sea in the first half of the nineteenth century. By 1851 there were 727,326 Irish-born people living in England, Wales and Scotland and no accounting for their children or the substantial numbers of temporary residents. In all 3 per cent of England's population and 7 per cent of Scotland's was Irish. These figures, if spread evenly across the nation, would not have occasioned the anxiety that in fact they did. But the Irish were concentrated in the disease-breeding urban ghettoes of the north-west counties of England and western Scotland. The Irish ghetto in Liverpool contained a quarter of that city's population. What the Irish bequeathed to the Victorian Englishman was a large mass of civic poverty characterised by drunkenness, swearing, fighting, and public disorder compounded by ignorance and either a foreign tongue —Irish—or a ridiculous dialect of English. This cultured revulsion extended to virtually everything about the Irishman, especially his religion : Protestant England was in one of its most strongly anti-papist moods. This fed the fires of anti-Irish prejudice and was reinforced by contact with the 'superstitious' immigrants. There was a practical side to anti-Irish feeling as the responsibility for the Irish poor fell upon poor relief and the ratepayer.

Totally out of sympathy and at times prepared to supplement the quiet expressions of religious and national hatred with anti-Catholic rioting, England's greatest fear was rational in comparison. The Irish made no attempt to hide their contempt or their hatred for the English government and Protestant ascendancy which lorded it over them from Westminster through Dublin Castle. What Irish radicals wanted was what Wolfe Tone had declared as long ago as 1791, 'to break the connection with England, the never-failing source of all our political evils'. Irish nationalism was added to a long history of Catholic sedition and in the 1790s the ideas and apparent success of the French Revolution again stirred the hopes and ambitions of many Irishmen. During the wars that followed 1789 the French made an abortive attempt to invade Ireland in support of the largely Protestant United Irishmen, who had assured them that a mass uprising was imminent. Committed to a radical reform of the Irish parliament as well as religious equality and liberty, the rebellion failed and its leader, Theobald Wolfe Tone, committed suicide in prison rather than face the English gallows. The Act of Union with Scotland, Wales and England in 1801 then deprived Ireland of its parliament and the centre of conflict shifted to Westminster. Over the next forty years some of the United Irishmen's goals were achieved by constitutional changes. The watershed proved to be Catholic Emancipation in 1829 which was stimulated by the fear that Ireland was again on the verge of rebellion. The government was unprepared to pay the price of savage repression or risk the loyalty of the British Army, of which one-third of the rank and file were Irish Catholics. Daniel O'Connell had precipitated the crisis, having been elected to a seat in parliament which because of his Catholicism he could not hold. After 1829 O'Connell as an MP fought unsuccessfully against both physical force and the Act of Union.

The growth of Irish influence, Catholic and Protestant, in Westminster through its MPs could not obliterate the continued demands for an independent Ireland. Responding again to the revolutionary activity on the continent in 1848 and Chartism in Britain, the heirs to the United Irishmen, the Young Irelanders, made a futile effort in that year to rebel only to be crushed with a quick swipe of the lion's paw. And yet this pathetic effort kept the revolutionary ideal alive and was a symbol of resistance during the darkest days of the Great Hunger—the potato famine. Defeat did not mean despair for the advanced nationalists. John O'Mahony escaped to France where he remained until 1854. Emigrating to the United States, he and Michael Doheny founded the Fenian Brotherhood (FB) in 1858. The name Fenian was derived from a legendary prehistoric Irish army named the Fianna. The other key figure of this decade was James Stephens, who had been closely involved with the French revolutionary republicans during their brief period of triumph from 1848 to 1852. On his return to Ireland in 1858, he established the Irish Revolutionary Brotherhood (IRB), later known as the Irish Republican Brotherhood. Dublin Castle had little difficulty in infiltrating the home organisation and in 1858–9 broke up the so-called Phoenix conspiracy which in part involved the threat of an invasion from America by the FB. In 1865 most of the IRB leaders were arrested and convicted on charges of treason felony and sent to prison. Stephens escaped and promised to personally lead the rebellion in 1866. He failed to unite the fractious FB and abandoned his leadership of the movement in December 1866. When the rising was mounted in March 1867 it failed totally, as the government's network of spies and informers had been forewarned. Hundreds of men were arrested and released shortly thereafter, but the leaders remained in prison as did former British soldiers who had taken part in the uprising.

Three-quarters of a million of the 'enemy' had been allowed to settle in Britain; the Greek entry into Troy via the wooden horse was insignificant in comparison. The enemy was within the gates in vast numbers. This is what terrified the English nation and drove the army and the hordes of Special Constables to their posts in the aftermath of the Clerkenwell explosion. Although the Irishman was thought to have cutlass and musket under his bed ready to rise up and massacre the English, the Irish in Britain as a whole were not to prove a threat to national security.

The cabinet met on 14 December and accepted the need for establishing a Secret Service Department to assist in the defence of London. Robert Anderson was brought from Dublin Castle five days later. He had earned a reputation concerning Fenian intelligence by writing an extensive report on Fenianism for the chief secretary, Lord Mayo, based upon the existent documents relating to the problem in Ireland and the United States. The Home Secretary nominated Lieutenant Colonel William Feilding, Senior Army Intelligence Officer in Ireland, to head the operation because of his success in checking the spread of the IRB within the British army. Anderson, recommended by the viceroy and the chief secretary, said that the original scheme was to take up quarters in a private house in some quiet street and to work in complete secrecy. This had not been practical in his view because of his responsibilities to the Irish government. Furthermore he could not imagine that it would be possible to maintain that degree of secrecy and argued for a display of apparent openness as a screen for secrecy. Thus while Anderson, as an assistant on Irish affairs, was installed in the Law Room at the somewhat ramshackle Irish Office on Queen Anne Street at a salary of £50 per month, Feilding and his deputy, another accomplished Fenian hunter from the Army, Captain Whelan of the 8th Regiment, RA, made a beginning in counteracting the anticipated Fenian bombing campaign. Careful consideration had led the Home Secretary Gathorne Hardy to keep the Secret Service separate from the Metropolitan Police, primarily because of Mayne's unfashionable methods which were seen to be distinctly out of date. Not wanting to hurt the seventy-one year-old Mayne's feelings because he was a close friend, the Home Secretary advanced the rationale that 'such a department should be the centre for secret information from all parts of the United Kingdom, and indeed the Continent' and as such should not be part of the Scotland Yard structure at least, he added, 'on its present footing'.[4]

Although in later years Anderson would claim that the scheme worked admirably, the need for the operation was viewed by him with extreme scepticism. This attitude was not appreciated by those politicians who were terrified at the prospects of an all-out bombing assault upon London. By Boxing Day the offices of the Board of Trade, Privy Council and other government departments had the flooring strewn with sand. Sand was also held in readiness in the event of the buildings being attacked by 'Fenian (Greek) fire'. On 17 December *The Times* printed the following advice from one of its readers.

> Sir,—To prevent damage occasioned by phosphorous or the liquid known as 'Fenian Fire', householders in exposed situations will do well to keep on hand a small supply of sand or dry ash dust, which if sprinkled over the burning substance, will absorb the liquid and probably extinguish the flame, even without the aid of water. Those who have a garden may remember that a few shovels full of earth will serve to check a fire equally well.
>
> Yours very truly,
> AN INSURED HOUSEHOLDER

The list of rumoured plots was endless, ranging from blowing up the Crystal Palace to bombs in the watermains, putting the street hydrants (water-plugs) out of action by filling them with strong cement, attacks on the Tower of London and Woolwich Arsenal, cutting the Atlantic Telegraph cable and blowing up ironworks. One letter threatened the life of the Queen in appalling grammar and rumours had two men on their way to the Isle of Wight to blow up Osborne House.

Then on Saturday 18 January 1868 a seditious placard appeared in front of the Mansion House, under the very windows of the Lord Mayor, in the place reserved for Royal proclamations. Wholly in manuscript it was headed with the date 1868, contained a pen and ink sketch of an Irish harp surrounded with a shamrock and below which were the words 'God Save Ireland'. On each side of the emblems were 'I.R.' for Irish Republic and the message read:

> The Irishmen of America are united! Irishmen of
> England follow their example! United; forward ye
> fearless sons of Ireland! Stand for the old country!
> Oh, that to England nailed Ireland should be
> Preserve her green flag of liberty,
>   Erin-go-bragh

The Times was hardly impressed by the sentiments and assumed that it was really a bad joke, while Constable 577, Newnham, of the City Police was deeply embarrassed about it having appeared on his beat which took him past the point every fifteen or twenty minutes.

By April it had finally become clear that the devastated wall of Clerkenwell was not a prelude to a national disaster and the Secret Service operation of Anderson, the two Army officers and three detectives was closed down. Anderson, however, remained in London and spent the next fifteen years co-operating with his brother, Samuel Lee Anderson, a law officer at Dublin Castle, in the monitoring of continuing Fenian activity. The Metropolitan Police and its chief commissioner came in for heavy criticism for the inept handling of the situation, although Mayne was not replaced until after his death on Boxing Day 1868.

Fenianism could be contained in Ireland by the work of the

Dublin Metropolitan Police and the Royal Irish Constabulary and no one, including the Supreme Council of the IRB, harboured any further hope of a proper Irish revolution. Britain had good cause, however, to look over her shoulder at the virulent form of republicanism being nurtured in the United States amongst those born of Irish parents as well as by the Irish who had found refuge from poverty and political repression. There was no discounting the importance to the IRB of men like Ricard O'Sullivan Burke and Thomas J. Kelly, men prepared to leave the freedom of a new land in order to bring freedom to their old homeland. What the British government had to accept was that the threat of life imprisonment under the most barbaric conditions would not deter them from their commitment to 'Erin-go-bragh'. There was a great deal of truth in Gladstone's assessment that where Fenianism was concerned its root was in Ireland but its branches were in America.

The Irish had come to the United States with their mass migrations during the great potato famine of the late 1840s. How many people died during the famine can never be known for certain. In the decade following the 1841 census Ireland's population dropped from just over eight millions to six and a half millions. During the same period, the recorded emigration was nearly a million and a quarter people. It is difficult to get absolutely accurate figures for the number of actual deaths, although good modern authorities seem to think that 800,000 is a safe figure for the number of deaths caused by hunger, 'famine fever' (which was typhus and relapsing fever), dysentery, and scurvy. The years of the famine saw much of Ireland's surviving population seeking refuge in Britain or the colonies and especially the United States.

What was left behind in Ireland was the deepest hatred. The failure of England to avert this national catastrophe did enormous if not ultimately fatal damage to the United Kingdom. Irish nationalists, according to Professor Patrick O'Farrell, were provided by the famine with the 'material for a most fundamental and emotional indictment of England—the charge that it contrived the extermination and banishment of the Irish on the scale of mass murder'. The cry was genocide; over three-quarters of a million men, women, and children were, according to popular belief, 'carefully, prudently, and peacefully *slain* by the English government'. And those that did not die were forced to emigrate.[5] Such was the nationalist interpretation of this terrible period in the life of a nation which had suffered for centuries from English domination and exploitation. It was not without reason that the Irish, turning from a traditional resistance to emigration, responded desperately to the prospects and promises of economic security and political freedom in the United States of America, a nation which had fought the English for freedom seventy-five years before and won.

In 1847 emigration to the United States exceeded 105,000 as compared to 44,821 in 1845; in 1848 figures rose to nearly 113,000. The American Republic had not always been so open to the needs of an overcrowded and subjugated Ireland. When the United States' minister to the Court of St James heard rumours that His Majesty's government was contemplating the deportation of Irish political prisoners after the 1798 uprising he said 'Absolutely No!' The United States was not going to become a refuge for 'hordes of wild Irishmen, nor the turbulent and disorderly of all parts of the world, to come here with a view to disturb our tranquillity after having succeeded in the overthrow of their own governments'. And yet several leaders of the Society of United Irishmen including Thomas A. Emmett found refuge in the United States.

The Irish continued to come, drawn by the promises of a young nation that had English as its national language, democracy as its government, no established religion to frustrate a man's personal advancement nor the practice of his Roman Catholicism. Even so he had to face exactly the same prejudices and appalling living conditions as his counterparts who had settled in Britain. In 'the land of the free and the home of the brave' the sign 'No Irish Need Apply' was the rule of the day. Between 1847 and 1855 1,300,000 Irish men and women came to the United States and by 1860 the Irish population amounted to 1,600,000, of whom nearly two-thirds lived in Pennsylvania, New Jersey, New York and the states of New England. One-third of the electorate of New York City, and 13.7 per cent of New York State's total population, was Irish by 1880. There was no discounting the effect that the Irish had upon those sections of the East where they concentrated in urban and suburban ghettoes. *The Times* (3 October 1865) critically assessed their impact upon the American political system :

> The happy institution of universal suffrage, the foundation on which American institutions repose, has given the ignorant and prejudiced Irishman a power which he could never possess under any other circumstances. The Irish vote had become a matter of consequence, and American newspapers and American politicians have not been slow to pander to the weaknesses and delusion of those who dispose of it.

If the Irish immigrant was 'ignorant and prejudiced', which for the most part he was, the responsibility lay with the British government, which had for centuries exploited Ireland, fastened upon it an established Protestant church, and ruled from the Castle by force. The Irish did not long remain in that condition, for the United States offered them free education for their children and the opportunity for self-education based upon a free press, which indeed courted the potential Irish readership, in addition to those papers edited by Irishmen, such as Patrick Ford's *Irish World*. A nation almost without heroes, much less successful ones, the Irish grasped eagerly for the names and virtues of George Washington, Thomas Jefferson, and particularly the populist Andrew Jackson. These were not 'hordes of wild Irishmen', but men prepared to, if not forced to, work in the most menial of jobs, but with their eyes lifted up from the 'muck rakes' in their hands to the economic, social and political security offered to the second generation and possibly to their own. It was a slow and painful climb to prosperity and middle-class respectability. The essential thing was that they were politically involved, but like the Roman God Janus, they looked in two directions, to both their new land and back to the 'auld sod'. They had breathed the air of freedom and been thrust into the greatest political and social experiment of the day and they rose to the challenge of nation building, committed to that pledge of allegiance which their children, repeated each day in their local free public school—'One nation indivisible, with liberty and justice for all'.

This was the ideal that countless Irishmen worked for in the 1860s and 70s and as part of this process contributed to a renewed sense of Irish nationalism. William V. Shannon, in *The American Irish*, suggests that the Irish nationalist movement was one of the ways in which the Irishman learned what it was like to be an American. The leaders of this movement advanced the vast numbers of immigrants, producing editors, teachers, idealists and voters committed to the great mid-nineteenth-century American ideals of democracy, universal male suffrage, compulsory free education, self-reliance, thrift, pride, hard work—the same ideals of Protestant America, which also included temperance. Patrick Ford refused to accept liquor advertisements in the *Irish World* despite the paper's shaky finances; the famous Father Mathew said 'Irish sober is Ireland free'. The Irish immigrant was not only united by his religion, but in his drive to give expression to his national roots; he desperately wanted to bequeath to his nation and its millions an Ireland made in the image of the United States. It should have surprised no one, when a Fenian Constitution for Ireland, presented at a convention in Philadelphia in October of 1865, was almost an exact replica of that written by the nation's Founding Fathers in the same city in 1787. It needed a 'George Washington' to drive the Protestant ascendancy from the shores of Ireland to establish a democratic constitution, representative institutions, universal education and, of central importance, an economy of independent yeomen farmers based on the Jeffersonian vision of an agrarian democracy, in place of the neo-serfdom of the land they had been forced to leave. The Irish population of America was a potentially fertile seedbed of revolutionary activity, even if the form that it might take remained unclear.

The Irish-Americans had the initial advantage over the other masses of nineteenth-century immigrants in that they spoke English and appreciated the cultural value of a system which was essentially that of a modified English culture. The timing of the potato famine brought the mass of Irish immigrants to the eastern seaboard immediately prior to the civil conflict that tore the nation apart. The war provided an opportunity for Irish military development, quite unlike that which had historically existed for the Irish Roman Catholic soldier in the British Army. In the years of the Civil War Irish units were raised with Irish-American officers, who organised and led their troops with

distinction and, although the Irish faced the inevitable prejudices, they often rose to high rank and conclusively proved their
patriotism as a people. Ricard O'Sullivan Burke of Clerkenwell
fame had begun the war as a private, ended it as a colonel,
and is claimed to have been in command of the fifteen miles
of Union earthworks surrounding Petersburg, Virginia. Irishmen also distinguished themselves in the service of the Confederacy. At the conclusion of the war Irishmen, regardless of which
side they had taken, found themselves in possession of military
experience and many of them continued their military association through the state militia units which were found throughout
the north. They had proved to themselves that they were
capable of being a military people and the skills with which this
successful experience provided them was enough to give them
the confidence to take on the British in neighbouring Canada.
Disputes over future policy led to the disruption of the Fenian
Brotherhood into three major groups; the most aggressive, the
Senate (or Robert's) wing led by Colonel John O'Neill, was
committed to an invasion of Canada.

The British government had access to the inner circles of the
O'Neill wing through the most extraordinary character of the
entire epoch of Fenian explosion and intrigue. Major Henri Le
Caron, dubbed the 'Prince of Spies' by the Irish revolutionary
John Devoy who was acquainted with him during these years.
Le Caron was neither French nor Irish-American, having been
born at Colchester, Essex on 26 February 1841 and christened
Thomas Billis Beach. Apprenticed to a Quaker draper in his
youth, he had finally run away from home to Paris at the age
of sixteen. Through a chance meeting at the English Church
in the Rue d'Aguesseau, he became a paid singer in the church
choir and found employment with a firm of stockbrokers. When
a number of American clients of the firm returned home upon
the outbreak of the Civil War, Beach, now bilingual and his
sense of adventure whetted, joined them, crossing the Atlantic
on Brunel's *Great Eastern* in 1861. On 7 August 1861 the
former choir boy enlisted, initially for three months, in the 8th
Pennsylvania Reserves as a private, using the alias Henri Le
Caron, nationality French. He rose to the rank of first lieutenant
in the cavalry, ending the war in Nashville, Tennessee, where
he married a local girl who had saved his life three years earlier.

It was in Nashville that he re-established his war time friendship with Colonel John O'Neill. Le Caron was soon aware of O'Neill's scheme to capture Canada and hold it as a base for attacks on England or possibly a ransom for Irish independence. Hearing the details of this decision taken at a convention of the Senate wing of the Fenian Brotherhood which met at Cincinnati, Ohio, Le Caron wrote to his father recounting the threat to imperial security. His father showed the letters to the Liberal MP for Colchester, John Gurdon Rebow, who took them to the Home Secretary, Sir George Grey. The British government was particularly grateful to have such inside information because it was becoming increasingly clear that this 'invasion' was being encouraged by the United States' Secretary of War, Edwin M. Stanton, who saw it as a means of extorting compensation in kind for the destruction of northern shipping by the CSS *Alabama* and other privateers built in Britain's shipyards during her years of obviously strained neutrality. Stanton was not interested in swapping Canada for Irish independence but in annexation, a popular theme in the United States since the beginning of the nineteenth century, and a contributory factor to the war of 1812. Although Le Caron was not privy to the thoughts of the American government he was able to glean various bits of information concerning the projected military activities of the Fenian Brotherhood.

'General' O'Neill's army crossed the Niagara River north of Buffalo, New York, in flat boats towed by a steam tug in the early hours of June 1866. Landing near Waterloo, Ontario, some 600 or 800 Fenian troops raised the Irish flag and marched on to capture Fort Erie. The Fenian troops, shrunken to 500 by desertions, then found their way blocked by the 22nd Battalion of Volunteers of Toronto. The Canadian forces conclusively defeated the Fenians at the battle of Ridgeway. The retreating Fenian army, now reduced to just over 300 men, were ferried back to American waters where the scow and tug were arrested by the USS *Michigan*. Three days later, 6 June, President Andrew Johnson ordered strict neutrality, seizure of the Fenian arms dumps and the sealing of the border. O'Neill and his army were arrested and soon released. The confiscated Fenian arms were later returned to the Brotherhood on the promise that they would not be used in another invasion of

Canada. Fenian losses were sixty killed and 200 taken prisoner.

Le Caron visited England in the autumn of 1867 where he was introduced to Rebow. Sufficiently impressed by the young man's potential as a secret agent, the MP discussed the matter with the Home Secretary. A meeting was then arranged with two Home Office officials in a house in Harley Street. Le Caron readily agreed to become a spy for his government. Upon his return to the United States he successfully offered his services as a 'military man' to John O'Neill, the recently elected president of the Senate wing of the Fenian Brotherhood. Promised a position in 'active warfare', Le Caron returned to Illinois where he began to seriously study medicine in Chicago. Then he founded a Fenian Brotherhood 'circle' in Lockport, Illinois. Becoming its 'centre' or commander he had access to all the reports and documents originating from the New York headquarters of the Brotherhood. He also organised a company of the Irish Republican Army. Upon completion of his medical qualifications he was appointed as the resident medical officer at the State Penitentiary, Joliet, Illinois. Le Caron immediately resigned the job when in the summer of 1868 O'Neill telegraphed 'Come at once, you are needed for work'. Travelling to New York, Le Caron was commissioned Major (ironically he used his Fenian commission, which was identical to one he held in the veterans' organisation, the Grand Army of the Republic) and Military Organiser for the Irish Republican Army. The date was 5 August 1868. He was now at the very centre of the conspiracy.

Although in October 1868 he came close to exposure, Le Caron continued his work, drawing a salary of $60 a month, plus $7 a day expenses from the Fenian Republic in addition to $150 a month from the Secret Service. Unknown to the Fenian Brotherhood he was in direct communication with the Canadian government's chief commissioner of police, Judge Gilbert McMicken. The next invasion of Canada, partly organised and wholly betrayed by Le Caron, began on 23 May 1870. It failed miserably, as did a subsequent effort the next year. Le Caron was earning his money. The hope for future Fenian attempts vanished when Gladstone's first government settled the *Alabama* claims for the sum of £3.5 million which was something like $19 million at the 1870 rate of exchange. The United States government no longer needed Fenianism as a lever in the negotiations. 'Brigadier-General' Le Caron, unsuspected by those whom he had betrayed, returned to civilian life, took an MD degree at the Detroit School of Medicine and set up a practice in Braidwood, near Wilmington, Illinois, a mining town fifty miles from Chicago.[6]

By 1871 American Fenianism was at its low-water mark, but it was to be revitalised by the introduction of a group of Irish exiles who had been deported from the United Kingdom as the result of an amnesty of 5 January 1871. Jailed as a result of their revolutionary activity, including an unsuccessful attack on Chester Castle in 1867, these men had languished in Portland and Millbank prisons until Gladstone decided to save the nation the expense of their imprisonment and the continued embarrassment of a vigorous campaign for their release. The first contingent arrived in New York on 19 January 1871. Composed of Jeremiah O'Donovan Rossa, Charles Underwood O'Connell, John Devoy, John McClure and Henry Shaw Mulleda, the group became known as the 'Cuba Five' after the Cunard ship which had carried them out of captivity. The *New York Herald* described the men :

John Devoy, in good health and spirits, five foot six in height with the square broad shoulders of a young Hercules, close-cropped hair surmounting a square massive forehead, small, deep-set blue eyes, giving an assurance of shrewdness to a face massed into firmness by a compressed mouth and strong chin. O'Donovan Rossa, six feet in height and as straight as a rush, with a fearless blue eye somewhat deep under arched brows, an aquiline nose sensitive as a warhorse at the nostrils; a high arched forehead, long brown beard and bronzed face indicative of the indomitable spirit within. Captain John McClure whose gentle face was marked with lines of undoubted strength, dark-haired and dark-eyed. Harry S. Mulleda, frank and fair, laughing eye and blonde moustache drooping at the corners, robust and hearty, a man about twenty-eight years old. Charles Underwood O'Connell, prematurely aged by the wear and tear of prison, hair almost grey, the tremulousness of physical debility in his hands, but a soul burning in dark eyes the chill of jail could never quench.[7]

The five men represented a good sample of the revolutionary activity of the IRB. Devoy had specialised in recruiting for the IRB amongst the British Army's Irish soldiers while, according to Devoy, O'Donovan Rossa had sworn more men into the IRB than any other ten men in Ireland. Devoy had been sent to jail for fifteen years and Rossa had been given life imprisonment because of his polemical personal defence during his trial. O'Connell had been arrested in 1865 when he had arrived in Ireland carrying papers dealing with the organisation of Fenianism in the United States Army; he received a sentence of ten years for his pains. McClure was serving a sentence of life imprisonment for taking part in the 1867 Rising in Ireland and Mulleda had received seven years penal servitude for gun smuggling. All five were British subjects.

A week later, 26 January, another Cunard ship, the *Russia*, brought nine more men, Thomas Francis Bourke, William Francis Roantree, Denis Dowling Mulcahy, Edmund Power, Edward Pilsworth St Clair, Patrick Lennon, Patrick Walsh, Peter Maughan, and George Brown. Bourke was a Civil War veteran from the Confederacy and had been sentenced to life imprisonment for his part in the 1867 rising. Pilsworth St Clair had been a close associate of Devoy's in British Army recruitment as were Maughan and Roantree. Power had been actively involved in both the raid on Chester Castle and the Manchester escape of 1867. Other leading revolutionaries to gain their freedom in the following months included John O'Leary, a chairman of the IRB Supreme Council and editor of the *Irish People* (20 years), Thomas Clarke Luby, a key IRB organiser (20 years), and four American citizens, William G. Halpin, a former officer in the Confederate Army, as was John McCafferty who had led the raid on Chester Castle (death sentence commuted to life imprisonment), Ricard O'Sullivan Burke (gun running) and finally another legendary gun runner William Mackey Lomasney, known as the 'little captain'.

If the exiles were not already aware of the extent to which American Fenianism was enmeshed in the jungle of American politics they soon were as both the Republican and Democratic political 'machines' sought to use their arrival to their respective advantages. Benjamin Butler, an Irish-vote-hungry Democratic Representative from the state of Massachusetts with its large

B

Boston Irish population, introduced a resolution of welcome to the exiles in the House of Representatives :

> *Resolved,* That the Congress of the United States, in the name and on behalf of the people of the United States, give to J. O'Donovan Rossa, Thomas Clarke Luby, John O'Leary, Thomas F. Burke, Charles Underwood O'Connell, and their associates, Irish exiles, a cordial welcome to the capital, also to the country, and that a copy of this resolution be transmitted to them by the President of the United States.[8]

The resolution was carried 172 to 21, the negative votes in a very thin House being cast by the Republicans. The triumphal progress of the exiles which had begun with a tumultuous welcome in New York was to come to a climax with a meeting on the White House steps on 22 February 1871. President Ulysses S. Grant could not afford to ignore the Irish votes either.

The exiles had strong opinions as to how future revolutionary activity in the United States had to be directed if a positive contribution was to be made to the eventual freeing of Ireland from continued English domination. On 4 February John Devoy wrote to John Boyle O'Reilly, editor of the Boston *Pilot*, giving notice of what was to come.

> Our aim will be to create an Irish party in this country, whose actions in American politics will have for its sole object the interests of Ireland. We will also hold aloof from all the different sections of Fenians. I may tell you that most of us are sick of the very issue of Fenianism, though as resolved as ever to work for the attainment of Irish independence.

The programme designed to achieve this breaking down of competition amongst the various Fenian organisations appeared six weeks later in the *Irish People*. It called for all Irish-American organisations to join a general council which would create an Irish Confederation. The constituent organisations would retain their own identity but would be represented on the general council by virtue of having donated 25 per cent of their income to the confederation. The Confederation would, however, be directed by a five-man committee composed of 'the men who have come here from English prisons'. A general council would represent the different States, Districts and Territories. The authors of the project concluded: 'One thing we have to guard against is treachery'.[9]

In the summer of 1871 there was the temporary establishment of an Allied Council containing two members of the Confederation, two from the Brotherhood, and a fifth elected by the four. The membership of the Confederation did not draw active Fenians so much as men who had, until that time, taken no part in the earlier organisations. The Fenian Brotherhood was almost moribund and confined to New York and a small section of Massachusetts around Boston. The Confederation's first convention was held in May 1872 and established a directory of twelve members including the executive of five 'exiles': Thomas F. Bourke, O'Donovan Rossa, John Devoy, James O'Kelly, and Thomas Clarke Luby. The future of American Fenianism, however, was not to lie with the Confederation, but in a secret organisation which functioned under the name of Clan na Gael or United Brotherhood. When the Boston *Pilot* summed up the efforts of Irish revolutionary societies in October 1872 the Clan was not even mentioned, but this secret society, upon the transference of the exiles' support to it, would be the basis for Irish-American revolutionary activity for the next decade and a half.[10]

Clan na Gael had been founded on 20 June 1867 in the house of James Sheedy on Hester Street, New York. The prime mover of this effort to avoid the factionalism which had characterised efforts at organisation over the previous decade was Jerome J. Collins, the scientific and meteorological correspondent of James Gordon Bennett's *New York Herald*. The new organisation also required the members to be Irish. The relevant clause in the constitution read as follows:

> All persons of Irish birth or descent, or of partial Irish descent, shall be eligible to membership; but in cases of persons of partial Irish descent the camps are directed to make special inquiries in regard to the history, character, and sentiments of the person proposed.

The Clan rejected the autocracy of O'Mahony and the Brotherhood and instead placed the governance of the organisation in democratically elected leaders. From another perspective 'Major' Le Caron said that the Clan was an 'off-shoot of the permanent conspiracy known under the name "Knights of the Inner Circle", which was joined by many Irish conspirators', including himself. At the end of 1869 the new Clan had absorbed the 'Knights' as well as some 300 members of the 'Brian Boru' Fenian Brotherhood Circle in New York City. Having seceded from the FB over a local political quarrel they had first operated as the 'United Irishmen'. Le Caron also mentioned P. R. Walsh of Cleveland, Ohio, as being known as 'The Father of the Clan', perhaps because of his development of the western areas of Clan na Gael. The first 'camp' (as distinct from the Fenian Brotherhood's 'circle') was the Napper Tandy Club in New York. Modelled upon the rites of the Masonic Fraternity, the Clan's members took a solemn oath to take up arms to establish an Irish Republic when called upon by their leaders. The republic would have complete political independence and guarantee full civil and religious liberty to all her inhabitants. Success could only be achieved by force of arms. Copies of Clan na Gael rituals do survive. A new hailing sign was put into operation in November 1876 :

> The Hailing Sign of Recognition, instead of being the passing of the hand down the cheek, will be in future : Placing the right hand carelessly under the left breast of the vest; reply by placing the left hand under the right breast of the vest.

The change occurred when the executive committee found that the sign announced at the beginning of the month was similar to that being used by the Ancient Order of Hibernians and that it was in the possession of two Massachusetts detectives 'operating against that order (and it is suspected against our own) in the Anthracite Coal Region of Pennsylvania. . . . The times require the utmost vigilance against betrayal.'[11] The Irish Confederation had collapsed for lack of support; the Fenian Brotherhood remained moribund; the future was to belong to Clan na Gael.

The Clan's rapidly developing organisation was soon to possess sixteen districts which were identified in code by letters of the alphabet.

A. New York City and Yonkers
B. New Jersey
C. Long Island and Staten Island

D. New York State and Vermont
E. Connecticut and Rhode Island
F. Massachusetts, Maine, and New Hampshire
G. Pennsylvania
H. Delaware, District of Columbia (Washington, DC), Maryland, Virginia, West Virginia, North Carolina, South Carolina, Alabama, Georgia, and Florida
I. Kentucky, Tennessee, Arkansas, Texas, Louisiana, and Mississippi
J. Ohio and Indiana
K. Illinois and Michigan
L. Iowa, Minnesota, and Wisconsin
M. Missouri, Kansas, Arizona, and New Mexico
N. Colorado, Nebraska, Dakota Territory, Wyoming, and Montana
O. California, Oregon, Utah, and Nevada
P. Canada

Over each of the districts was a District Member or EN; with the districts divided into camps of 'Ds' each having its own officers, treasurer and trustees. The officers for each camp were designated Senior Guardian (SG) and the Junior Guardian (JG) and they alone knew the name of the Treasurer and Secretary of the national executive and the District Member. The management of the Clan was a secret to the vast majority of its members, knowing only the names of each other and their camp officials. The initiation fee was a minimum of $1 and weekly dues were not less than ten cents, with the Treasurer of each camp retaining not more than 25 per cent for contingent expenses, the remainder being deposited in the bank in the name of the local trustees. Each camp was required to submit numerical and financial statements in October, February and June; 10 per cent of all money received was sent to the Secretary of the national executive for application to the Percentage Fund, which was the basis of the national organisation's operating expenses. By 1884 the accounts of the national organisation would show a membership in the United States of 20,000 men. Audits on membership and the Percentage Fund were made quarterly with one copy to each camp with its security and safety being the responsibility of its Senior Guardian.

By 1876 Major Le Caron had recognised the necessity of finally accepting the offers made to him to join Clan na Gael. In order to satisfy its 'Irish clause' he claimed his mother was Irish and his father French. Convinced that he could not easily ingratiate himself into the rough and tumble of the Clan's Chicago power structure, and repeating his Fenian Brotherhood tactics, he founded his own local camp (D 463) in Braidwood, Illinois. The camp grew to have a membership of over 200 members. As the Senior Guardian of the camp he received a copy of all Clan documents which he then, whenever appropriate or possible, passed onto London. He recalled :

> A stringent regulation of the Executive required that all docu-
> ments—when not returned to head-quarters, as many had to
> be—should be burned in view of the camp, in order that the
> most perfect secrecy should be secured. It was, of course,
> impossible for me to retain the originals of those which had
> to be returned, and of them I could only keep copies. With
> those requiring destruction in the presence of my camp, I was
> enabled to act differently. Always prepared for the emergency,
> I was, by a sleight-of-hand performance, enabled to substitute
> old and unimportant documents for those which really should
> have been burnt, and to retain in my possession, and subse-
> quently transmit to England, the originals of all the most
> important. I was, of course, shaking hands with danger and
> discovery at every turn, and yet so marvellous was my success
> that I not only escaped betrayal, but that which would un-
> doubtedly have led to it, namely suspicion.[12]

Le Caron's access to the documents was made possible only by the Junior Guardians trusting Le Caron with the key to the second lock (in addition to his own) on the strong box. The double locks were supposed to guarantee that it could not be opened without both the Guardians being present.

The National Executive (FC) of Clan na Gael included a chairman, secretary, treasurer and eleven of the sixteen District Members, who were elected by the biennial conventions. Although the Fenian Brotherhood Central Committee talked of re-establishing links with the Irish Republican Brotherhood and pursuing an active policy against the British, it was the Clan's executive which carried out the policy. Provision was made for a secret Military Department which would initially remain on paper until activated by a rising in Ireland. But most importantly was the establishment of the Revolutionary Directory (RD) consisting of seven members; three of whom were nominated by the Clan executive, three by the Supreme Council of the Irish Republican Brotherhood and a seventh who was to come from the Australia–New Zealand area. This latter representative proved impossible to find so that the six members took to choosing a seventh who might come from either side of the Atlantic and was known only to the RD. The members held office for six years with one man retiring annually and the replacement being made by the relevant organisation. This committee of seven had charge of all preparations for a war with England, power to declare war, negotiate with England's enemies, and to assume all the powers, functions, and authority of a provisional government in Ireland after the declaration of war. The RD was the supreme authority in all Irish revolutionary affairs and was financed by Clan na Gael. Plans and operations required the approval of the Clan's FC and the IRB's Supreme Council in addition to justifying its use of men, money and materials. If the Clan and IRB executives were convinced that the RD's activity was not 'directed solely to the attainment of the complete independence of Ireland' they could remove its members and replace them or abolish it altogether.

Although there may have been an initial tendency for men to belong to both the Fenian Brotherhood and the Clan, apparently the Brotherhood reclaimed the allegiance of some of the key Irish exiles now that the Confederation alternative had failed. In 1874 the Brotherhood's Central Committee of ten men (in addition to the Head Centre John O'Mahony) included Thomas Clarke Luby, Thomas F. Bourke, O'Donovan Rossa and William Mackey Lomasney. The committee addressed the Irish–American community that September in what promised to be a renewal of the fight against English imperialism.

> The hour has arrived when . . . we should awake to fresh and strenuous exertions, and rise and rally round the old standard of our fathers. . . In the recent Convention of the Fenian Brotherhood, energetic measures have been adopted for the revival of our glorious struggle. . . . Immediate steps are to be

taken once more, after so long and pernicious an alienation, to a fraternal communication with the Irish Revolutionary Brotherhood at home. . . . There is ample room . . . for all existing Irish national organisations to work for the old land without jostling against each other.

A series of secret resolutions were passed at the convention and not written into the minutes. The Fenians were sworn not to disclose the numerical and financial strength of the Brotherhood, the name of the Legion of St Patrick (its military arm) was changed to the Irish Legion, but most significantly a committee on home organisation was formed. Composed of O'Donovan Rossa, Luby, George Smith and the leader of the attack on Chester Castle in 1867, Captain John McCafferty, it made the following recommendation : 'We are strongly of the opinion that it is our duty not only to make every possible effort to rescue our brothers, still incarcerated in British dungeons, but also to render some pecuniary assistance to their destitute families'. The group of prisoners whose plight attracted the greatest attention were those Fenian soldiers from the British army who had been transported to Western Australia.[13]

The concluding comment of the Central Committee's call to arms concerning co-operation with all of the 'Irish national organisations' might be a reference to a decision already taken at the Clan na Gael convention at Baltimore in July 1874. Its concern for the six Fenian soldiers still held at the penal colony near Fremantle because the Duke of Cambridge had objected to their release with the political prisoners five years before led to the creation of an Australian Prisoners Rescue Committee of ten men. Five of these, James Reynolds of New Haven, Connecticut, Patrick Mahon, Rochester, New York (treasurer), John C. Talbot of San Francisco, John Goff of New York City and John Devoy were to take the leading roles in the organisation and financing of the rescue, which would be known about by eighty-six camps and close to 7,000 members. The organisation which was not yet ten years old now claimed the allegiance of the majority of the militant Irish-American community. The rescue of the Fenian prisoners would bring a further expansion of membership as the Clan demonstrated that it was prepared to act and not simply pass resolutions. What is extraordinary is that the British government remained unaware of the projected rescue, which from inception to completion spanned more than fifteen months. John Devoy wrote to James Reynolds on 3 February 1875 suggesting that if they bought a ship and fitted it out for whaling, it would cost about $12,000. By doing some whaling and carrying cargo they could break even by the resale of the ship upon its return if it realised $4,000 or $5,000. While the preparations were taking place and the money being raised, the detailed plans were being made by John J. Breslin, famous for his part in aiding the Irish patriot James Stephens in his escape from Richmond gaol, Dublin in 1865. The revolutionary fervour of the Irish-American community was now finding an outlet, but the proposed rescue was only one aspect of a policy which had turned completely away from the traditional preoccupation with the capture of Canada.

On 27 April 1875 the whaler *Catalpa* sailed for the South Pacific and after doing the whaling that the Clan financing required effected the rescue of the six men on 17 April 1876. Successfully evading the Royal Navy's ships by flying the Stars and Stripes, Breslin brought his cargo of patriots into New York harbour on 19 August to be met by that city's leading politicians as well as those men who led the various Fenian organisations. The message of this little victory seemed quite clear to John Boyle O'Reilly, editor of Boston's *Pilot*: 'England will now begin to realise that she has made a mistake that will follow her to her death-bed, in making Ireland so implacable and daring an enemy. This is only an earnest of what will come when the clouds of war are over her. The men who sent out the *Catalpa* to Australia are just the men to send out a hundred *Catalpas* to wipe British commerce from the face of the sea.' While England was engaged in an international war with one of her many continental opponents the Irish would strike from their neutral base with privateers against the empire's shipping. The *Alabama* example required the co-operation of the United States' government and, since the settlement of the claims arising out of its destruction of American shipping, its co-operation was far from certain. And yet what other course was left? This problem of how best to strike at the enemy dominated the Fenian discussions.

On 19 September 1874, in the *Irish World*, Patrick Ford suggested the following policy:

> This country is Ireland's base of operations. Here in this Republic—whose flag first flashed on the breeze in defiance of England—whose first national hosts rained an iron hail of destruction upon England's power—here in this land to whose shores English oppression exiled our race—we are free to express the sentiments and to declare the hopes of Ireland. It is your duty, revolutionary chieftains, to realise these hopes! If you are but true to this duty—if you are but true to nature—there are those among you who, perhaps, will yet live to uplift Ireland's banner above the ruins of London, and proclaim with trumpet-tongued voice, whose echoes shall reverberate to the ends of the earth—'The rod of the oppressor is broken! Babylon the great is fallen!'

The policy which evolved replaced the unfulfillable dream of an Irish rebellion of the sort which brought independence to their adopted land in 1776. In its place came the revolutionary chieftains who were to be known as the skirmishers. Military science defined skirmishers as small groups of select troops operating at great risk in advance of the main forces, probing for weaknesses in the enemy's defences and then leading in their subsequent exploitation. On 10 October 1874, the *Irish World* stated that

> We want some band of men to pioneer the way—sometimes to skirmish, sometimes to act as a forlorn hope, sometimes to give martyrs and confessors; always acting, always showing that we have still amongst us brave men ready to do or dare all that brave men ever did and dared for the salvation of a fallen land. If no one society will supply this want, it is, undoubtedly, the duty of every society to give a helping and an encouraging hand in providing it. Let there be no unworthy jealousy, no petty enmity in this matter. There must be action and preparation before a revolution, and some little skirmishing, too, before the general battle comes on, and there must be some body of Irishmen specially devoted to this work. . . .

The skirmishers' target was England.

2

Skirmishers by
Sea and by Land, 1876-1881

The Irish cause requires Skirmishers. It requires a little band
of heroes who will initiate and keep up without intermission
a guerilla warfare . . .

Irish World, 4 December 1875

SINCE the failures of the Canadian invasions of the 1860s the
various Fenian organisations had been searching for a strategy
which would make an active contribution to the freeing of the
home from which so many of them had been forced to flee
starvation and political oppression. The Irish were not the only
European minority group harbouring in the freedom of the
United States but without any question they were the group
which most easily integrated. Yet they seemed eternally restless.
In the five-year period following the success of the *Catalpa*
expedition American Fenianism would mature, but in its
maturation it would nevertheless display the old weaknesses of
disunity produced by internal suspicions and rivalries. The
Skirmishers would take to the field under the banner of
O'Donovan Rossa, to be followed later by Clan na Gael; the
first bombs would be detonated on English soil in 1881. The
British government would vainly try to enlist the support of its
American counterpart to stop the organisations and their
'dynamite press' which supported the transatlantic dynamite
offensive.

At the reception that followed the tumultuous welcome of
Breslin's *Catalpa* expedition in the summer of 1876, John Devoy
had been introduced to the inventor of a secret naval weapon.
He remembered that the inventor was 'well informed of Irish
affairs and was anti-English and with clear and definite ideas
of the proper method of fighting England. He was cool, good-
tempered, and talked to us as a schoolmaster would to his
children'. In fact he was a schoolmaster by the name of John

Philip Holland. John Holland had been born in Liscannor, County Clare in 1841, taking his initial vow to become a member of the teaching Order of the Irish Christian Brothers in June 1858. From then until May 1873, when he withdrew from the order before taking his final vows because of ill health, Holland taught in its schools. His mother and elder brother Alfred had already emigrated to the United States in the wake of a younger brother, Michael J. Holland, who had left Ireland to escape possible arrest for his nationalist views. In the autumn of 1873 John Holland packed his few possessions and took steerage passage for Boston, where Michael lived. In his baggage was the sketch of his first submarine design. Recalling this important moment in his life from the distance of 1900 he said :

> I knew that in a country where coal and iron and mechanical skill were as plenty [*sic*] as they were in England, the development of large armour-plated ships must come first. Therefore I must get to a place where mechanics in shipbuilding were less advanced and the available material for the big iron-clad vessels scarcer. Then, too, I was an Irishman. I had never taken part in any political agitation, but my sympathies were with my own country, and I had no mind to do anything that would make John Bull any stronger and more domineering than we had already found him.[1]

Soon after his arrival in Boston, Holland had the opportunity to review his work on the submarine boat when a slip on Boston's icy pavements in November 1873 left him with a broken leg, a slight concussion and time for study. After recovering from his injuries he moved south to New Jersey where he took up a post with the Christian Brothers as a lay teacher in the boys' division of St John's Parochial School in Paterson, near New York. In years to come he was to spend countless evenings at his classroom blackboard with an engineer friend, William Dunkerly, working out the principles and design modifications necessary for successful underwater navigation. He unsuccessfully submitted a submarine design to the United States Navy Department in February 1875. Almost a year and a half later his brother Michael, a member of Fenian Brotherhood Circle No. 159, arranged for Holland to meet O'Donovan Rossa.

Rossa and others had recently been seriously considering the idea of attacking England on the high seas. Patrick Ford had suggested in the *Irish World*, 19 September 1874, that it would take only ten Irish-manned privateers to sweep the seas of English commerce in six months. It must have seemed obvious to Holland that Ford's dreams—that the Irish could do to the English what the Confederacy's raiders had done to Federal shipping during the American Civil War—was quite unrealistic. The Royal Navy was too large to be taken on with a few privateers. If, however, one was able to adopt an unorthodox approach based on a secret weapon of advanced naval technology, then British commerce might be attacked successfully. In theory a submarine could lie in wait, decks awash and unseen, at the conjunction of shipping lanes outside territorial waters near harbours. There it would strike its devastating blows, with torpedoes sending the enemy's naval ships and merchant marine to the bottom. This was the tactic, but the submarine and its associated weaponry had to be developed and could only work if this vision could move from St John's blackboards into the financing, construction and testing of such a boat.

Rossa found Holland's ideas convincing enough to give him a letter of introduction to Jerome J. Collins at the *New York Herald*. The letter was dated 6 July 1876, only five weeks before the return of the *Catalpa* from Australia. Collins, who was to die five years later on De Long's ill-fated *Jannette* polar expedition, was the obvious man to vet Holland's scheme because of his scientific reputation, as well as being one of the Clan na Gael founders. It was subsequently agreed that Holland would provide a demonstration of the submarine's principles as proof of the soundness of his proposals. Holland had a model submarine built which was thirty inches long, metal-hulled with rudder and diving planes, and powered by a clockwork motor. The model was successfully demonstrated at Coney Island later that year before John J. Breslin and a small group of Clan observers.

Granting the feasibility of the project the problem of financing it immediately came to the fore. Breslin was a trustee of a fund which had been created recently by O'Donovan Rossa—the Skirmishing Fund. The previous year, under the

question 'Can Ireland be made free?', Patrick Ford had continued his development of the Skirmisher theme along these
lines in the *Irish World* on 4 December 1875 :

> We are not now advising a general insurrection. On the con-
> trary, we should oppose a general insurrection in Ireland as
> untimely and ill-advised. But we believe in action nevertheless.
> A few active, intrepid and intelligent men can do so much
> to annoy and hurt England. The Irish cause requires Skir-
> mishers. It requires a little band of heroes who will initiate
> and keep up without intermission a guerilla warfare—men
> who will fly over land and sea like invisible beings—now strik-
> ing the enemy in Ireland, now in India, now in England
> itself, as occasion may present.

Rossa was doubtless aware of the Clan na Gael and Irish
Revolutionary Brotherhood conversations in progress throughout 1876. These eventually led to the establishment of a joint
Revolutionary Directory with responsibility for 'striking the
enemy'. But who would bear the cost of such an effort? If men
and women of the Irish-American community could find
$12,000 or so in nickels and dimes to finance the *Catalpa*
expedition to rescue six soldiers, what would they give to do a
proper job of fighting the English?

Rossa's letter of December to the *Irish World* suggesting the
establishment of a 'Skirmishing Fund' was held back until a
leading article appeared in the newspaper on 4 March 1876
giving the idea its blessing.

> England will not know where or how she is to be struck. A
> successful stroke or *any* stroke that will do her five hundred
> thousand dollars' worth damage will bring in funds enough
> to carry on the work. . . .

The goal of the new fund was set at $5,000. Rossa offered him-
self as the secretary for the first year, and named James J.
Clancy, an *Irish World* editorial writer, as treasurer with
Augustine Ford, the editor's brother, as the third trustee.
Patrick Ford refused to be a trustee himself but put in the
relatively unknown Clancy. Devoy identified the 'very good
fellow' as 'Ford's principal man and it is rather cool of him
to put in a man he can order'. As the third trustee was Ford's
brother the editor of the *Irish World* was set on controlling the

fund.[2] All contributions were to be listed in the *Irish World*. Reactions to the fund were mixed. John O'Leary, a leading figure in the IRB, wrote from Paris on 27 March repudiating what he saw as a horrible dream of grotesque proportions. He personally did not 'mean to have hand, act, or part in the burning of cities, towns, barracks (by *dynamite* or anything else) while Ireland is not in open insurrection against England'.[3] Nor was the Clan na Gael executive pleased to have the initiative pass from them and such a proposal thrust before the public without prior consultation. Dr William Carroll, a prosperous Philadelphia physician, who was the Senior Guardian of Camp 48 and chairman of the national executive from 1875–1880 wrote to John Devoy on 29 March asking him to arrange for Rossa to meet with the FC on the matter of the Skirmishing Fund. The meeting with Rossa seems to have agreed that when the collection reached its goal of $5,000 then Clan na Gael trustees would assume responsibility. This was very much in line with John Devoy's thinking, which, like O'Leary's, reacted strongly against Rossa's allusions to 'capturing Princes, rescuing prisoners, etc., in a sufficiently direct way to give a British lawyer ample proof against any man who should fall into their hands'. What Devoy desired was a public revolutionary fund 'placed in the hands of a committee who should have full control of it, but such a committee should be of men of undoubted revolutionary ability and also have the confidence of our people'. Devoy strongly objected to the use of the word 'skirmishing' which Rossa insisted must remain in the fund's name. Devoy said they should not proclaim their intentions to the world.

John Devoy was quite right in his prediction that the *Catalpa* 'skirmish' would provide the advanced nationalist movement with an 'immense lift' and the Skirmishing Fund had exceeded its goal by the spring of 1877. The new trustees were Clan members but not under Clan control. The name was changed to the National Fund and its reconstituted group of trustees included Rossa, John Devoy, Thomas Clarke Luby, James Reynolds, William Carroll, Thomas Francis Bourke and John J. Breslin. They announced the beginning of a new campaign for funds in the *Irish World*, 21 April 1877. The 'Special National Fund' was to 'aid the work of Ireland's deliverance'.

By the end of the year Dr Carroll was writing to Devoy warning him that the Fenian Brotherhood's Central Committee would make an attempt to capture 'at least' part of the Skirmishing Fund, probably because just prior to the death of the Brotherhood's founder John O'Mahony back in February, Rossa had been elected Head Centre of the FB.

O'Mahony's death had served to accentuate the differences within the American Fenian organisations. In addition it pointed to the problems of Rossa's intemperance and his refusal to serve anyone's interest other than his own. The death of the founder of the Fenian Brotherhood led naturally to the suggestion that he should be interred in Dublin's Glasnevin Cemetery. Rossa, who ran his European Steamship and Railroad ticket agency from the *Irish World* offices at No. 263 Broadway, secured free shipment for the casket on the William and Guion Steamship Line. The official mourners included Dr Denis Dowling Mulcahy and William Roantree, both exiles whose prison sentences had expired while in the United States and were thus able to return freely to Ireland. According to Mulcahy the Dublin funeral was in the best Irish tradition of setting more 'value on the dead patriot's bones than on his living brains'. There were, however, serious difficulties concerning who was to cover Mulcahy's expenses. Carroll had written to Devoy at the end of February enclosing a letter from Rossa which implied that Carroll had committed the Clan to pay the mourners' expenses. Denying that he had done so, Carroll offered to raise a fair proportion of the sum from his Philadelphia camp. The *Irish World* (21 April 1877) carried a letter in which Rossa said that he had received permission from Augustine Ford and James Clancy to promise the money to Mulcahy and $2,030 had been received from the Skirmishing Fund for the funeral and the Clan and the Fenian Brotherhood would refund the money. The picture was extremely confused and of the $1000 Mulcahy had apparently been promised from the Fund, he received only slightly more than half, leaving him in financial ruin, stranded in Dublin, and so embittered that he would eventually bring legal action against the Fund's trustees to recover what he was convinced was due to him.

Despite all of these difficulties the decision had been taken after the *Catalpa* success to finance the development of John

Holland's submarine torpedo boat. The Skirmishing Fund's trustees arranged that the boat be built by Handrin and Ripley, Albany Iron Works, New York. The projected boat, the *Holland I*, was perhaps the smallest submarine ever built, being but fourteen feet six inches in length, three-foot in the beam and only two feet six inches in height, not including the turret. The trustees were aware that this first boat was not the secret weapon they had contracted for, but an experimental prototype. Their hopes for the future did not rest solely upon Holland's dreams, for while the small boat was being built, Dr Carroll (X) was keeping Devoy posted (1 February 1877) on plans designed to get 10,000 men organised, armed and drilled under the Clan's Military Board, in addition to a scheme guardedly referred to as the 'salt water venture'. This was most likely plans for a fleet of Fenian privateers which would operate against Britain if the Anglo-Russian tensions of 1877–1880, turned to war.[4]

Although the boat was being built in New York, Holland continued teaching in Paterson across the Hudson River in New Jersey. Breslin supervised the boat's construction under the alias of Jacobs, Jr, the Skirmishing Fund was Jacobs and Company, and the importance of O'Donovan Rossa in 1876 was illustrated by his alias, Jacobs, Sr. Sometime in the spring of 1878, the *Holland I* was moved from New York yard to the shops of J. C. Todd and Company (later Todd & Rafferty) in Paterson. It was in this machine shop that the primitive petroleum engine, patented by George Brayton four years earlier, was installed. This engine was hoped to provide vastly improved performance over the foot-pedal power of the previous Holland designs.

On 22 May the boat was launched on the Passaic River near the Spruce Street bridge in Paterson. The two-and-one-quarter-ton 'wrecking boat', as the local people christened it, slowly disappeared under the water; either the buoyancy had been calculated for salt water rather than fresh, or intake valves or hatches had been left sufficiently open to allow water to pour in. The submarine was quickly towed to shore and after two days of trim and buoyancy adjustments she was launched again; this time sinking by the stern because of faulty riveting to her iron-plated hull.

By 29 May the boat was floating on an even keel but the

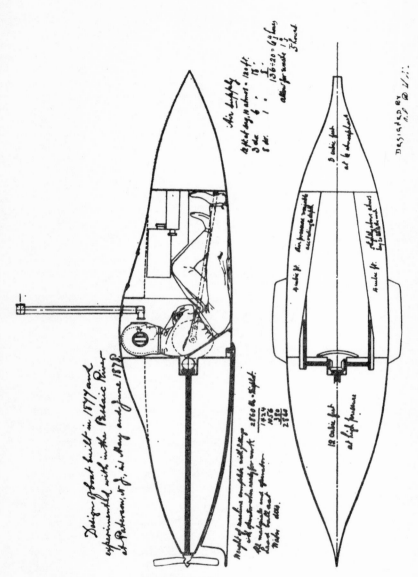

Early Design for the *Holland I*

four h.p., two-cylinder Brayton engine refused to fire and Holland was forced to connect a live steam line from an accompanying tender to the engine's pressure chamber, which then operated the boat's single screw propeller. On 6 June Holland crawled into his tiny turret, put the boat into drive and slid out into the Passaic River where he proceeded to take the boat down some twelve feet, still connected to its umbilical-like steam hose. The accompanying steam launch carried his assistants, O'Donovan Rossa and two other local Fenians. That evening the boat was to remain submerged for an hour. The results of these tests over the summer of 1878 were sufficiently encouraging for the National (Skirmishing) Fund's Trustees, led by Dr Carroll, to advance funds for the construction of a larger and more sophisticated boat. Unlike the *Holland I* it would be armed. Rossa had just been forced by the Fund's Trustees to give up his secretaryship on 23 May because of a deficiency in the accounts.

James J. O'Kelly, writing from Boston on 11 October 1878, told Devoy that he had had a long talk with John Boyle O'Reilly about the National Fund during which he had explained to the editor of the *Pilot* the 'intelligent use' that 'we hope to make of it'. O'Kelly recorded the surprise expressed by O'Reilly—he had assumed from 'Rossa's raving' that the fund was to be used recklessly during times of peace rather than against England when she was seriously engaged in the impending conflict with Russia. While in Boston, O'Kelly was going to visit Ben Butler, one of the Massachusett's Representatives, to ask for a subscription of $500 to the National Fund, pointing out that such a 'proof of real sympathy with our people would be likely to aid himself in his political aspirations'. There was also a short undated note saying : 'That "Skirmishing" idea must be dropped if we want to get money—the well-to-do respectables won't touch it, and with a little diplomacy they may be induced to come out handsomely I think.'[5] Most importantly, the money continued to flow in and it was very much needed, for while the original fund was closed at $5,000, the new appeal had initially to cover the cost of Holland's new boat which would require close to $20,000.

John J. Breslin continued his supervision of the boat's construction and Holland reluctantly resigned his teaching position to devote full time to his second boat. *Holland I* had its machinery and engine removed and Holland scuttled her in fourteen feet of water near to her first launching site. The contract for the hull construction of what John Fitzgerald referred to as the 'big cigar of J.J.B.'s' was placed with the Delamater-Robinson Iron Works at the foot of New York's West 13th Street. Work began on the submarine (later to be christened the 'Fenian Ram' by a New York journalist) on 3 May 1879. The owners and workers at Delamater's yard were convinced that they were building an unfloatable craft; Clan na Gael saw it as an unbeatable naval weapon. Holland continued his work amidst a steady flow of visitors to the shipyard in which the foreign observers included representatives of the Sultan of Turkey. Refusing offers to build submarines for Turkey, he kept his mind firmly set on his boat. How much he knew of the tremendous tensions within his backers is not known. The story of the Skirmishing Fund is one of the most confused and contradictory parts of the Clan story, one which continued to haunt John Devoy into the 1920s when he finally won a libel suit against Patrick Ford's nephew over allegations that he had improperly benefited from his association with the fund. The early story is important for within it lies the wedge that split the Irish-American revolutionary movement.

When the accounts of the Skirmishing Fund were turned over to the new trustees, appointed at the Clan's Providence, R.I. Convention in July 1876, its balance stood at, according to John Devoy's recollections, $23,000. The new fund over the next four years then raised an additional $55,000 leaving the trustees of the Fund something over $78,000 with which to conduct their activities on behalf of Ireland's deliverance. The original $23,000 seems to have been in Registered United States bonds. After O'Donovan Rossa's fall from grace in the spring of 1878, he remained a trustee but was replaced as secretary by John J. Breslin. Breslin was instructed to convert these bonds to 'coupon bonds' which were negotiable without record, thus protecting the Fund and its revolutionary activity from 'English spies'.

The next crisis in the operation of the Fund came when John Devoy was in Ireland in 1878–79 on behalf of the Clan. During his absence Patrick Ford, who obviously felt a right to call upon the Fund to reciprocate in kind for the support he had given it, approached both Carroll, the senior trustee, and Breslin for a loan of $12,000. Ford was acting on behalf of his newspaper's paper supplier, Mr Hoag, who was in urgent financial straits and required immediate collateral for the payment of a debt. Since the end of April of 1878 Ford had been in Hoag's debt, sharing his office on the third floor of No. 10 Spruce Street, having moved out of the Broadway office across from the old city hall in New York. Carroll and Breslin agreed to Ford's request, but rumours of the secret transaction were soon out and there was a demand for an audit of the National Fund at the Clan convention which met in Wilkes Barre, Pennsylvania in July of the next year, 1879. The resultant admission proved to be deeply embarrassing; Thomas Clarke Luby resigned from the Fund while Breslin and Carroll reluctantly went cap-in-hand to Ford to ask for the return of the bonds. He proved to be unwilling to do so and did not return them until sometime early in 1881. In the meantime the *Irish World* took a highly critical view of the trustees' application of the fund, thus supporting the sniping being carried on by O'Donovan Rossa.

The Fund's trustees were committed to 'honourable warfare', which meant attacking England, not with skirmishers, but taking part in a proper war while England was distracted by a foreign enemy—whether it was the Zulus, the Russians or the Boers, it mattered not in the least. But Rossa warned : 'You want "honourable warfare". Well wait till England will let you have it, and you'll wait till you'll lie down and die.' Some attempt had been made to compromise when Augustine Ford was invited back to the Trustees to be Secretary, but he did so reluctantly. The fragile unity of the movement had broken over control of the National (Skirmishing) Fund, and O'Donovan Rossa was not one to accept this situation in silence or inactivity.[6] What was to develop was reminiscent of the Fenian Brotherhood split of the late 1860s, except that perhaps it had even more serious consequences for the Irish-American movement. The Clan completed the break with Rossa and his supporters when it accepted Michael Davitt's 'New Departure' in Irish agitation, which put the stress of effort into the Irish agrarian problem. Michael Davitt proposed 'an open participation in public movements in Ireland by extreme men, not in opposition to Mr Parnell or moral-force supporters, but with the view of bringing an advanced nationalist spirit and revolutionary purpose into Irish public life, in a friendly rivalry with moderate nationalists. . . .'[7] The Clan underwrote Davitt's tour of the United States in the autumn of 1878 and was the only Irish-American organisation with the financial strength to support such an effort. The Clan continued to finance arms smuggling into Ireland but in addition undertook to support Davitt's Land League and the non-violent policy of Parnell's party at Westminster. Both Devoy and Carroll had made visits to Ireland both to assess the situation and to encourage the rejuvenation of a sadly demoralised home organisation. The American version of the Land League was organised in May of 1880 composed chiefly of members of the Clan and the Ancient Order of Hibernians. The Irish Land and Industrial League would function as a political wing of the Clan and provide a link with the Irish Land League. In 1879 the strength of the Clan was 11,539 members of whom 7,377 were in good standing.

Rossa was not the only person who disapproved of this shift in tactics. Dr William Carroll (an Ulster Presbyterian by birth) resigned as chairman of the FC over the issue but remained a member of the RD and a trustee of the Skirmishing Fund.

Rossa's alienation was completed by Ford's decision to support the New Departure in the *Irish World* which thus deprived Rossa of a forum for his own flamboyant opinions and predictions of the future. The *Irish World* continued its criticism of the Skirmishing Fund's failure to 'skirmish', but Rossa had to find a newspaper and an organisation to support his ideas. Since the National Fund had officially dropped the word 'skirmishing', Rossa immediately resurrected it. During late June of 1880 the *United Irishman* appeared under his editorship, claiming the support of the United Irish Clubs, which according to Clan sources were for the most part remnants of the Fenian Brotherhood. This was followed by a convention of 120 which founded a 'Revolutionary Directory'; Clan sources were unimpressed. The convention was really only attended by 43 men, of whom 30 were residents of Philadelphia, a city which William Carroll was known to have called the 'most Irish city in the nation'. The public announcement of this convention in April produced a circular from the Clan's FC reminding its members that Article XI, Section 3 of the Constitution forbade members to belong to other Irish organisations on pain of expulsion. If Devoy's appreciation of Rossa's character was correct, he accepted his latest martyrdom happily. Rossa counterattacked, demanding an accounting by the National Fund Trustees. Failing to receive a reply from the Trustees, he raised his own United Irish Reserve Fund. Archibald, the British consul in New York and in charge of dealing with Irish-American informers, could not find it in himself to take Rossa's 'new departure' seriously, telling the Foreign Office that the respectable American press saw such fund-raising as only a way to extract money from credulous Irish labourers and servant girls for selfish ends: 'The idea of any practical movement by these agitators towards weakening British power in Ireland is regarded as purely quixotic' (9 July 1880). Robert Anderson's estimate of money available to all of the American revolutionary groups in 1880 was some $8,000; enough for mischief but not rebellion.[8]

Rossa was convinced that Clan's National (Skirmishing) Fund was not intended to finance development of submarines, however bright their future prospects might have been, but to cause explosions in England. He put this position clearly in a letter which found its way into the possession of John Devoy.

> Look at this Skirmishing matter—I am not in their way these two years, and yet we haven't a blow-up anywhere. We heard about some operations on the continent, perhaps it was they that did that dynamite affair at the Court of Russia, but I don't know, I go in for commencing nearer home first. When we have our own affairs fixed, it would be time enough for them to commence destroying tyranny elsewhere.[9]

The remainder of the letter expressed great hopes for the summer convention of the United Irish Clubs, anticipating that it would be the 'biggest thing ever held in America'. The convention however turned out to be a damp squib. When Anderson calculated the financial resources of what Davitt called the 'advanced nationalists', he could not have known just what 'mischief' money in the hands of O'Donovan Rossa could achieve. Rossa was no sooner banking the response to his United Irish Reserve Fund appeal, than he was preparing to send his long overdue Skirmishers into the field against the English tyrants. He was about to prove the folly of dismissing him too easily.

Unknown to Rossa, the Clan's Revolutionary Directory, part of an interlocking directory with the National (Skirmishing) Fund trustees, was planning a series of dynamite attacks against English targets to balance off against the Clan's official policy of New Departure co-operation. The attacks were to be planned and led by Captain William Mackey Lomasney.

Lomasney had been born in 1841 in Cincinnati, Ohio of Irish parents, who had emigrated from Co. Cork. His father had been an active Fenian, while his great grandfather's memory was honoured in the family, for he had been killed in the uprising of 1798. Still in his early twenties, he went to Ireland, joined the Irish Republican Brotherhood, becoming famous for his daring arms raids on gunshops and coastguard stations. He was also one of the leaders of the famous attack on the Royal Irish Constabulary barracks at Ballyknockan in 1867. His luck ran out while raiding a Cork gunshop in February of the next year. A police-constable was shot in the struggle for Lomasney's revolver and he was arrested and tried for attempted murder. The trial judge was Judge Thomas O'Hagan, a former 'Young Irelander', who sought to lecture Lomasney on the enormity of the crime. Lomasney responded by saying he was simply following O'Hagan's example of 1848! He became a close friend of John Devoy in Millbank Convict Prison and was released in the amnesty in 1871. Returning to the United States, he settled down in Detroit at 96 Michigan Avenue as a stationer and bookseller. John Devoy's description of Lomasney fits the bookseller image better than the revolutionary.

> A small man of slender build, who spoke with a lisp, modest and retiring in manner, one who did not know him well would never take him for a desperate man, but no one in the Fenian movement ever did more desperate things.[10]

Lomasney's reputation as the 'little captain' died hard. When the RD decided to begin an active campaign based upon England's impending involvement in a war with Russia he was their natural choice, having actively served on the Clan's Military Board. His importance was underlined in a letter of late March

1878 to Devoy. General F. F. Millen strongly suggested that the time had come for doing something to 'arouse the military spirit of the useful portion of the VC'. Millen felt that Lomasney should go around the districts and address the 'military men *in secret session*'.[11] By 1880 Millen had resigned as head of the board to be replaced by Colonel Michael Kerwin. Lomasney's responsibility was soon to be far heavier than recruiting for the Clan's 'army'.

On 3 November 1880 Lomasney, whose Military Board work had been covered by the code letter 'K', agreed to accept the Revolutionary Directory's call to arms and adopted the *nom de guerre* of 'Waldron'. First he asked for a 'couple of hundred dollars' with which to experiment with dynamite. Originally it was planned that he would work with Captain Edward O'Meager Condon. As the leader of the Manchester Rescue in September 1867, Condon had been condemned to death; three of his accomplices were executed but Condon's American citizenship saved him. Released by amnesty in 1878, Condon's value to the Clan's scheme lay in his familiarity with English cities and his well-earned reputation as a 'desperate man'. Yet he was not prepared to support the New Departure policy, vacillating over plans for dynamite campaign. By mid-December 1881 Lomasney told the RD that he was not prepared to use Condon. Lomasney told Devoy:

I scarcely think there will be need for what I am preparing for, but it is best to be ready, and none will be better pleased than myself if there never happens to be use for what I am preparing till the firm is ready to go thoroughly into business.[12]

The latter point was a reference to a full scale Irish revolution. If forced to use Condon, Lomasney was prepared to resign. He was wholeheartedly committed to a policy which would not give the British government an excuse for adopting coercive measures against Ireland. The RD provided sufficient funds for experiments and arrangements for 'such work while there [France and England], should I deem it expedient'. 'I will however', Lomasney continued, 'put this statement in such a way as not to commit the RD, should I hereafter (which, of course, will only be with the consent of the RD) adopt retaliatory measures. Now I am satisfied events may cause us to do so, and for this reason

I wish to be most careful'.[13] Lomasney was anticipating that coercion might be applied to Ireland because of the exertions of the Land League. In those circumstances the RD was prepared to mount a campaign of dynamite attacks in retaliation. According to Major Le Caron some years later, Lomasney had an excellent chance to escape detection.

> Though of youthful appearance, his face was a most determined one, and the way it lent itself to disguise was truly marvellous. When covered with the dark bushy hair, of which he had a profusion, it was one face; when clean-shaven, quite another, and impossible of recognition. Acting, as he constantly did, as the delegate from the American section to the Fenians at home, this faculty of disguise proved of enormous service, and may very well have had disastrous effects on police vigilance. I have seen Lomasney both shaved, on his return from Ireland, and unshaved, in his American life; and in all the men I have ever met, I never saw such a change produced by so easy a process.[14]

Lomasney was still in Detroit on Saturday 15 January 1881, but on the verge of departure for New York via the New York Central Railway, for he was in Paris on Friday 11 February. Lomasney left for Europe knowing that O'Donovan Rossa and his United Irish Reserve Fund had already put the first Skirmishers into the English field.

The first attack of the dynamite war took place in the midst of a dense fog which covered the Manchester area on 14 January 1881. A ventilating grid at Salford Barracks had been removed from the wall abutting on a side street and a bomb was placed inside. When it exploded at 5.20 p.m. it destroyed a butcher's shed, killed a boy of seven and injured three people, one seriously. Strangeways Prison was put on alert and the outer wall was patrolled first by police (seriously under strength because of riots in the colliery districts) and then by troops as the prison officials prepared for a Clerkenwell-type assault. A troop of cavalry left Preston for Hindley near Wigan and one hundred infantry took up positions at St Helens, an important rail junction. Despite expectations the Town Hall and Exchange were not bombed and the panic subsided as quickly as it had arisen.

William Vernon Harcourt, the Home Secretary, wrote to Howard Vincent, Director of the Criminal Investigation Division, at Scotland Yard on Sunday 23 January:

> The reports that come into me as to the probability of explosions under the auspices of the 'Skirmishing Committee' become more and more alarming. I am much disturbed at the absolute want of information in which we seem to be with regard to Fenian organisation in London. All other objects should be postponed in our efforts to get some light into these dark places. If anything occurs there will be a terrible outcry.[15]

The Criminal Investigation Division (CID), created four years before, was one of the reforms initiated during Sir Edmund Henderson's time as chief commissioner of the Metropolitan Police. At first Henderson had expanded the Detective Branch from fifteen to nearly two hundred men under the command of Superintendent Adolphus 'Dolly' Williamson. The efficiency of the Yard improved but the famous trial of four detectives on corruption charges ('conspiring to obstruct justice') in 1877 led to radical action. In August of 1876 a Home Office Departmental Commission had been set up to assess the need for further reorganisation of the Detective Division. Howard Vincent, then a young lawyer, intrigued with the possibility of being the first assistant commissioner of a revolutionised detective branch, made a hurried visit to Paris to study the French detective system. He later submitted a report on the findings of his trip to the commission, which led to his being later successfully appointed as the first Director of Criminal Investigations.

The powers of the CID director were severely restricted in comparison with his Parisian opposite number. Although responsible to Vincent, detectives were attached to Metropolitan divisions where they had to report to and co-operate closely with Divisional Superintendents. 'Dolly' Williamson was the Chief Superintendent of the department and by 1883 its manpower would reach six hundred men. Vincent's acknowledged success at the Yard was largely dependent upon diplomacy for, although directly responsible to the Home Secretary, he had no statutory or disciplinary authority over his department. This did not dampen his enthusiasm as he organised the division, raised salaries, improved training standards for recruits, simplified the criminal record system, compiled a Police Code, and updated the *Police Gazette*. Vincent's reforms prepared Scotland Yard to face the Fenian onslaught, in addition to the more usual demands placed upon it by the ingenuity of London's criminals.

As early as August of 1880 Vincent had submitted a memorandum to Sir Edmund Henderson pleading for the Chief Commissioner to authorise preparations to deal with Fenianism and co-operate with the RIC. 'Henderson', however, wrote Vincent, 'always slow to move, preferred to wait for orders from the Secretary of State'. The orders had not come from the outgoing Conservative Home Secretary, Sir Richard Cross. That autumn William Vernon Harcourt, his Liberal successor, asked Robert Anderson to attend to the Irish side of the expected Fenian campaign; Vincent, relieved for the time being of all other duties, was responsible for Great Britain. He managed the whole business of the CID for nearly three years without any help, not even a secretary, working ten- to fourteen-hour days. He wrote to Harcourt on 1 August 1881 : 'I have not broken down yet, and I hope I shall not'.[16]

Harcourt would make his own position quite clear regarding his own appreciation of the problem of the CID when he gave the address at prize-giving for the children of the Metropolitan and City Police Orphanage at Strawberry Hill, Twickenham, in late June 1881. Howard Vincent, as the host on the occasion, was amongst those who heard the work of the London police forces lauded by the Home Secretary. He must have been especially pleased when Harcourt continued by saying that 'he knew it was complained that there were many defects in our detective system. Those who complained of the faults of that system were often the first to denounce the very methods by which it could be made effectual. The country was jealous, and justly so, of any organised system of espionage. But people must remember if they were called to play an above-board game against those who played against them with loaded dice and marked cards, against the midnight marauder, the skulking assassin, and the secret society, they must expect to be baffled and defeated'. Harcourt judged that the present system of detective work was 'fair, just, and proper'; he was obviously not prepared to rule out the necessity of espionage if the demands

upon the police changed drastically. The newspapers reported
that the Home Secretary's speech was greeted with cheers by the
policemen and their families.[17]

Life as a London policeman was hard. There was no doubt
about the magnitude of the difficulties under which the 'man on
the beat' laboured. One of the most vivid contemporary descriptions of Scotland Yard itself was provided by an Irish-American,
John McEnnis:

> A group of dingy old houses surround the courtyard, all of
> them built on different levels and in different times, with
> modern passages cut through. So that the sightseer is always
> going up or down two or three steps or losing himself in blind
> hallways that lead nowhere, or coming unexpectedly back to
> where he started from. The stone stairway leading to the
> upper offices has been channeled in the centre by a flood of
> four centuries of passing shoes, so that it is worn away
> almost to an inclined plane instead of a flight of staccato
> steps. Over everything, in everything, and through every-
> thing there are grime and gloom. The little windows are
> smokey; fog lies in the courtyard, and even the diffused day-
> light by which the Londoner distinguishes night from day is
> more vaporous and unsatisfactory here than elsewhere.[18]

Immediately after the Salford attack Vincent requested information on local Fenianism from the various police authorities,
hoping that such intelligence make it possible to discover plots
and allay 'panic'. While the Chief Constables were still free to
address Harcourt directly, Vincent was to be used as a clearing
house with assurances that full credit would be assigned to the
source of information. Arrangements proceeded for the protection of London's major buildings with Superintendent Gernon
of A Division having special responsibility for the Houses of
Parliament; six uniformed constables in two reliefs guarded the
Tower of London and extra precautions were taken by H Division at the Royal Mint. Fearing an IRB attempt to steal
weapons, the various volunteer arms stores, such as the Third
Middlesex Artillery, were either distributed to the individual
soldiers or the breechlocks removed and sent to police inspectors
at their private addresses. Chief Constables were requested by
the Officer Commanding Home Forces to patrol the outside of

army barracks; on 28 January Buckingham Palace had six additional constables added to its normal force. Harcourt had already written to Commissioner Henderson notifying him that he had asked the Chief Secretary for Ireland, W. E. Forster, to send an inspector to London to work with Howard Vincent on the anti-Fenian effort.

On 1 February 1881 the Cabinet withdrew Michael Davitt's ticket-of-leave which had been issued in 1877. The government, preparing to remove one famous Fenian from its midst, then had to face the legal limitations placed on the use of the army for civil duties. Troops in the Home District could not go out to assist the civil power without a written request from, and accompanied by, a magistrate, nor could they fire unless required by that magistrate. It was decided that if troops were required the situation should be reported to the Home Office and one of the Metropolitan Police magistrates would be made available. On 4 February Davitt was arrested on a Metropolitan Police warrant. The Secretary of State subsequently received a bill from the London and Northwestern Railway for £33; the cost of running a pilot engine from Holyhead to Euston to protect the train carrying Davitt back to London.[19] Davitt was sent back to prison apparently to complete the final seven years of his fifteen-year sentence.

Lomasney, meanwhile, was in Paris. Writing to Devoy on 23 February, he made his opinions very clear.

> Those foolish affairs in England are believed to be the work of O'D.R.'s men. The amount of folly and bungling in connection with these attempts are simply disgraceful. They will have to clear out at once. Osborne [John O'Connor of the IRB] has men on their track and is determined to stop such nonsense. If allowed to go on confusion and anarchy would be the result. Some of them have been trying to inveigle our men into their crazy schemes, and if they are not compelled to leave here immediately, we might as well have no organisation at all.[20]

Despite efforts of both the Clan and the IRB to stop the Rossa Skirmishers, two men, probably Patrick Coleman and Edward O'Donnell, slipped past their 'friends' and the detectives of Scotland Yard to plant their bomb at a building across from the Royal Exchange and the Bank of England which had long been a target for frustrated Londoners, the Mansion House, residence of the City's Lord Mayor. As early as 1848 special watchmen had been hired to protect Mansion House from the beggar women, who milled outside on its filthy footpaths. The women had been known to carry baskets of paving stones from some distance to smash its windows, as well as spending them on nearby banks and counting houses. The windows were eventually wired up but continued to be broken by the women by jabbing through the wire mesh with the steel busks from their stays.

Late on a foggy Wednesday night, 16 March 1881, Rossa's men headed for a carefully selected spot at the Mansion House to plant their bomb. They moved stealthily into the narrow alley of Church-passage. The target was the 'Egyptian Hall', designed by the Earl of Burlington and so-called from its similarity to the Egyptian Hall described by Vitruvius. The stained-glass windows of the hall were illuminated by large gas fittings set on the outside of the building and would have been lit had the Lord Mayor's banquet scheduled for that night not been cancelled because of the assassination of Czar Alexander II three days before. The hall would have also been filled with dignitaries of the city and nation.

The bomb constructed for this grand occasion was a flat wooden box twenty-four inches square and five inches high similar to a common deal packing case, filled with fifteen pounds of coarse blasting powder. Strongly bound with iron hoops, the box was pierced in the middle where a fuse had been inserted. An obviously heavy parcel, it was carefully wrapped in brown paper and placed in a recess fenced in by an iron railing immediately below the east window of the Egyptian Hall. The recess, formerly a window, offered a convenient ledge for the parcel. The fuse was lit under the unexpectedly empty hall and the bombers fled with only a matter of minutes in hand because the beat of the duty constable took him past this 'very lonely and deserted' spot every quarter of an hour.

At 11.30 p.m. Constable Samuel Cowell discovered the parcel and smouldering fuse. He hurriedly put out the burning wrapping paper and fuse only an inch from the powder, and carried the unexploded device off to Bow Lane police station. The attempt had failed.

The Commissioner of the City of London Police, Colonel James Fraser, offered the Corporation's reward of £100 for the capture of the culprits. But nothing was known about them except what might have been surmised from the bomb itself. The powder was found to be at one end of the box, while stuffed into the other end to take up the remaining space were remains of an old carpet bag, some brown paper, two American newspapers, one Glasgow and one Irish newspaper of recent date, and a linen bag in which the powder had evidently been purchased. The bombers had hoped to provide the unforgettable event of a lifetime for the diners, and even if aware of the cancellation they presumably decided that they must act that night, possibly because of the travel arrangements designed to spirit them out of Scotland Yard's clutches.

It was immediately obvious that the abortive outrage had been the work of a group connected with Irish independence. *The Times* (18 March 1881) suggested that the choice of the target might have been connected with the current Lord Mayor, Mr Alderman M'Arthur, an Irishman, being in residence at the Mansion House. He had, according to the paper, angered his Lambeth Irish constituents by supporting the recent Irish Coercion Act. Exactly a week later *The Times* identified the bombing as the work of Patrick Coleman, Edward O'Donnell and possibly Thomas J. Mooney; only Coleman's name was associated with the attempt in O'Donovan Rossa's paper the *United Irishman* (23 April). The British Consul in Philadelphia, Clipperton, sent the Foreign Office a cutting from the *Philadelphia Times* (12 April) implicating Coleman and O'Donnell, while Mooney's name was associated with the attempt by the *New York Herald* (17 April). There was little doubt that the United Irish Reserve Fund had attempted to make its second payment. Sir Henry Ponsonby came to the Home Office on Friday 18 March to say that the Queen was nervous about Buckingham Palace being blown up and wished to have precautions taken about it. It was also clear that the violent death of the Czar had made an impression upon the Queen.[21]

The Queen was not alone in her concern, for Lomasney, still in Paris, notified the Revolutionary Directory that he was ready to begin the proposed 'work' if required. He also made it quite clear that at least twenty times the sum initially allocated would be required to do the job properly. Two draft receipts in Lomasney's hand dated 26 January indicate that the sum was $5,500; Lomasney was talking of $100,000 for a dynamite campaign of the intensity required to achieve Irish freedom.²² Lomasney was deeply concerned about the terrible revenge which would be exacted upon the Irish living in England if such a campaign took place. Personally he did not judge the time right for such an attack either in means or resources. If however the threats of mass eviction in Ireland were carried out he was prepared to proceed, noting that the 'difficulty would be in stopping when once we commence and defending and protecting those on whom vengeance would be wreaked'. Explosions had to be used as a force of retaliation and not allowed to precipitate violence. The 'little captain' appears to have been in Ireland during the excitement following the attempted bombing at the Mansion House, for he claims that it had been severely condemned by 'the most patriotic and sensible portion of our country people, not alone because they were ridiculous and stupid in the manner of carrying them out, but because they were wholly, or nearly so, unjustifiable at present'. He was clearly relieved that the explosion had failed because the 'loss of life and numbers of good men would have suffered in a way that certainly you [Devoy] and I would ever deplore'. The philosophy of war which Lomasney was prepared to defend was summed up simply: 'the act is not only justifiable but that it will be conducive to the welfare of our cause'. On those grounds alone would his revolutionary activity be judged and when his acts conformed to his philosophy, as they must, he was prepared to defend his work in the dock even with death or imprisonment before him.²³

Looking at Ireland, and the tremendous build-up in Land League activity, from the safety of Paris, he felt that although it was wholly justifiable to resist eviction, had the 'governing body' (RD or the IRB Supreme Council, more likely the former) considered whether it was conducive to the cause in the long run? Lomasney's opinion was that it was best to work on quietly until the people of Ireland were adequately armed and thus in a position to defend themselves. Guns were being smuggled into Ireland (paid for by the Clan) and distributed through the IRB channels even though the recent effort to recruit John

c

J. Kelly as the principal agent had failed; the $10,000 advanced for the project was to be returned. Lomasney stressed that the Clan had to provide the arms direct or send a great deal of money for purchasing arms on the continent. Until they had a good stock of arms on hand it was 'folly to be talking of revolution or even thinking of engaging in anything that may force a crisis'. Efforts were still being made to get 'pipes'— cannons. Regardless of Lomasney's detailed plan of action he makes it quite clear in his correspondence with John Devoy that he was prepared to do the job which he had agreed to do before leaving the United States. And yet he would not consider any other enterprise unless there was a marked deterioration in the situation in Ireland for 'to do so would be mad, criminal and suicidal'. Resignation would be his answer to an unjustifiable change of plans.

He was less worried about what the RD might or might not do than the futile efforts of Rossa's men, 'men incapable of carrying out his insane designs'. Rossa had to be stopped in his criminal acts because they compromised the Irish Republican Brotherhood 'without their knowledge or consent'. Upon his return to France from Ireland, Lomasney had sought permission from the RD via telegraph, to 'run these fellows right back again'. His greatest fear was that such idiotic attacks made the cause appear 'imbecile and farcical'. Irish revolutionaries appeared to be a 'lot of fools and ignoramuses, men who do not understand the first principles of the art of war, the elements of chemistry or even the amount of explosive material necessary to remove or destroy an ordinary brick or stone wall'. Lomasney, with the disgust of a professional, asked what could be more pitiful than using common blasting powder to 'scare and shatter the empire'?[24]

One person who took his absence from Detroit very seriously was his wife Susan—Mrs 'Waldron'—who wrote to her William regularly care of Dr John O'Leary, Hotel Corneille, Rue Corneille, Paris. O'Leary had the task of getting 'Mr Waldron's' mail to him, which on occasions took rather a long time. At the end of April, O'Leary complained to Devoy that Lomasney's wife was flooding him with letters about delays and although he would do a great deal more for Lomasney, 'I don't want to do what is quite unnecessary even for him'. If she knew what he was doing in Europe she had reason for concern. In addition to moving about Ireland and Britain selecting potential targets for attack and worrying about Rossa's men, Lomasney was continuing his dynamite experiments as well as producing and stockpiling explosives, probably in French and English depots. Concern about the Rossa men reached such a level that on 20 April he telegraphed his RD contact, William Connolly, from London :

> 'CONNOLLY LABOUR BUREAU, CASTLEGARDEN, N.Y.
> Barrow [Devoy] request statistic late shipping emigrants fast as possible with funds can now carry out agreements within time specified, all departments working well.'
>
> (no signature)[25]

The cover for this message was quite plausible in that Lomasney was posing as an emigration agent representing the Connolly Labour Bureau. As such it would have been his job to recruit emigrants and to be responsible for their travel arrangements to the United States where they would have been found employment by the bureau. This service would have been part of the overall cost of their immigration. The message to John Devoy was an urgent query as to who the Rossa agents were and any information as to descriptions. The phrase 'with funds can now carry out agreements within time specified' may have been part of the business 'cover' and without any code meaning; while 'all departments working well' was the agreed assurance that all was well in Paris. No record of a reply remains. On Friday, 15 July John O'Connor, the IRB representative on the RD and Lomasney's associate, wired Devoy that they were leaving for the United States on the following Tuesday. Not a bomb had been detonated by them in anger. What the two men left in France, England, and Ireland in terms of organisation and explosives is a matter for speculation, but the implications are that the work which had taken them five months to complete had been done to Lomasney's satisfaction.

At this time Clan na Gael was also taking further steps to put the organisation on a war footing. The closing accounts of the National (Skirmishing) Fund of 31 May 1881 were presented to the Clan's national convention which met in the first week of August at the Palmer House in Chicago. The accounts showed that the total costs of the submarine development amounted to $27,387.57, to which was added John Breslin's salary of $2,090.20. The submarine was valued, along with torpedoes, as an asset of that sum, plus the balance on hand of $38,545.82, thus giving total assets of $65,933.39. To this sum was added a loan of $12,000 to the *Irish World* to repair the rift between the Clan and Patrick Ford. Expenditures were listed at $13,520.10 for various revolutionary purposes, which would have included contributions to the IRB for administrative needs, money for smuggling guns into Ireland, trips to Ireland by Devoy and Carroll to co-ordinate activity with the Supreme Council of the home organisation, and the recent reconnaissance carried out by Captain Lomasney and John O'Connor. Major Le Caron sent a copy of the audit to London and for the first time the British government had evidence of the existence of a Fenian submarine.[26]

With the election of a prominent Chicago lawyer, Alexander Sullivan, as the new president of the Clan came the beginnings of a new era within the secret organisation. Prior to this convention the executive body (FC) had been composed of a chairman, secretary, treasurer, and eleven district members. Adopting the position that future operations would require the strictest secrecy, the executive would be limited to five men, plus an *ex officio* secretary. There would be no ENs (district members) represented in the future. The tightening of security against lurking British spies required some explanation to the rank and file of the eleven districts. The FC therefore had sent a circular to the membership 31 August/1 September 1881 with instructions that it should be read twice and then burnt. Significantly the Revolutionary Directory (RD) of the Clan/IRB provided a covering statement approving the changes in the organisation. The new five-man executive was composed of Sullivan, Michael Boland of Louisville, Kentucky, James Feely of Rochester, New York, Dr John D. Carroll of Brooklyn, New York, James Reynolds of New Haven, Connecticut and James Treacy of New York, who was the secretary. The main point of the circular was to assure the members that the FC and the RD were doing their respective jobs in a most efficient manner, the

money in the National Fund was being used on behalf of the
achievement of Irish independence, and that in the future a
shroud of secrecy must fall over the work of the Clan to protect
its revolutionary agents from detection by the enemy. The Clan's
membership had to be patient, silent about what they did know,
zealous in their continued financial support, and confident in
their democratically-elected leaders.[27]

After its launching in May 1881, Holland's new boat had
been towed from the New York construction yard across the
Hudson River to the Morris Canal Basin where she remained
until 3 July during which time the first set of tests were carried
out. The boat, leaden in colour, was thirty-one feet long, six
feet in beam, and drew seven feet four inches with a gross
displacement of nineteen tons. An improved Brayton petrol
engine was installed and produced something like fifteen h.p., and
drove the boat at about nine miles per hour on the surface.
Having sought to build his boat as nearly like the lines of a
porpoise as his rather primitive engineering permitted, the boat
may well have been able to exceed five or six miles per hour
submerged. The three-man crew was located in a central compartment and the 'ram', which conceivably could have been used
to 'hole' an enemy ship below the water line, was armed with a
pneumatic gun with a nine-inch tube, some eleven feet long.
The weapon was a six-foot projectile designed to carry a 100 lb
charge of gunpowder fired with a four hundred-pound charge
of compressed air. Even when firing the projectiles of Captain
John Ericsson, famous for his association with the USS
Monitor, the weapon proved to be a failure. From 3 July the
boat did trials in New York harbour and with all of that activity
there was no longer any secret concerning the existence of the
craft and the British consulate in New York had merely to read
the newspapers.[28]

At the end of July, little more was known about the actual
boat than its colour. This ignorance continued throughout
August and the chargé d'affairs in Washington, Drummond,
informed Lord Granville that, since Captain R. C. Clipperton
appeared to be 'completely in the inside track', he recommended
that Clipperton's present informers have their pay continued.
Clipperton was prepared to apply to the Federal authorities to

have the boat detained if it appeared in the Delaware River at Philadelphia.

At the end of July the Washington legation was able to provide some details on the submarine and its movements. Delamater's in New York was identified as the builder; the boat had then been taken to the Morris Canal near Jersey City. Later it was found five miles from New York in a secluded spot on the bay partially submerged and almost hidden from view. The British report sent to the State Department stressed that 'this is presumably a Fenian enterprise for the purpose of an attempt to blow up British war vessels'. John Breslin had been identified as one of the men taking part in the vessel's tests. Since the boat was claimed to have the 'most wonderful power as a destructive machine' the British government requested that US Marshals be called out to prevent the ship from leaving United States' jurisdiction. The federal government did not reply.[29] Drummond had a personal interview with the American Secretary of State, James G. Blaine, on 31 August during which the British diplomat was assured that if the boat did exist the American government would take action. Blaine added that if bombs or ships killed American citizens, no Irishman's life would be safe. Nevertheless, despite such assurances, most Americans in responsible positions considered that 'the whole business was nonsense and nothing worse than Irish vapouring'.[30]

In November 1880 evidence had emerged that Fenians were prepared to build a submarine for use against Great Britain. At least that is what James McClintock told Consul Crump and Captain Arthur, the British Naval Attaché in Washington. It was McClintock who, along with Baxter Watson, had built the CSS *Hunley*. Although operating on the surface, it was the first submarine to sink an enemy vessel, the USS *Housatonic* at Charleston, South Carolina, 17 February 1864. McClintock told his British contacts that he had been approached by un-named 'Fenians' in hopes that he would build a submarine and torpedoes for them. Instead he offered his services to the British government for $200 per month. A plan was suggested in which the American would make the torpedoes, sell them, and then give the British agents information as to where they went and to whom. In addition to his salary, he would have received a reward if the plan succeeded. The idea was rejected presumably because if it had been discovered by the United States government, McClintock would have been gaoled and Crump and Arthur expelled for spying. The Foreign Office was looking for co-operation, not a *cause célèbre*! If McClintock had received a serious offer then it was most likely from Rossa's United Irish Fund's Skirmishers: even more likely is the possibility that the Fenian 'offer' was simply another hoax.[31]

The Philadelphia Consulate had also reported (24 March 1881) that a wrought ironsmith had invented explosives in the form of coal loaded with dynamite to be thrown into Her Majesty's warships' coal bunkers and other steamers and that the only thing holding up the production of the bombs was Rossa's lack of money for the project. Then came the explosion which sank HM Sloop *Doterel*, off Sandy Point in the Straits of Magellan. Only eleven of the crew survived the tragedy out of a complement of one hundred and fifty-six officers and men. When Rossa claimed responsibility there were many prepared to believe him, even though an Admiralty Court of Enquiry suggested that the cause was a gas explosion resulting from badly ventilated coal bunkers. Whatever the cause it doubtless encouraged contributions to Rossa's own skirmishing fund.[32]

The search for other Skirmishers by Lomasney and O'Connor had failed to locate James McGrath, living in Liverpool under the alias of Robert William Barton. McGrath was twenty-seven years old and had been born in Glasgow of Irish parents. Living in Dundee for some time, he found work as a steward on a ship operating between Scotland and London. Eventually he emigrated to the United States where he initially lived in New Orleans before moving north to New York. Although McGrath himself was never to admit it, *The Times* of 11 June 1881 reported that he then came under the instructions of Rossa to mount a series of attacks in the north of England. It is probable that McGrath was the bomber of Salford Barracks, using gunpowder in that instance. Sometime after his arrival in Liverpool, McGrath contacted a thirty-two year old Liverpool dock labourer, James McKevitt, born in Warrenpoint, County Down. McKevitt had worked in the docks since 1870 and was now living at 11 Naylor Street where the postman delivered McKevitt's personal copy of Rossa's *United Irishman* newspaper, still freely circulated in England if not in Ireland itself. Posing as a cattle dealer, McGrath was to share lodgings with McKevitt from 15 April.

Their first target was to be Liverpool's main police station on Dale Street. Since the attacks at the Salford Barracks and London's Mansion House the public buildings of Liverpool had been under close surveillance especially since the city justifiably considered itself to be the most vulnerable in the kingdom as the main port of entry from North America. No building was better guarded than the main police station but then again that made the bombers all the more eager to penetrate the security. After careful observation, they decided they could do it by placing the explosive device in the doorway of the 'section-house' or barracks which was attached to the main building on the Hatton Garden side. The bomb was a piece of iron pipe sixteen inches long and three inches in diameter with each end firmly plugged up with a fuse inserted through one of the plugs which had been drilled and set with tar. The time chosen was just before midnight on the night of Monday 16 May 1881. McGrath, finding the doorway deserted and the patrol which was responsible for its security on another portion of its beat, lit the twisted wick fuse and placed the bomb in the doorway between the vestibule and outer door. Its explosion shook the building but because the gunpowder had been loosely poured in, rather than tamped hard, the pipe did not disintegrate : only the end of the devise blew out, causing limited damage to the door and windows. It was assumed that the device was meant to 'harass the police, who have already been put to much inconvenience by reports of Fenian intentions'. At least this was the opinion of *The Times* (18 May 1881). There was no sign of the bomber or bombers and while the police continued to search, particularly amongst the city's large Irish population, McGrath and McKevitt began preparations for a more serious attack.

This time they prepared to use the commercial dynamite which had been smuggled in from the United States. One of their first acts was to change lodgings to a house in the Kensington district on about the first of June. Here they collected two large sections of cast iron ($\frac{5}{8}$ inch thick) water or gas main, which had recently been renewed in the neighbourhood, one of which they proceeded to plug with two inch sections of deal after having filled the interior cavity with slabs of dynamite.

Detonator cartridges were inserted and a fuse admitted through a hole in one of the end plugs. The extremely heavy device was then packed in a large canvas seaman's bag and tied, leaving only the fuse exposed. The target was Liverpool's Town Hall.

In the early hours of Friday 10 June 1881, the two men, both armed with revolvers, carried the heavy load from their lodgings and up the steps of the west door of the Town Hall; they prepared to light the fuse. At 4 a.m. a cab driver named John Ross, searching for a fare, spotted the men as he was driving up Water Street. Thinking them to be sailors because of the large canvas bag he turned his horse along Exchange Street West, drew up and asked them if they wanted a cab. They said 'no' and he proceeded to the cab stand on Castle Street in front of the Town Hall. At almost that moment a twenty-six year old police constable, George Reade, a native of County Wexford, came around the corner from Castle Street in time to see a match being applied to the fuse. The constable immediately began blowing his whistle for assistance; McGrath and McKevitt ran for safety with Constable Reade close behind. When Reade dashed into Chapel Street he met Constable Creighton whom he told : 'Go back to the Town Hall, it is being set on fire. I saw them strike the match and heard the fuse'. Creighton, a former RIC officer, dashed back to the Town Hall where, with two other officers, he pulled the bag, which he could not lift by himself, down the steps on to the pavement. As one officer attempted to cut the string binding the bag, they suddenly took fright. Retreating just in time, the bomb exploded with a report described by one former artilleryman as that of a thirty-two pounder cannon. Reade had reached the point of exhaustion when the pursuit of the two fugitives was taken over by twenty-six year old Constable Casey, the son of Irish parents. He soon found McKevitt hiding under a wagon. Taken into custody, the bomber tossed a ten-shot pistol over a nearby wall. Casey turned the prisoner over to Creighton who, along with the other officers, had miraculously survived the explosion. Casey, a former soldier, now armed with McKevitt's pistol, carried on after McGrath, who had fallen into the nearby canal and then tried to hide in an empty coal barge. It was there that Casey captured him without a struggle.

McGrath at first gave his name as that of 'Barton' but later admitted his real name, refusing to give any additional information. In his pockets were found two bronze medals linked together. The larger one commemorating the Fenian Brotherhood carried on the obverse in large letters 'Ireland and America', with the date 1866 and a hand-in-hand emblem; on the reverse the emblem of a ship surmounted by 'Irish' and below it 'Republic', and the letters 'F' on the left side and 'B' on the right. The other medal was the smaller 'O'Connell medal' which carried the inscriptions of 'Ireland for the Irish', 'The Irish for Ireland', and 'Repeal Year, 1843'. One of the two men also carried a Roman Catholic prayer book in addition to dynamite detonators.[33]

The two prisoners were escorted to Walton Prison with a large police guard armed with Colt revolvers. Prison officials, responding to rumours of an escape attempt on Sunday, took special precautions. The area around the prison always attracted large gangs of men on Sunday mornings 'playing pitch-and-toss and indulging in questionable amusements' but the police put a stop to the projected cock fight of that morning. The concern was heightened by the large number of Irish navvies about, due to the construction of the Walton tramways.[34] On Wednesday the fifteenth Chief Inspector Williamson of Scotland Yard arrived to see what he could learn from Liverpool's good fortune. Although McGrath carried a notebook with Fenian addresses and information there were no further arrests. Williamson's primary job was to see if he could link McGrath with Coleman and Mooney, the two men connected with the Mansion House attack. Scotland Yard sent another inspector to Liverpool together with a couple who lived in Spring Street, Marylebone who made unsworn identification of McGrath as a man who back in April had asked for Coleman.[35] A search of the ashpit at the lodgings of McGrath and McKevitt revealed the other bomb, a piece of iron pipe with an internal diameter of four inches and eighteen inches long with plugged ends but lacking its dynamite charge. The landlady had thrown it there after having discovered it in the men's room. The ashpit was then dug up by the police in an unsuccessful effort to find additional dynamite. There had also been an explosion at the police station at Loanhead near Edinburgh on Sunday morning the twelfth but it was attributed to pranksters rather than having any Fenian significance. McGrath was sentenced to life imprisonment and McKevitt received twelve years. Police investigations had come to a dead end but at least there was common agreement that McGrath and McKevitt were two of O'Donovan Rossa's Skirmishers.

The Philadelphia Consul, Captain Clipperton, had been approached in mid-January by an informer offering information concerning the construction of five 'infernal machines' locally. They were to be built for Clan na Gael and delivered on 15 February 1881.

> These 'infernal machines' were described to me as being made of galvanized iron, not quite the $\frac{1}{16}$ of an inch thick, and measuring overall eight inches in length by three and a half inches square, weighing when not charged two and a half to three lbs. The interior of each case contains twelve tubes five inches in length, each one containing about one lb. of explosive mixture. In the end of the outer case is left a space for the machinery which is set in motion by a very simple kind of clockwork.

He estimated that each tube could contain the destructive force of up to eighty pounds of gunpowder, providing a bomb that had the explosive force of 960 pounds of gunpowder. Clipperton requested $1,000 in order to penetrate the plot and prevent its spread to England or Ireland; a small price, he noted, compared to the possible damage of life and property if the plot succeeded. Clan na Gael was reportedly paying as much for each of the five bombs. The British Minister to Washington, Sir Edward Thornton, sanctioned the payment of the informer and by 9 July, Clipperton informed the Foreign Office that he still had confidence in the man's reports. The informer was the 'manufacturer of the torpedo and infernal machine samples' which Clipperton had sent through the legation on 30 March. The situation was serious for the bombs had apparently been shipped from Boston in late June by a man named Charles Mills for the Phoenix Manufacturing Company. The real shippers were in fact Patrick Burke and Patrick Coleman. If this were true then the bombs had been made for the Skirmishers and not for the Clan, as Clipperton's informer reported. Three of the machines had been shipped separately, one on the *Ethiopia* for Glasgow, another on the *James Grice* for Plymouth and the third on the *Canada* for Le Havre. Clipperton telegraphed the following in cypher from Philadelphia at 8 p.m. on 7 July to the Foreign Office:

> Knowledge of seizure must be kept from the Press in view of further seizures. Interior chambers must not be examined. They are fitted with friction fuse certain to explode. Three more have been sent. Fifteen others to be delivered to conspirators next week.[36]

There was no mistaking the urgency of the matter and copies were sent to Gladstone, Harcourt and W. E. Forster, the Chief Secretary for Ireland.

Clipperton's warnings plus the knowledge that McGrath had smuggled the Liverpool dynamite in from America brought increased customs surveillance at Liverpool. On 30 June they found six 'infernal machines' in barrels marked 'cement' on board the SS *Malta* out of New York. This was followed by the discovery of two more bombs of the same variety on the SS *Bavaria* on 2 July. As in the instance of the McGrath bomb, Professor J. Campbell Brown was called in to do the analysis of the new 'infernal machines'. The device was the most sophisticated yet seen for it involved a zinc cannister containing eleven slabs of Atlas dynamite and was to have been detonated by a built-in pistol device actuated by a clockwork mechanism. One of the barrels was returned to the Boston shipping agents for identification but the inquiry proved fruitless despite the fact that Consul Edwards in New York had discovered an instrument maker in the city who claimed to have made some clockwork mechanisms of the variety found in the Liverpool bombs. Edwards did not know how far Her Majesty's government was willing to go in pursuing a matter which was really in the jurisdiction of the United States.[37]

The infernal machines of Consul Clipperton never arrived, because the whole matter turned out to be a hoax. Nor was it the only hoax, for Sir Augustus Paget, the British Ambassador in Rome, received the translation of a letter sent to the acting consul in Leghorn. The anonymous author of the letter claimed that a respected 'friend' talking to four workmen from the province of Lucca found that they had just returned from Boston where they had been involved in turning coal dust into bricks which contained glass or tin tubes and small tin cases which had been inserted with utmost care. They also drilled holes in large lumps of coal and filled the cavity with a greenish heavy liquid. Both of these items were explosive designed to be deposited in the coal stores of British steamers. The Home Secretary received a copy of this information from the Foreign Office on 3 November.[38] It was becoming increasingly difficult to sift the true threat from the hoax. The problem of explosives was serious enough in Great Britain where reports coming into Scotland Yard established that there were 100,000 lbs of high explosives at Nobel's Explosives, 149 West George St, Glasgow, alone, not to mention that held by other companies and private individuals.

Scotland Yard detectives attempted to keep watch over the activities of the Irish and Irish-American 'plotters' in Paris who frequented the Cafe du Rond Pont, Avenue de la Grande Armeé and the English & American Bar, Rue Royale, which was kept by a Fenian named Reynolds. There was also an Irish Club on the Champ de Mars. The scattered reports suggest little more than the detectives pathetic dependence upon elderly female window cleaners. The situation regarding co-operation from the United States government was even bleaker. The only glimmer of hope arose out of the celebration commemorating the centenary of the British surrender at Yorktown during the War of Independence. The British minister had found it diplomatically inconvenient to attend the festivities in person but that did not prevent the Americans from saluting the British flag during the ceremony. Granville took the opportunity to telegraph Her Majesty's government's appreciation of the act and received the reply that Secretary of State Blaine was pleased to receive it, mentioning that 'one of the reasons for doing so was to show the Irish here, the true feelings of the American government for England'.[39] Far more tangible expressions of Anglophilia would however be required if the combined threat of Clan na Gael and Rossa's Skirmishers was to be defeated. Granville must have wondered if there was any way of getting the American government to take the requisite action against the bombers' home organisations. Thornton, before he left

Washington to take up the post of Ambassador to St Petersburg, had offered him the following advice:

> Americans are so exceedingly vain about their Country and at the same time so sensitive that they immensely appreciate any compliment that may be paid to them from England, especially by any member of the Royal Family. So that, although it is certainly necessary firmly to maintain any principle when we are sure that it is right, I have never met with people who are so open to the flattery of a little courtesy from the higher classes of the old country.[40]

Only time would tell.

3

Spymaster-general

Few Governments in the world have been so badly served
with particular information concerning the identification and
pursuit of criminals as that of Ireland. . . .
Illustrated London News, 17 June 1882.

THE political confrontation of the autumn and winter of
1881–2 had been for the most part provoked by Parnell. Despite
what seemed in retrospect clear warnings from the prime minister
that he must moderate his criticism of the government's new
Land Act, Parnell continued his unrelenting attacks upon the
Liberals. Gladstone issued a public warning in a speech he gave
at Leeds on 7 October 1881 in which he said that Parnell
desired 'to arrest the operation of the Land Act, to stand as
Moses stood, between the living and the dead; to stand there,
not as Moses stood, to arrest but to extend the plague'. Parnell's
response was to characterise the prime minister as 'a masquerad-
ing knight-errant'. Any doubts that had existed in the mind of
the cabinet were temporarily suspended and on 13 October the
government ordered the arrest of Parnell, John Dillon, and John
J. O'Kelly. They were jailed at Kilmainham along with other
'suspects' under the provisions of the Coercion Act.

Regardless of the Land League's opposition to the Land Act
which it saw as wholly inadequate, the act had in its way
largely beaten the League. Parnell intimated to his mistress,
Katharine O'Shea, that a few months in prison would not be a
bad thing as far as his political leadership was concerned. He
also anticipated that Land League agitation would be replaced
with rural violence led by the 'moonlighters' and 'Captain
Moonlight'. Between January of 1881 and Parnell's arrest in
October there had been nine murders, five cases of manslaughter
and thirty-two instances of 'firing at the person'. The statistics
rose dramatically in the next six months, producing fourteen

murders and sixty-one cases of 'firing at the person'.

The implications of this acceleration in violence were 'clear' to Gladstone and a strong body of British public opinion; the coercion policy so favoured by the viceroy, Lord Cowper, and W. E. Forster, his chief secretary, was inadequate. As it happened, a set of reciprocal needs culminated in the formation of a new policy. Gladstone needed Parnell's aid to stifle Irish opposition to the government's land reforms, and the Irish leader could be courted for his own political need to regain personal control of the Irish members at Westminster. Furthermore, his daughter born to Mrs O'Shea on 16 February had just died and Parnell had good cause to want to be by her side. Largely, therefore, through the efforts of Joseph Chamberlain, the Kilmainham treaty emerged, whereby the government for its part agreed to deal with the question of those tenants who were in arrears with their rent, often through no fault of their own, while extending the coverage of the act to leaseholders; and Parnell for his part agreed to accept the Land Act of 1881 as a practical solution and to use his influence to depress the level of violence in the countryside. Accordingly, on 2 May 1882, Parnell, Dillon and O'Kelly were released from Kilmainham jail—W. E. Forster resigned from the Cabinet in protest over the 'deal'—and there seemed to be signs of hope that the confrontation between Gladstone's government and the Irish nationalists in the Commons might be resolved and the agrarian crisis averted before the viceroy and his Irish government had a proper revolt to suppress.[1]

At that moment Major Le Caron was preparing a report for Robert Anderson at the Home Office noting that an influential American Fenian had just received a letter from the treasurer of the Land League, Patrick Egan, promising to visit the United States in the near future. Le Caron's information gave Anderson the impression that the Kilmainham agreement would have the effect of undercutting the arrangements reached earlier in 1881 between the Land League and Clan na Gael's American equivalent. He surmised that if Egan was subjected to pressure in the United States, remembering that most of the League's budget came from transatlantic donations, it might lead to the abandonment of the present policy of conciliation. The policy had been agreed upon without reference to the Americans, who clearly wished the struggle to go on unabated. On the other hand if the League did not respond to the anticipated American initiative, Anderson guessed that it would provoke a 'revival of [American] Fenianism pure and simple before the close of the year, and a demand probably for special powers to enable the govt. to cope with it'. Either way, 1882 looked to be a severely trying time for both Ireland and England.

Gladstone, tiring of coercion, was prepared to replace not only his chief secretary for Ireland but also his viceroy, having already accepted Cowper's resignation of 29 April. Cowper's resignation had been agreed before the Kilmainham Treaty and was unconnected with the prime minister's policies. The choice of a successor was a particularly apt one : Gladstone selected the lord president of the council, Earl Spencer, who had served in that post during his first Liberal government of 1868–74. Accompanying Spencer to Dublin was the engagingly 'whiggish' younger brother of Lord Hartington, Lord Frederick Cavendish, who reluctantly accepted Gladstone's invitation to be the new chief secretary. Cavendish almost missed the train from Euston to Holyhead on the evening of 5 May, a Friday.

Also in the party was Edward George Jenkinson, one of Spencer's private secretaries. Educated at Harrow and the East India Company's Haileybury College, he had gone out to India as a young man arriving there in 1856 on the eve of the Mutiny. Decorated for bravery during those months of atrocity, he had remained for twenty-three years, serving as joint magistrate and deputy collector of Benares and afterwards Farukabad, divisional commissioner of Jhansi and afterward Oudh. A distinguished career in the company and later in the viceroy's administration had been brought to an abrupt end by failing health. Jenkinson had been forced to return to England in late 1879. His family connections did not fail him and he soon found a position for the next two years as private secretary to his first cousin, Lord Northbrook, then at the Admiralty; it was a post which provided him with employment commensurate with neither his needs, his ability, nor his aspirations. That was not the life for a self-assured governor of men from the empire's furthest frontier.

Dublin was oceans away from Delhi and the pageantry of the

raj could not be compared with the festivities associated with Spencer's official arrival in Dublin on the next day, Saturday. Was it possible for Jenkinson to compare the problems that faced the viceroy in keeping a vast subcontinent or a relatively small island in subjugation under the British crown? Ireland had never suffered a bloodbath of the magnitude of the Indian Mutiny in 1857, but even as India remained superficially tranquil because of the coercion of the British regiments and the British-officered native Sepoys, Ireland was also a nation suppressed by the force of arms. Comparisons and contrasts were inevitable in the mind of Jenkinson, a man who moved with the air of one accustomed to authority. Whatever the differences between these two ends of the empire, Ireland offered him an escape from the frustrations of Westminster where he was condemned to wander rootless in the corridors of power; he needed a seat in power. While he could not return to the Oudh or the Jhansi, Ireland, the nearest of the imperial frontiers, made it possible for the forty-seven year old Jenkinson to begin anew. Although arriving as a secretary to the viceroy, he was in the cockpit of power from which a man of his proven ability and ambition was bound to achieve a position of eminence. He knew how to govern backward peoples even when they resisted the benefits of British rule.

Jenkinson soon learned how those benefits were dispensed from Dublin Castle, the centre of Irish administration. Situated in mainly eighteenth-century buildings above the southern banks of the Liffey, Ireland's government was headed by the lord lieutenant or viceroy, usually a politically active member of the English protestant aristocracy. He was assisted by his chief secretary (sometimes a cabinet minister at Westminster), a number of law officers, including a lord chancellor and an attorney-general, all political appointments. The chief secretary was in Dublin for about six months out of the year. His power depended in part upon the strength of the viceroy and his own political acumen, since he was minister with parliamentary responsibility for Ireland. He in turn was assisted by an under secretary, who was effectively Ireland's head of executive government. As a former magistrate, Jenkinson was particularly interested in the men immediately responsible for the maintenance of law and order. These were the eighty-one Resident Magistrates scattered across the island—nine of whom had been appointed since the agitation began in 1879—and since 1881 six Special Resident Magistrates located in the most difficult counties. The Special RMs had been selected from the body of the Resident Magistrates and had been directly responsible to the former chief secretary, W. E. Forster. Behind the magistrates stood the para-military Royal Irish Constabulary of 14,500 men, the Dublin Metropolitan Police, and, at time of grave trouble, 30,000 soldiers. The investigative organisations available for ferreting out crime were the 'G' Division or detective force of the DMP, led by the famous Inspector John Mallon, and the Crime Branch of the RIC located in Dublin Castle's Lower Yard. These organisations were constantly involved in solving and preventing the crimes and atrocities which characterised Ireland in the minds of the English.

Late on the afternoon of Saturday, 6 May 1882 when Spencer and his party arrived to the crowds and parades of the official ceremonies, the forty-six year old Cavendish left the Castle on the south bank of the Liffey, which divided Dublin from east to west, determined to walk home the two or three miles to the chief secretary's lodge in Phoenix Park. He knew the city well because he had been there during his brother's tenure as chief secretary. Covering almost one-half of the distance and just entering the gates of the park, the largest enclosed park in Europe, he began the steady climb along the footpath which bordered the wide avenue. He was then joined by the permanent under secretary for Ireland, Thomas Burke. Burke, the government's senior administrator, also lived in the park, in an official residence with his sister, and had taken a cab from the Castle but got out just beyond the park entrance.

The two men continued up into the park in close conversation, passing the cricket grounds and the polo field. When they reached a spot almost directly in front of the viceregal lodge, a cab pulled up beside them, four men leaped out and stabbed them to death, scrambled back into the cab and escaped through the park's southern entrance leading to Chapelzod Bridge. The assassins left black-edged cards at the newspaper offices announcing that the murders were the work of the 'Irish Invincibles', a group unheard of until that moment.

Earl Spencer had earlier left the Castle with an aide-de-camp and a groom and returned to the viceroy's residence, later going out with same escort 'to ride for exercise'. He rode down to see Burke's sister about a half mile to the northwest and as he was passing through the park on his way back to the lodge, he recalled (seven years later): 'I thought should I take a canter down the grass, or should I take a short cut home. I was very tired and took the short cut. I did not see Mr Burke and Lord Frederick Cavendish, but they were actually walking down the very piece of grass which I should have cantered down and the murderers were lying in wait for them at that moment. I had stopped to see a polo match and had got off my horse for a short time and stood within a few yards of [James] Carey who was on his way to the ambush.

> I had gone upstairs in the viceregal lodge and was looking out of the window over the Park talking with a member of my family when I heard a wild cry and saw a man running towards the house and waving his hands and shouting out murder. We all ran down to the door and he came up and said two men had been stabbed close by. He pointed to the place, which we could see quite distinctly. . . . I wished at once to go out to the place and see for myself what had happened, but my staff refused to have this as they thought it might be a mere ruse and that someone might be lying in wait to do me an injury, and in a very few minutes I learned the dreadful news of whom it really was that was killed. I could not but think that had I cantered down the turf I should have passed the band of murderers almost at the very time Lord Frederick Cavendish and Mr Burke reached them, and that the whole thing would have been stopped for they must have dispersed in the presence of three mounted men.

Spencer told Gladstone : 'They were killed about ten or sixteen yards apart. Mr Burke defended himself and his gloves were cut. He was stabbed in the face and neck and two other places, Freddy about the heart and in three other places. . . . They both, the surgeon says, must have died almost instantaneously. Freddy's face I hear was as if he was asleep; poor Burke showed the agony of a struggle'. The surgeon's assurances of an 'almost' instant death did little to overcome Spencer's painful conviction that he might have prevented the murders if he had followed his intention to take a 'canter down the grass'.[2]

The news of the assassinations was telegraphed to London that night and reached several members of the government at an Admiralty reception. They immediately left for Downing Street where a cabinet meeting was arranged for Sunday afternoon. By 11 p.m. most of London had heard the news. The next day the strawberry beds crowding the banks of the Liffey near the Phoenix Park were combed by police looking for the murder weapons while navy divers explored the river bed. Doctors who had seen the wounds assumed that they were made by 'bowie knives' used with deadly skill learned in the United States. Rumours were heard that the murderers were identifiable as Americans because of the 'cut of their clothes and whiskers'.

What was Robert Anderson at the Home Office to make of all this? He knew that he would have to prepare himself to speculate upon what group of men were responsible for the attacks, particularly if the attacks did bear the hallmarks of an Irish-American plot. When would he be summoned to the offices of the secretary of state, William Vernon Harcourt? Certainly he must hear from the Home Secretary before the 3 p.m. Cabinet. There was precious little information coming through from Dublin, certainly nothing he could add to the memorandum which he had sent to Harcourt the day before, predicting a 'revival of Fenianism, pure and simple, before the close of the year'. What could have been more prophetic?[3]

His secret work, which had been taken up during the Fenian panic of 1867–8, had promised him both financial security and professional advancement. In early 1868 he had accepted the opportunity to remain in London at the Irish Office, to liaise between Dublin Castle and the Home Office on Fenianism. Since the work came to involve almost exclusively English interests, he was eventually employed in the Home Office at the Prison Department. Six years Jenkinson's junior, Anderson had witnessed since that time the failure of all of his efforts to achieve increased salary or a more prestigious position, regardless of which party was in power. Finally reaching the limits of his patience, he had decided during that winter of 1881–2 to give up his unpaid and politically unrewarded secret service work, taking up the responsibility of advising an unnamed individual on the question of tariff reform. Now, however, the years of governmental indifference promised to be swept away and it would be to Anderson that the leaders of the Liberal government must turn. He was still in contact with Major Henri Le Caron who, although miserably paid for his efforts, occasionally sent personal reports to Anderson's home address. The ties of espionage had not yet been cut.

Gladstone's cabinet, which met that Sunday afternoon, faced the immediate requirements of Irish security. Earl Spencer, often referred to as the Red Earl because of his beard, had two security forces at his disposal, the Royal Irish Constabulary led by Colonel George E. Hillier and the Dublin Metropolitan Police under its Chief Commissioner Captain George Talbot, which included Inspector John Mallon's 'G' Division. The *Illustrated London News* characterised the RIC as 'an excellent but rather military force whose fidelity and bravery have recently been acknowledged by the distribution of special rewards to the amount of £180,000'. It was felt that this force was not suited to the demands of investigation and apprehension. On the other hand this journal could not find much of a complimentary nature to say about the DMP either:

> It seems questionable whether the Dublin Metropolitan Police be equally efficient; but neither one nor the other appears capable of the service of detective investigation. Few Governments in the world have been so badly served with particular information concerning the identification and pursuit of criminals as that of Ireland, under the system prevailing till the recent assassination. . . .[4]

To a large extent the viceroy shared these reservations in correspondence with Gladstone, indicating that he had asked for Hillier's resignation, who was by this time an invalid; Spencer expected to receive it the next day, 9 May. Not prepared to promote Hillier's deputy, Colonel Robert Bruce, he had written to him explaining the position and was most favourably impressed with Bruce's gentlemanly acceptance of the situation. As soon as he had received the resignation of the present inspector-general, Spencer planned to appoint in Hillier's place, Colonel Henry Brackenbury.[5]

At this time the British military attaché in Paris, Brackenbury's police experience had been limited to a successful tour of duty in Cyprus in 1878 when the Congress of Berlin had sanctioned the transfer of the island from Turkey to Great Britain. Brackenbury had been Military Secretary to Sir Garnet Wolseley, and accompanied the general when he was appointed chief commissioner of the island. He went out to Nicosia at the end of July 1878 as chief commandant of police and inspector of prisons. After setting up the Cypriot police he returned to London in April of the next year, subsequently declining the offer of the chief secretariat of Cyprus. Wolseley soon returned to London to go out to South Africa to deal with the Zulu War in early 1879 and again took Brackenbury with him. Following the conclusion of that imperial skirmish, Brackenbury became private secretary to the viceroy of India, Lord Lytton, and subsequently returned with Lytton to England after Lord Beaconsfield's government resigned in March 1880. On 1 January 1881 Brackenbury was appointed to the Paris embassy. As a member of the 'Wolseley ring' of bright young officers, with experience leading a military-style police force like the RIC, he was an obvious man to turn to, especially with Wolseley's recommendation. Arriving in London on leave at Charing Cross Station on Sunday evening, 7 May, he learned of the murders from a ticket inspector. Informing the War Office of his arrival, he arranged to call on the adjutant-general on Tuesday morning on the chance that the Duke of Cambridge, commander-in-chief of the army, might wish to see him. Brackenbury recalled:

Arriving at the Club [in Charles St, St James Square] on Monday evening, I heard that several messages had come during the day desiring me to call at the War Office, and there was a note for me from Mr Childers, the secretary of state, saying he wished to see me early on Tuesday. I called as desired and was shown into Mr Childers' room. He said, 'The government wish you to go to Ireland'. I asked in what capacity, and was told it was to take charge of the police. I did not wish to go, and said so. I said that my one wish was to see active service. I thought there would be war in Egypt, and hoped to be allowed to go. Mr Childers said 'It is war in Ireland, the government have selected you, and I do not think you can refuse'.[6]

The message was very clear. Brackenbury was on his way to Dublin Castle, his own preferences notwithstanding.

He was not the only person sent to Ireland to bolster Spencer's force of administrators : G. O. Trevelyan was selected to succeed Cavendish as chief secretary for Ireland after Charles Dilke's refusal because the position did not carry a seat in the cabinet; R. G. C. Hamilton was to be the acting chief under secretary while another India veteran, Colonel J. F. Bradford, went to the chief secretary's department. Spencer also forced the resignation of the chief commissioner of the DMP, Captain Talbot. Whether Robert Hamilton, who only a matter of days before had been appointed by Northbrook as under secretary of the Admiralty, had quite the same qualms about his appointment as Brackenbury is not known, but then he was a professional civil servant and not a soldier whose *raison d'etre* was war. The changes had been completed to Spencer's satisfaction by Tuesday night. He wrote to Gladstone the next day, the tenth, saying that he did not require further help.[7]

Within four days *The Times* (13 May) was in possession of the not unreasonable rumour that the government was calling for an unnamed, but experienced Indian official to organise a detective force—it could have been Jenkinson, Bradford, or as it turned out to be, Brackenbury, all having been in India at some time or another. The newspaper felt that it was the right move to make since it also had serious doubts about the ability of the RIC to perform that particular police function. Anxiety for the Queen's safety was apparent; the previous evening she returned to Windsor Castle with the route from the railway station protected by the borough constabulary. The international situation continued to deteriorate and it appeared that Great Britain was on the verge of intervening militarily in Egypt because of the palace coup which had brought the nationalist leader Colonel Arabi Pasha to power, thus threatening the heavy Anglo-French financial investments in the country. Brackenbury watched these developments keenly, as the papers carried the news that two ironclads had been ordered to Alexandria to take part in a show of force directed at intimidating the nationalist regime.

Brackenbury arrived in Dublin on Saturday 13 May without an official position, for Spencer had reconsidered his plan to appoint the English officer to the inspector-generalship of the

RIC. After receiving Hillier's resignation, Spencer decided to see Brackenbury before making the appointment. Spencer wrote to Gladstone that day saying that he had met Brackenbury and had found that he was 'able, intelligent and ready to do what the Public Service requires of him'. Four days later Spencer concluded that Brackenbury, with the title of Chief Special Commissioner, would be better used to set up a national detective force specifically to counter Fenian activity. Colonel Bruce, the deputy inspector-general of the RIC was to be promoted, preventing further anxiety and unrest in the constabulary. Much to the surprise of Bruce he found himself promoted to a position which ten days before had been denied him, a fit reward for loyalty and good manners.

What Spencer proposed was the creation of an effective detective service from the disjointed resources of the RIC and DMP. It was to be directed by an assistant under secretary for police and crime (Gladstone having rejected the original request for a Chief Special Commissioner) to be involved in all major executive problems including the use of troops on personal protection duty. On 17 May Spencer was still waiting for Treasury approval for the creation and funding of Brackenbury's new job. The Treasury said 'yes' and Ireland had its first 'spymaster-general'. *The Times* (22 May) was certain that Colonel Bruce's promotion would be 'regarded with confidence and satisfaction by the force and public' and that he was an officer of great experience and tried ability. Four days later the same paper reported Brackenbury's arrival in Dublin adding: 'Ten constables have been appointed to the detective department lately formed with Colonel Brackenbury at its head, and each stipendiary magistrate will have a detective to protect him and be in his vicinity at all times'. Brackenbury's job was to 'take charge of the police' (his words) from his newly created job and co-ordinate and supervise all of security agencies in Ireland while creating a secret intelligence section directly responsible to him—an expensive operation. This first stage alone would require an initial allocation of £5,000, an overall estimate being £20,000. Brackenbury threatened to resign if the money was not available, for without sustained investment on that scale the initial sum would be wasted; both Spencer and Trevelyan agreed. Money to be spent on spies and informers was not easily obtained and Spencer reminded the prime minister that over the past year or so, much more money than that for which Brackenbury had asked had been on offer in the form of un-collected rewards for information leading to the capture and conviction of Fenian agents. On 19 May a telegram from Spencer pleaded for action: 'Pray get necessary Cabinet sanc-tion to request of Brackenbury for Detection money'. Approval was given that day by telegram. It was followed by a request from Spencer on the twenty-first asking for written confirmation be put on the record but not through routine channels.

Brackenbury was finally appointed assistant under secretary for police and crime on 25 May. Lacking first-hand experience of Ireland's security problems he set out to pick the brains of the two Andersons, Vincent of Scotland Yard's CID, the head of Dublin's detectives, John Mallon and RIC County Inspector Reed. The secret report (31 May) that he then drew up for the consideration of Spencer and the cabinet stressed the strength and organisation of the Irish secret societies both in Ireland and the major cities of Great Britain, including London, Man-chester, Birmingham, Darlington, Tyneside, Glasgow and Dundee. In addition to a Fenian 'operational centre in Paris' the American cities of Chicago, Philadelphia and New York also bore watching with care. The present lull in Fenian activity, it was agreed, could be ascribed to an effort to aid the Irish parliamentary party's efforts to weaken the Crimes Bill then in passage through the House by making its stringency seem un-necessary. Brackenbury's brief association with the DMP and the RIC brought him to the same conclusion as that earlier cited by the *Illustrated London News*: that they were excellent at their particular jobs but unable to mount the required secret counter-offensive against Fenianism. Thus Brackenbury recom-mended the establishment of an extensive, secret and separate organisation which would break the nerve of the secret societies by infiltrating them, exposing them and then destroying them: 'If we can break up one secret society—if we can once make the leaders feel that there is no safety, that they are being betrayed —these terrible combinations will fall to pieces'. The counter-Fenian organisation would operate in total secrecy with its personnel chosen and directed by Brackenbury. The agents would be recruited from the RIC and DMP along with informers.

Police agents would never be allowed to commit illegal acts but informers would be promised protection and impunity for any acts short of felony. The cost, £20,000 per annum the colonel noted, was small compared to the many small imperial wars which had cost thousands of pounds. Gladstone was not prepared to pay the price and initially offered £5,000, which was rejected by Brackenbury as wholly inadequate. A compromise was finally reached whereby £25,000 would be available for two years. Thus began, with Gladstone's suggestions, a new departure in British police work.[8]

Spencer had as much reason as the Queen to fear assassination but he seems to have been little affected by the threat. He assured the prime minister on 26 May that he was optimistic and sleeping and eating quite well. His ability to cope doubtless had much to do with a lively sense of humour, if not of the ridiculous. Four days after this letter to Gladstone, he wrote to Harcourt enquiring if he had realised how nearly he had inadvertently caused Robert Hamilton to be shot? The Home Secretary had sent a coded telegram to Dublin describing a man reported by Edward Archibald, consul-general in New York, as potentially dangerous. Hamilton, as the under secretary, received it at 1 a.m. and not having the key to the cypher, got up, and accompanied by his principal secretary and two messengers 'drew up to the lodge' in Phoenix Park. While Hamilton and his entourage were apparently trying the windows(!), one of Spencer's ADCs was awakened to find two men with their faces hidden by mufflers up to their eyes trying to get in his window. His pistol was loaded and ready but fortunately they moved on before he got at the 'supposed robbers'. He then, quite beyond belief, went back to bed. The story was truncated in the telling, but Spencer used the selected details to chide Harcourt for sending an unimportant message in cypher. He concluded with some delight, 'but you may picture to yourself what an Irish ADC might have done'.[9]

The Home Secretary was doubtless amused by this and willing to concede the point especially since he himself was highly critical of much of the information secured through the consulates. He urged Spencer to warn Brackenbury that the purchase of information in the United States exposed one to the 'great danger of being the victim of deliberate plants ... for the sole

purpose of obtaining money by the very persons who have contrived [the crimes].[10] To some extent Harcourt's opinion had
been informed by Francis Percival Dewees' book, *The Molly
Maguires, The Origin Growth and Character of the Organisation* which had been published in Philadelphia in 1877. Dewees
described how the Pinkerton Detective Agency had infiltrated
the secret Irish-American society which terrorised the coal
region of Pennsylvania. Harcourt, impressed by the success of
the 'Pinkertons', recommended that Brackenbury (with the assistance of Archibald, the New York consul-general, who could
work out the arrangements) meet with one of their best secret
agents for advice on organisation and training, in addition to
employing the agency both in the United States and the United
Kingdom. Yet Brackenbury may have had reservations as to
how successful such undercover penetration would be in the
present circumstances, particularly since such an operation was
time-consuming as well as expensive: what was required were
quick results. The strategy that he adopted finally was to use
bribes and payoffs to undermine the Irish Republican Brotherhood and other secret societies, hoping to achieve success within
two years. Edward Hamilton recorded the results of a long
conversation with Brackenbury in his diary on Tuesday 20
June. While Hamilton found the estimate quite convincing, it
had risen from £20,000 to £50,000, which was not as much as
Lord Rosebery had spent gaining re-election at the last general
election. 'I have far more faith in this mode of going to work
to break up the secret organisations', wrote Hamilton, 'than in
such measures as the Crime Prevention Bill.'[11]

When Robert Anderson was asked to represent Brackenbury's
department in London, he twice refused 'in the most definite
way'. Harcourt then put on the pressure, which might have
included threats with reference to his continuance at the Prison
Board and provided encouragement in the form of 'liberal
remuneration'. Anderson then undertook the renewed role with
enthusiasm, apparently delighted with the prospect of some first-
hand sleuthing, as opposed to simply filtering information from
Le Caron through to the Home Secretary in a suitably disguised
form.

Brackenbury sent a Cork RIC officer to Paris to infiltrate,
hopefully, the Irish revolutionary circle which used the Third

Republic's capitol as a safehouse. Charles Mayne arrived in Paris on 21 June, notifying Brackenbury that he had taken Room 395 at the Grand Hotel du Louvre. Contact had been established with Mr Plunkett of the British Embassy who would act as his postbox. Anderson was now to be notified to send out his agent, who knew the famous Fenian James Stephens by sight, having associated with him in the late '60s. He arrived a week later and Mayne noted that he thought the man's salary of £2 a week was too small; he was finding the £1 a day allowance too little for Paris, even though it might have done in Dublin. Two days later photographs of some of the leading Fenians arrived to aid in identification. Anderson's 'friend' got on quite well and Mayne felt that he was also making progress, particularly having the previous day met E[gan] at a cafe, recognising him immediately from his photograph. There were three other unidentified men in the group, one with a long foxy beard. Mayne and his associate were still in Paris as July closed.[12]

The Home Secretary, having seen to Anderson's co-operation, also had to deal with Edward Archibald. He was then in London attempting to retire from the Foreign Service. The seventy-two year old Archibald was prepared to stay on in New York for the time being in order to carry out the intelligence function, while Harcourt went ahead with plans to bring Archibald and Brackenbury together with Sir John Rose. Rose was willing to 'spy out the land' as part of a scheduled trip to North America, prior to the establishment of a secret service operation there in conjunction with the Pinkertons.[13]

Rose had been an obvious man to turn to for advice since he had been in charge of the Canadian anti-Fenian operation in the central and eastern United States during the 1860s and '70s and was thus the only person in London with any first-hand experience of the problems of transatlantic Fenianism. Rose was asked to submit a secret memorandum on what he personally described as an 'efficient detective system in the United States and Canada' based upon a 'very free use of Secret Service money'. He had received confidential help from the then American Secretary of State, Hamilton Fish, as well as New York City authorities, while the consulate had carried on its intelligence work with direct links to the Canadian representatives in Washington, as well as Ottawa. Rose was unable to recall the names of his 'chief officers' but remembered that they were connected with both the State and Federal governments as well as the New York City police. Furthermore he was sure that Mr Fish could be counted upon for renewed aid, as well as the current Secretary of State, Frelinghuysen. Through their combined influence the Mayor of New York could be counted upon for co-operating with British intelligence. Fenian lodges from Buffalo, New York and the west had been under the scrutiny of Ottawa, and thus Sir John A. MacDonald would know far better how that end of the system operated. This memorandum came to the Home Office with a covering letter dated 13 May suggesting that the American authorities were 'accessible to flattery, though not of course to money'.[14]

Gladstone's cabinet was also seeking to deal with the increasingly difficult situation in Egypt, for the show of force by Admiral Seymour's fleet had provoked Arabi's forces into strengthening the defence of Alexandria threatening the Anglo-French fleet in the bay. On 3 July Seymour was authorised to silence the guns and flatten the fortifications unless the construction ceased. The Egyptians ignored the ultimatum and at 7 a.m. on 11 July the British squadron, operating without French assistance, opened fire on the six miles of forts lining the Alexandria shore. The ten-and-a-half-hour bombardment accomplished the cabinet directive.

During this first fortnight of July Brackenbury was in London to brief Trevelyan on the current security situation; he wrote asking 'leave to resign, hoping to be allowed to go with Sir Garnet Wolseley to Egypt'. Although the cabinet had not as yet decided to send in the army, it was obvious to Brackenbury that such a move was imminent. Despite the colonel's assurances that the counter-Fenian organisation was now so well organised that it could be run by the Anderson brothers and RIC County Inspector Reed, Brackenbury's request was met with amazement. He was told in clear and unequivocal terms that the situation in Ireland was critical and while he could be spared from an Egyptian campaign, for which there was doubtless a surplus of unemployed officers eager for glory, he was engaged in creating an Irish secret service, which in his own words held the key for future peace on that island. Brackenbury withdrew his request, but the matter was referred to Spencer. Spencer accepted his resignation.[15]

On Thursday 20 July 1882, the day the cabinet decided to send the army into Egypt—the invasion came on 16 August—Spencer sent the following letter to Gladstone.

> I was glad to hear that you approved of my decision about Colonel Brackenbury. I felt that I would have no real confidence in a man ready to throw up duties of such vast importance as these which he did undertake to carry out after so short a time, & for purely selfish objects.
>
> It gave me however a great deal of anxiety & I was relieved when I learned that you and others of my colleagues (felt?) that my stern decision was just.[16]

William Vernon Harcourt was one of those colleagues that supported Spencer's decision to remove Brackenbury. The Home Secretary said that Brackenbury had behaved 'infamously' and 'deceitfully' in discussing plans for organising the intelligence system in the United States while preparing to go to Egypt. Furthermore, he had personally urged Childers that '*on no condition shall he be employed at present in any post of distinction*' (Harcourt's emphasis); advice which was acted upon.[17] And yet Spencer's decision had been open to criticism since there appeared to be no obvious successor as under secretary for police and crime. On the very day that Spencer was thanking Gladstone for his support he was begging Harcourt for help, since Colonel Bradford had refused the opportunity. Would it be possible for him to have the Director of London's Criminal Investigation Division, Howard Vincent? Recognising that this was not possible he raised the name of one of his private secretaries, E. G. Jenkinson. He had been Spencer's 'right hand' since his arrival in Dublin and was a very able man with good 'India experience', though not with the organisation of the police. Spencer adopted the procedure of putting Jenkinson's name to one side, although he was highly recommended by both Colonel Bradford and Brackenbury, and proceeded to eliminate all the other candidates.[18]

On 31 July Harcourt wrote to Spencer enquiring as to Brackenbury's replacement, as well as asking if he had any news of the colonel since 'we hear nothing of him here'.[19]

Brackenbury could have answered that question, as he did in his autobiography many years later, because Childers had taken Harcourt's advice and Brackenbury 'was refused permission to go to Egypt in any capacity, and was placed upon the half-pay of a major. . . .' So much for one whose resignation 'gave great offence to Her Majesty's Government'. Spencer had finally arrived at Jenkinson's name in the elimination process and settled on the appointment on the first or second of August. Harcourt was notified on 2 August and the prime minister the following day. Harcourt was told that after careful consideration and discussion with Robert Hamilton and George Trevelyan, Edward George Jenkinson had been chosen for the most difficult job in Ireland. There was simply no question in Spencer's mind of having to improve the detective system if they were to survive: 'We depend in Dublin on one man Mallon, were he to die or be killed we have no one worth a row of pins'.[20]

Although not as well known as the other names on Spencer's list of candidates, Jenkinson was well connected, being Northbrook's first cousin, and his mother a sister to Sir George Gray, a former Home Secretary under Palmerston. Spencer told Gladstone that Jenkinson reminded him at times of Sir George, but that most importantly, 'He will not leave his post'. Jenkinson, as the newly appointed under secretary for police and crime, arrived in London on 4 August for consultation.[21] Jenkinson did not however arrive unannounced, as he preferred, because in the House of Commons on 3 August, Frank Hugh O'Donnell railed against the 'spymaster-general' appointment of this man 'trained in the despotic school of India officialdom'. G. O. Trevelyan vigorously defended Jenkinson, one of the 'Mutiny Magistrates of India', strongly denying that he had been one of those involved in the 'nameless and horrible atrocities' of that period.[22]

On 8 August Spencer wrote to Harcourt with the news that the RIC at Limerick were agitating for an improvement in their pay and pensions, in addition to the payment of the promised £180,000 in reward money. Spencer suggested that the solution might involve bringing English constables into Ireland. Harcourt rejected the idea as being utterly impracticable. Spencer sent E. G. Jenkinson and Colonel Bruce (the recently appointed

RIC inspector-general) to Limerick to take charge of the negotiations. Their instructions were that if the police had not
returned to their duties by 9 a.m. on 12 August they would be
discharged. By the end of the month sections of the Dublin
police were also in open disobedience and Spencer was again
pleading for English constables. He had been told that Scotland
Yard had some 500 Irishmen who had previously served with
the RIC—could they be encouraged to volunteer for Irish
service? Harcourt was willing to at least consider the possibility
in the light of the present difficulties, particularly since Gladstone was supporting Spencer's request. He thus asked the assistant commissioner, Colonel R. L. O. Pearson, to make the
necessary enquiries, which turned up only thirty-eight Irishmen.
It was estimated that there might be as many as sixty, of whom
probably not more than six had ever served on the Dublin
force. The report to the Home Secretary noted that double pay
would be required as customary, for serving out of one's district.
Even under those conditions, Pearson estimated that not more
than a dozen would volunteer and these would not be constables
but inspectors and sergeants. By 16 September the troubles
were over, with all but seventeen policemen reinstated, and
other members of the force who had resigned had by then withdrawn their resignations. Harcourt gave the credit to Spencer,
who with typical modesty said it belonged to Hamilton,
Jenkinson, and Trevelyan.[23]

Howard Vincent, Director of London's CID, for the most
part carried the anti-Fenian responsibilities in England. One
of the men he had been concerned with was Michael Davitt.
As part of the Kilmainham agreement, he had been released
from Portland prison on 6 May and was escorted back to
London by Parnell, John Dillon and John J. O'Kelly. Five days
later Davitt was interviewed by Vincent and he undertook 'to
assist the authorities by every means in his power and if
earnestness of manner is any guarantee he will do so'. Davitt
succeeded in convincing Vincent that, although he had tried to
subvert the British government in the past, he was no longer a
Fenian. The comments made by Vincent to Harcourt with
reference to the Phoenix Park murders were most perceptive,
however, for he was convinced that it was the result of a long

D

existing plot to kill Burke and Forster and was not an American plot. He did not feel that O'Donovan Rossa had the courage to do it.[24] The Foreign Secretary, Lord Granville, was at the same time being told by his minister in Washington, Sackville West, 'I believe now that the Dublin Crime was instigated on this side of the water by the irreconciliables or Fenian Section of the Irish Land League Party here'.[25] As it turned out Vincent was correct in attributing the crime to a few desperate 'ruffians' and not part of a large plot with American direction and backing. On 27 May Vincent asked Davitt to see him at the Yard about a conversation the Irish leader was to have had with a man called Brennan. The detectives found that Davitt had left for Ireland at 9 a.m., a clear violation of his licence, which required that he not leave the police district without notifying the police. Furthermore, he had also made a 'solemn promise' to write to Vincent and not move without warning. While Vincent was not terribly worried about Davitt's 'escape', he nevertheless suggested to Harcourt that if 'he becomes troublesome in Ireland a judicious communiqué to a discreet newspaper upon his communication with me would impair his influence'. One wonders if Vincent did not also consider such a suggestion as an invitation to Davitt's murder. It is, at any rate, an indication as to how this policeman's mind operated.[26]

Nearer at hand, Vincent had far more difficult problems than keeping his eye on Davitt. During the fortnight previous to Davitt's exit, Vincent had been trying to discover who had made yet another attempt to dynamite the Mansion House on 12 May 1882. Previously, O'Donovan Rossa's 'Skirmishers' had made bombing attempts on the Barracks at Salford, and the Police Station and Town Hall at Liverpool, but like the earlier attempt on Mansion House they were easily characterised as of a 'very miserable character'—the words of Major Henri Le Caron. Nevertheless the threat was very real. One of the Irish-American newspapers which Dublin Castle and the Home Office watched most closely was *The United Irishman* which described itself as an Irish National Journal and was published in New York City with the intention of making Ireland an independent republic: its editor and publisher was O'Donovan Rossa. A typical editorial suggestion was that if the $30,000 recently (late 1881—early 1882) contributed to the Land League had gone to an 'active policy' it would have equipped sixty men with sixty boxes of matches, or something better, who would have burnt down the neighbourhood of St Paul's Cathedral. The 'something better' was understood by all of Rossa's readers to mean gunpowder or dynamite.[27] One interesting point that emerges from that estimate is that Rossa's own experience with 'active service' suggested a budget of something like $500 to get a dynamiter in and out of London, in addition to the cost of the explosives.

Regardless of the cost it became fairly clear to Howard Vincent that Rossa's men were back in London. At 9 p.m. on Friday 12 May a parcel wrapped in brown paper had been discovered in one of the kitchen windows of the Mansion House, sited along a narrow court between the mayor's residence and St Stephen's Church, Walbrook. Inside the parcel was a white lead cannister with the zinc label *Buckshot Ellis*. The cannister was twelve inches long by six inches and contained blasting powder and a piece of rag for a fuse, which had been lighted but went out before igniting the charge. Strangely enough, it is difficult to know if the bombers had really intended the charge to explode, for the cannister carried an inscription claiming that the Irish landlords were the chief recipients of the Defence of Property Fund raised at the Mansion House. Special Constables were immediately stationed near the Lord Mayor's residence and the Home Secretary directed Vincent to 'beat up' the Irish sections of London. Telegrams were immediately sent to the Superintendents of B to Y Divisions of the Metropolitan Police (A Division was Westminster). Vincent asked that the 'resorts of the lower classes of Irish are to be visited as far as possible tonight (13 May) by the most experienced officers'. The police were reminded to keep a careful watch for the three known Rossa men associated with the attempt on the Mansion House in March of the previous year, Thomas J. Mooney, Edward O'Donnell and John (Patrick?) Coleman. A reward of £400 was offered for information on the previous explosion; £10,000 was currently being offered for information leading to the conviction of the murderers of Cavendish and Burke. Vincent assured Harcourt later that evening that his instructions had been carefully given out but requested an authorisation for £100 reward money for information leading to conviction, thus giving his officers the chance to 'broadcast' the offer during the evening's searches. Detectives were also consulting the 'copper's nark'—their informants.

The next day, Sunday, Vincent reported to Harcourt that the raids had gone off without mishap and that while two or three men had been apprehended they had later been released. Vincent was very interested in the press's attitude which pointed to the plot as a hoax and Inspector Williamson's best informant tended to substantiate the opinion that there had never been less Fenianism in London than at that moment.

Harcourt wrote to Spencer in Dublin offering such wisdom as he had on the matter. 'The attempted explosion at the Mansion House', he said, 'was a Fenian scare of the old clumsy kind. I made it a reason for having all the Irish quarters in Lond. beat up last night. My police report very little Fenianism in London but of course it may be imported any day either from America or Ireland'.[28]

Even while the City reacted by putting out a reward of £500 the Home Secretary's son and private secretary, Lewis Harcourt, recorded Queen Victoria's reaction to the 'clumsy' affair in the following diary entry:

> The Queen is in a great state of fuss about the situation in general and finance in particular and is constantly telegraphing about the Mansion House explosion; recommending that English detectives should go to Dublin (which has already been done). . . .

Young Harcourt could not avoid seeing some of the humour in the Queen's current demands that special precautions be taken for her journey to Scotland, while at the same time she complained because the railway companies charged £100 for patrolling the whole line from Osborne to Balmoral with 1,200 platelayers. This was in addition to the pilot engine running ahead of the royal train to ensure an unbroken line. One can only speculate as to the number of Irishmen, loyal or otherwise, who stood along the rail line that day.[29]

The most enheartening news of that bleak spring and early summer of 1882 was the discovery of an IRB arms cache at 99 St John's Road (Rydon-Crescent), Clerkenwell, not far from the site of the House of Detention, bombed in 1867. The story

as it emerged in the third week of June was that an export
agent giving the name of 'Sadgrove' had hired a stable located
at the back of a house belonging to one of the many Swiss watch
and chronometer makers in the district, William George Schoof.
Schoof recalled that 'Sadgrove', an Irishman, had looked at
the stable towards the end of 1881, but did not rent the
premises until 6 February. He did not move packing cases into
the stable until two months later on 6 April. 'Sadgrove' was then
not seen again for a month, re-appearing at the stable on the
night of Thursday 11 May, the night before the abortive explosion at the Mansion House. He was reported to have taken a
black bag from the stables and to have given Schoof a forwarding address at 37 Charles St, Birmingham. The rent of £2 per
month fell into arrears and Schoof's letter to 'Sadgrove's'
forwarding address was returned by the dead letter office. The
landlord's suspicions were now aroused and he informed the
police of the curious behaviour of his tenant.

On the afternoon of the sixteenth the police entered the stable
on Rydon Crescent with a ladder, forcing a window at the rear.
Thus almost by chance a major arms haul was achieved. Within
the stable was found between 70,000 and 80,000 rounds of
ammunition, 400 rifles with stocks marked with the shamrock,
bayonets, and sixty revolvers; in all Howard Vincent estimated
some £4,000 worth of arms. This was certainly a serious blow
to Irish hopes of a successful insurrection. A description was
telegraphed to all police divisions. The man 'Sadgrove' was
middle-aged, about six feet tall, stalwart build, determined
expression, small moustache and beard, and a smallpox-marked
face.

William Peel, Inspector of 'G' Division, had led the raid on
the stable. Having determined that the crates contained illegal
arms he had staked the building out until 6 a.m. on Saturday
morning. The arms and ammunition, upon Vincent's instructions, were then removed as quickly as possible—the ammunition, according to the usual practice, being sent to the
Plumstead Magazine. The arms went to the nearest police
station, the lock was changed and the watching continued. At
10 p.m. 'Sadgrove' appeared, found the lock changed, demanded
a key but Schoof refused and ordered him off the property.
The suspect was followed by two detectives who arrested him

at his home a mile to the south, at 12 Charles Street, Hatton Garden, where he lived with his wife and three children.

When the home was searched some old revolvers were found and some 400 cartridges for Colt revolvers. Taken to King's Cross police station, 'Sadgrove' (John Walsh) was charged with 'feloniously receiving and fraudulently dealing with certain rifles, bayonets, and other fire arms, believed to be the property of Her Majesty's government. . . .' Harcourt's first inclination seemed to have been to make the charge treason felony, which could carry a life imprisonment as the maximum penalty. Walsh, who was thirty-eight years old and of an 'imperfect education' as the police report put it, had thus far managed to elude the police for at least two years. Harcourt was all too aware of the possible consequences of the 'unbaited trap', for Walsh could have taken to his heels and remained free to continue his work. The Home Secretary suggested to Vincent that the stable should have been left as it had been found in order not to alert the gunrunner. Vincent, smarting under this criticism of his professional judgement, justified the removal of the arms because Schoof would not agree to having the arms remaining on his property. Although this excuse was weak, Vincent was convinced that even if, as Harcourt also suggested, the removal of the four crates and twenty-four cases in the two four-horse vans had aroused local interest, in 'such a district' the news would soon have been out even without additional excitement. The CID chief also was concerned that there might have been dynamite in the store and under such conditions public safety had to be of prime importance. Vincent must have realised that he had come very close to losing Walsh. The store appeared to have been deserted and the landlord had not seen Walsh for six weeks: there was also the matter of the returned letter and the rent. In conclusion Vincent justified himself not on method but results, reminding Harcourt that the Royal Irish Constabulary had been trying to make a breakthrough in the arms traffic for two years without success and now the CID had produced both weapons and the man reputed to be the leading agent.[30]

Lewis Harcourt had been at Scotland Yard when the vans brought in the china crates with French markings from King's Cross police station. He noted that one of the unusual things about the twenty 40 calibre Colt revolvers was that they bore the test mark of Liege; the result being that a detective was immediately despatched to Belgium with a specimen for identification. Obviously if the CID could locate the suppliers of arms to the Irish Republican Brotherhood, intercepting such shipments in transit would be made easier, even lacking co-operation from police on the continent.[31] There was no way of knowing if the Clerkenwell cache was the extent of the arms in transit to Ireland or whether Walsh and his associates had other such stores in major cities awaiting shipment to Ireland.

Vincent wrote to Harcourt on Monday 19 June to say that he had written to Dublin asking Robert Anderson for assistance. Colonel Vivien Dering Majendie, the Home Office's Inspector of Explosives, was to conduct an examination of the ammunition, while Childers at the War Office was to provide an Army officer to trace the history of the old government Enfields which had been converted into Sneiders and bore the Tower proof marks.[32] Anderson subsequently made visits to both Liverpool, Manchester and Dublin Castle. As one of his central tasks Anderson interviewed the RIC men stationed in Manchester and Liverpool. From these conversations it became evident that the RIC carried on too much ordinary police work, to the detriment of their primary function which was dealing with Irishmen who escaped to England in order to avoid arrest and prosecution under the coercive legislation. Anderson wanted these men to be the 'detectives' in Fenian investigations and suggested a new system to Jenkinson, but there had been no decision on the matter.

E. G. Jenkinson as Assistant Secretary for Police and Crime in Dublin and Robert Anderson, Fenian affairs advisor in the Home Office in London, began their association in the autumn of 1882, a working relationship which was to last for the better part of three years and was to be based primarily upon mutual distrust and jealousy. Anderson now found himself working for Howard Vincent and Jenkinson. He told the Home Secretary that he was personally surprised to find that so little was known of what was 'going on under the surface, in Ireland', and that Jenkinson was 'counting' on his being able to help in that respect. Anderson, considering himself the expert on Fenian affairs, was smarting as a result of having been passed over twice in the previous weeks for the post of 'spymaster-general'. On the other hand he and Vincent appear to have worked reasonably well together, although their efforts were continually frustrated by their inability to find 'underground contacts' with the Fenian organisations. They very much wanted to send an agent to Dublin, but they could not find anyone to send who both wanted to go and was worth sending.

> An Inspt. feels safe here in London, & in fact he is perfectly safe, if only he be prudent; but in Dublin this work is full of danger, & the recent assassination of men suspected of having given information has produced an impression which must die before others will be found willing to come forward.

Nevertheless Anderson had found two men who would be willing to go to Dublin for a few days but they would insist on communicating only with Anderson in London.

> All agree that there is nothing of any importance doing at present in Fenian circles; but yet there seems to be a very general expectation that 'something will be done shortly'. I believe this impression is the result of the talk of a general movement, wh[ich] was common before the battle of Tel El Kebir; & I feel sure that political & agrarian outrages are alone to be feared.

Anderson's appraisal was summed up with the impression that over the past six months there had been a marked change for the better in Ireland. He did however fear what the winter might bring and he had told Jenkinson that only information on political offences could be expected from him.[33] Anderson's letter did manage to convey quite clearly his own low opinion of the state of Irish intelligence under Jenkinson. Harcourt brought this opinion to Spencer's attention and enclosed Anderson's confidential letter promising to see Anderson when convenient. A week later, after having received the 'Anderson Memorandum', which dealt with intelligence-gathering on both sides of the Irish Sea, Harcourt played down Anderson's opinions, commenting to Spencer that : 'I am so used to those of his brother [Samuel Lee Anderson] that I am not profoundly moved or convinced by them'.[34]

Robert Anderson's penchant for secrecy clearly annoyed the

Home Secretary. His reports, whether to the Home Office or to the Director of the CID were carefully edited, in order to protect his sources from discovery. His cardinal rule was never to divulge the identity of an informant and to withhold the information until such time as the police reaction would not point to the informant. This method was not peculiar to Anderson, for Jenkinson was also totally committed to the protection of informants upon whom the process of intelligence-gathering primarily rested. Anderson remembered on one occasion being taken to task by Harcourt for refusing to tell him the names of certain informants. Anderson said that he immediately asked him to be relieved of his share of the secret service work of the Home Office. The Home Secretary backed down and was then prepared to overlook the ignorance in which he was to be kept and took to quipping that 'Anderson's idea of secrecy is not to tell the secretary of state'. Anderson defended his position on the grounds that one Irish informer had been murdered by Fenians upon his arrival in New York two or three years earlier. The man's name had been mentioned to Lord Mayo, the chief secretary, who passed it on in conversation to the lord lieutenant during dinner at the viceregal lodge where it had been overheard by a Fenian sympathiser on the domestic staff. Such a lapse in security would give serious second thoughts to anyone willing to give information on the Fenian organisation either in the United States or the United Kingdom.[35]

Sir John Rose had carried out his North American reconnaissance in August. His report on *Secret Consular Agencies in the United States* was submitted on 13 September 1882. After arriving in New York, Rose had interviewed those men currently involved in the gathering of intelligence, stressing that in the future payment would depend upon results and that salaries in comparison would be trifling. He judged that the supervision of agents was competent, the agents had been judiciously selected, and the various reports were being sifted with discrimination. The consulates in New York and Philadephia filed independent reports with the Foreign Office but did not communicate with each other, nor did they receive comments in return concerning either the accuracy or the effect of the information. While Rose felt that the eastern seaboard was adequately covered by the current arrangements, the mid-west, with Chicago at its centre, was relatively ignored, being operated as a sideshow to the other work the Philadelphia consulate had in hand. Noting that Chicago was an area 'where the [Fenian] organisation is equally active and dangerous as in New York if not more so', he recommended that the Chicago vice-consul, John Dunn, be given responsibility for setting up an intelligence system in the city. As the first step towards its realisation Rose had seen Gilbert McMicken, Speaker of the Manitoba legislature, who had been responsible for secret service work in the mid-west for the Canadian government during the years of the Fenian invasions. McMicken in turn encouraged Rose to contact 'one of the most efficient' agents of those days, 'a Doctor H. Le Caron —who had been physician to some of the Irish societies'. When Anderson read this part of the report he must have been deeply concerned, for here was the identification of his personal 'secret agent' and even a current address: P.O. Box 129, Braidwood Illinois. Arrangements had been made for McMicken to organise a meeting with Le Caron upon receipt of a prearranged message from either the consulate in New York or Philadelphia. The establishment of the Chicago network was extremely important because of the city's large Irish population and, whether Rose was fully aware of it or not, its functioning as the administrative centre of Clan na Gael. Le Caron, according to Rose, was all that was left of the previous system and he alone gave promise of 'real usefulness under the altered conditions'. The current expenditure of money and men was adequate but there must be no thought of relaxation. The possibility of sending agents from Ireland to the United States was qualified with the need to alert the three consulates to their presence. The report concluded with the following recommendations: that the New York consul should be the head of the American operation collating all information derived from the other consulates; the consulates would in the future use their own discretion as to what information they shared; the consulates should receive information from the Home Office via the Foreign Office as to the effect and accuracy of their information; finally the expenditure and efforts must remain at the present level. The only recorded reaction to the report was that of Samuel Lee Anderson, who noted that Archibald should have overall responsi-

bility in the United States and that his brother should co-ordinate the work in London, keeping the consulates informed as to
the progress of their work.[36]

One of the first problems that faced E. G. Jenkinson was
that of the proposed intelligence network in the United States.
Rose's preliminary memo had been shunted from Robert
Anderson at the Home Office to his brother at Dublin Castle.
Samuel Lee Anderson had acted as Brackenbury's deputy and
continued to do so for Jenkinson. Sam Anderson's comment to
his brother concerning the disposition of the memo (24 July
1882) was: 'I presume nothing is to be done on this!' Robert
replied that earlier in the summer he, Brackenbury, and Harcourt had met Rose at Harcourt's home on Grafton Street
where the matter had been fully discussed. The reason for not
implementing the memorandum was that Rose's schemes were
'utterly wild and extravagant. Enormous sums of money were
spent, without any important result'. E. G. Jenkinson closed the
matter with 'put away' in the margin of the memo.[37]

Archibald, the New York consul-general, eventually agreed
to defer the matter of his retirement until the end of 1882 and
returned to the United States. The Pinkerton Detective Agency
was already involved in a covert operation in America, as was
indicated by a memorandum which Harcourt had sent to
Spencer at the end of August. Although Lord Granville was
prepared to keep Archibald in New York, subject to Harcourt's
concurrence, such an arrangement could not solve the long-
term problem of the gathering of intelligence concerning American Fenian activity. Anderson felt that even after his retirement
in December, Archibald should remain in the United States
'for it is of the very highest importance that he sh[ould] keep
the charge of Fenian inquiries during the transitional period
when the new consul-general is learning his work'. Could
Archibald be persuaded to stay in a private capacity until 1
April 1883?[38]

Archibald was at that very moment being kept extremely
busy by the discovery of an almost unbelievable plot to sink
the SS *Castalia* of the Anchor Line; its cargo of 499 mules was
destined for the British Army in Alexandria. A Colonel Swinley
had been sent to St Louis to purchase the mules which had then
been sent by train to New York, with periodic stops for feed

and water in public stockyards. Archibald had received information from 'Mr Edwards' (his code name for all of his informants) that the famous O'Donovan Rossa bomber Patrick Coleman intended to fix a wooden keg bound with iron to the hull of the *Castalia* and sink her at her New York quayside. Coleman was said to be working as a bar-keeper in a tavern on 43rd Street near to the Hudson River where the ship was docked. The informer claimed that there was no connection with either the Clan or Rossa, and Archibald found the New York police unwilling to search the tavern for the alleged bomber. The ship sailed safely on 8 September without any apparent attempt to sink her. The informer, who was apparently paid nothing for his trouble, found that the keg had disappeared, yet he still possessed the fuse for the device. Concurrent reports that the 'Dynamite Council' of Rossa composed of Dr Shien, George Spearman, and Frank Byrne, were going to fill the ship's coal bunkers with 'coal shells' proved to be unfounded, as did another rumour that Rossa would poison the animals.

Archibald may not have taken any of this too seriously because his report was not dated until 14 September. Furthermore there is no record of a telegraphic alert to Anderson. Rather the Home Office appears to have received the report from the normal diplomatic pouch service via the Foreign Office. Anderson in turn forwarded it to the Irish Office on 4 October; Jenkinson read it the next day and ordered it to be copied, which was done by Samuel Lee Anderson, returning it to his brother at the Home Office on the eleventh. Apparently this closed the matter except for the fact that they had failed to recognise that they, for one brief moment, had been close to the centre of a major conspiracy. Archibald had seen and described in his report the prototype fuse which would be detonating the lignine dynamite bombs of O'Donovan Rossa's Skirmishers within four months. He noticed these details in his report:

> ...two metal tubes about a foot long and an inch in diameter. The outer of these tubes (the bottom of which is closed with a good sized percussion cap) was to be charged with a combination of potassic chlorate, 2 parts; pulverised sugar, 1 part; and sulphate of arsenic, 1 part...

This was inserted into the larger diameter tube leaving room for the second tube to be inserted inside. It contained several perforations in the end carefully sealed by layers of porous paper glued down and secured in place with pack thread. This tube was to be filled with a powerful acid, which eating its way through the paper would in about an hour come in contact with the outer chemicals causing an explosion which would detonate the percussion cap, in turn exploding the dynamite or gunpowder into which the detonator had been inserted. It may not have sounded very convincing in October 1882 but it was chemically correct and took little extra imagination for its developers to provide an improved model which, using brass taps, made it into a serviceable detonator for 'field work'. In the light of this information it is all the more remarkable that Anderson's next letter to the Home Secretary, not written until 14 October, made no mention of this development, and stated that he had not written recently since there was nothing to say. This then was the state of the Secret Service operation in the autumn of 1882.[39]

4

A state of Emergency: Glasgow, London and Liverpool

... the Houses of Parliament are searched as if continually on the eve of a GUY FAWKES plot....

The Times, 19 March 1883

NEW YORK'S British consul-general sent a cypher telegram to E. G. Jenkinson at Dublin Castle on 28/29 January 1883 advising him of the need to take special care of Lord Hartington. The message also reported that O'Donovan Rossa had made 'some significant remarks' about William Vernon Harcourt and thus Earl Spencer, the Irish viceroy, encouraged the Home Secretary to take every precaution. Harcourt's reply was typical of his wit: 'O'Donovan Rossa has so long sworn to take my life that I have almost ceased to believe in him, nevertheless I take precautions and see that Hartington is protected'.[1] Leading members of the government and royal family, including the Duke of Cambridge, were protected by both uniformed and plain-clothes policemen but precious little security could be afforded for the virtually limitless number of potential public targets. 1883 would see a state of emergency in force in Britain as the anticipated Irish-American attacks came not against individuals but upon the public buildings of England and Scotland.

What O'Donovan Rossa needed was the simple combination of men prepared to take the risks as bombers and the money to pay their way. Clan na Gael also needed brave men but at least still had access to the Skirmishing Fund. However, most of the fund's assets were committed to Holland submarine development and supporting the IRB; new money had to be found for the dynamite strategy. Changes in the Clan's leadership and organisation in 1882 marked a turning point in its relations with the IRB. The Clan's new president, Alexander Sullivan, found that the

IRB was not prepared to support the use of dynamite against British targets. Thus he led the move within the Clan executive FC to cut off the flow of money to the IRB, allocated for organisation and arms which 'for all that was known to the contrary, were simply rusting away in Ireland'.

The position of the IRB's Supreme Council was forcefully put by James J. O'Kelly in a letter to John Devoy. Writing from Budapest at the end of September 1882, O'Kelly was deeply worried about rumours he had heard in London suggesting that William Mackey Lomasney was about to bomb Dublin Castle. Pleading for Devoy to stop the attempt, he offered two good reasons not to extend the dynamite war. The first was simply that it was doomed to failure because the Irish government already had the details. Secondly, if the plot did succeed it would do the Irish nationalist movement immense harm. Public opinion was against military operations and if something was done by Clan na Gael that cost a hundred lives the reaction would be a hundred times worse than the backlash to the Phoenix Park murders. It would produce a reign of terror against the Irish in Britain and in Ireland similar to that which preceded the insurrection of 1798. They had already seen the results of Michael Davitt's violent speeches and the blatherskite of *The Irish World*—a curfew law and Orange Juries of the good old type. The blowing up of the Castle would probably lead the Irish to the pitch cap and the triangle! O'Kelly also rejected the American assumption that such an attack would stimulate an uprising; rather it would merely induce further emigration. Irish-Americans had to realise that their old homeland had five million residents of whom one and a half million were Protestants and at least a half a million Roman Catholics were hostile to independence.

To further increase the Clan's war chest, Alexander Sullivan managed to divert large sums of money collected in the United States for the Irish Land League. During the tour of the United States in the spring of 1882 by Patrick Egan, the treasurer of the Irish Land League, he had contributed $100,000 of Land League money to the Clan's dynamite activity—that was what the current rumours reported and there certainly was some truth in it, despite the amount being obviously inflated. In a letter to John Devoy that July, Sullivan talked of taking $25,000 out of Clan funds 'for some work is on foot', cashing a cheque for that amount in Paris later that summer.[2]

Much of the money raised for revolutionary activity came via the dynamite press, which initially included *The Irish World* and its more radical counterpart, *The United Irishman*, edited by O'Donovan Rossa. Rossa printed the following letter which he received from Monroeville, Ohio.

> Dear Sir, Inclosed find $3; $2 for my yearly subscription for the 'United Irishman', and $1 for dynamite. I think it the most consistent remedy for old tyrant England.
> Wishing you and the 'United Irishman'
> success, I remain, etc.
> (signed) Thos. O'Neill.[3]

O'Neill and his fellow contributors were about to see the 'consistent remedy' applied in 1883. The first bombs of that year were delivered by O'Donovan Rossa's Skirmishers and not by Clan na Gael.

Rossa's first target was Glasgow Corporation's Tradeston Gas Works in Lilybank St (now Gourock St). The works closed for the day on 20 January 1883 at 6 p.m. leaving only an inspector on duty at the governor's house. He did not see the bombers moving towards gasometer no. 4, which contained 350,000 cubic feet of town gas.

Four hours after the workers had left the site two loud explosions were heard and the gasometer collapsed in sheets of flame into the surrounding bank. The force of the explosion was so great that it was heard and felt by people in the vicinity of Queen's Park, over three miles away. Flames spread to a nearby carpet-beating works and a ropery, causing considerable damage and injuring eleven persons, one seriously. Within an hour the reverberations of another explosion were heard in Glasgow, this blast destroying an unused coaling shed at the Buchanan St station of the Caledonian Railway. Then, at about 2 a.m. a group of young people, including a gunner of the Royal Horse Artillery, found an oval shaped ladies' tin bonnet box on the parapet of the stone aqueduct carrying the Forth and Clyde Canal over Possil Road. The soldier opened the box and put his hand into what appeared at first to be sand; the contents exploded, severely burning him, slightly injuring his companions, but leaving the aqueduct untouched. The destruction of the aqueduct would have flooded the entire area. Glasgow's magistrates had offered a reward of £100 shortly after the first explosion and subsequently increased it to £500. There were no eye witnesses or informants to betray the bombers and the reward went uncollected.[4] Seven weeks later the bombers struck again and this time the targets were in London itself.

On Thursday evening, 15 March between 7.20 p.m. and 7.30 p.m. Rossa bombers moved into Playhouse Yard, a few yards east of the Blackfriars railway bridge. Moving to the rear of *The Times* publishing offices which faced on to Queen Victoria Street, they placed an oval japanned tin ladies' bonnet box on one of the ground-floor window ledges. For almost thirty minutes the box rested precariously on the ledge and at 8.00 p.m. detonated and fell on the pavement. A City of London police sergeant on duty in Printing House Square heard the sound of a 'fog-signal' from behind the building. Dashing up the adjoining alley into Playhouse Yard he saw the box on the ground with smoke pouring from it: 'I kicked the box and stamped out the fire with my feet. I saw something fall out of the box—pieces of paper and pieces of towelling'.

The bomb was the same variety as that found on the aqueduct in Glasgow—a hat box filled with about ten or twelve pounds of lignine dynamite. The sawdust (lignine) base contained a concentration of close to 30 per cent nitroglycerine. The failure of the bomb to detonate properly resulted merely in a blackened window. The fuse, a brass tube, was also recovered but later lost. The evidence was sent to Colonel Majendie for examination.[5]

While the City police were dealing with their explosion, the Duke of Edinburgh was seated in the gallery of the House of Commons, a mile and a half away. The MP for Sunderland, Mr E. T. Gourley, was speaking to an almost empty House (it was the dinner hour) about the Duke's recent report on the Naval Reserves and the Coast Guard. Just as Big Ben was striking 9 p.m. the chamber reverberated with the shock waves of a nearby explosion. The second target that night was a set of new government office buildings on Parliament Street surmounted by a statue of a triumphant Britannia. The block housed the Home

Office, the Foreign Office, the India Office, Colonial Office and the Local Government Board. Moving to the entrance of the last office facing towards Charles St (now King Charles St) the bomber set the parcel down, removed the paper, opened the tap on the brass fuse which he inserted into the mass of lignine dynamite. Setting the box behind the stone balustrade on the ledge of Room No. 8 (one window from the door and the third from the southeast corner of the building) he went as he had come, undetected. The sulphuric acid began to eat its way through the paper wrapping of the fuse. The estimated time of detonation was forty minutes.[6] The 'infernal machine' exploded between the prime minister's residence on Downing Street and the House of Commons, an explosion which was claimed to have been heard by the Rev. W. D. Parish, Vicar of Selmeston, Sussex, forty-six miles away. That night O'Donovan Rossa's Skirmishers destroyed, in the words of *The Times,* 'one room in a thousand'. The 'A' Division police station on King Street was severely pelted with debris from the explosion, which mostly comprised sections of the building's balustrade. The hoarding surrounding a nearby construction site was blown down and, according to *The Times* of 17 March, from 'the appearance of the block of Government offices a lawless mob might have been wreaking vengeance upon them. Scarcely a whole pane of glass remained'. 50,000 handbills were distributed, announcing a £1,000 reward for information leading to arrest and conviction of the bombers. The Home Secretary also promised a pardon for an informing accomplice.[7]

When daylight came, Colonel Majendie had laboriously picked through the debris and managed to collect several fragments of the bonnet-box bomb. Gladstone, accompanied by assorted government officials, was then given an on-the-spot appraisal of the situation by Superintendent Gernon of 'A' Division. Gernon had also been responsible for the external security of the Clerkenwell House of Detention when it was bombed in 1867. The scene was photographed and then came the task of cleaning up and evaluating the damage.

The guard on the Bank of England was doubled and a total of 355 men were finally pulled from their beats to guard public buildings, ministers and their residences, and members of parliament to and from their houses. Of this total sixty-five constables

Secret.

House of Commons
Friday
March 16ᵗʰ '83

My dear Spencer

You will have heard by this time of the first act of retaliation in London. I was at dinner in the H. of C. when we heard a loud report, several of them at the table said "It is an explosion". I rejoined "I have heard so much of explosion "I have almost ceased to believe in them". In about ¼ of an hour the office-keeper of the H.O. came over with the news. It is now quite clear what happened. The * marks the place of the explosion.

India Office

King St.

* Local Govt. Board
Home Office
Whitehall.

Harcourt's letter to Spencer following the explosion at the offices of the Local Government Board.

were protecting the homes of ministers, three inspectors, two sergeants and 285 constables protecting public buildings, including twelve men at Buckingham Palace and six at Westminster Abbey. Worried about the state of siege implied in the MEPO (Metropolitan Police) report assessing the situation, Harcourt minuted that while it was to be read to the police force it was *'not to be used or quoted'*.[8] The strain upon the Metropolitan Police threatened to be unbearable, since even in normal conditions Henderson's total force of 12,000 men had a city of five million people in which to maintain law and order. No more than 6,000 men could be on duty at any given time and Henderson wrote to Harcourt on 17 March for an immediate addition of twelve inspectors, fifty sergeants and 500 constables, suggesting the latter could be enlisted from a large number of men on the waiting list. Henderson's request for 500 men was based upon the assumption that a trained battalion of infantry would be used to mount guard on many of the key buildings. The area of Whitehall alone required 102 constables and thirty-seven inspectors according to the 'A' Division estimates (see diagram page 111).[9]

Citizens unashamedly began to offer advice to the government. Mr G. Bark of Godalming wrote immediately to the prime minister warning him that the electric lighting wires in the Houses of Parliament and Windsor Castle could be used to explode devices. The Home Secretary was sent an advertisement from a 'Practical Chemist and Inventor' concerning bottles of fire-extinguishing fluid at 30s per dozen, cold comfort to say the least.[10] Harcourt, like most members of the House, had been at dinner when the explosion had occurred. One of his companions said, 'It is an explosion', and the Home Secretary rejoined with a phrase often on his lips, that he had heard so much of explosions that he had 'almost ceased to believe in them'.

Spencer was also given a description of the old bonnet box found at *The Times*—about a foot in diameter with a rough hole broken in the lid to admit the fuse and detonator. It was obvious that the box and explosives were similar to those used in Glasgow.[11] Why Rossa's men had chosen the Local Government Offices as a target was probably best explained by the *Pall Mall Gazette* when it observed that on many maps of

London the Local Government Office was marked as the Home Office.[12]

News of the explosions was immediately telegraphed to the United States. The next day, 16 March, a *New York Times* correspondent interviewed O'Donovan Rossa:

'I can't say anything about the explosion', remarked Mr Rossa, by way of introduction: 'I have been advised by my friends not to talk on the subject. Some of my friends have insinuated that I can't keep a secret, and I will show them that I can this time. I received a telegram this morning from Major Horgan, late of the sixty-ninth Regiment, in which he says: "Do not open your lips to mortal man or woman today on the subject of the explosions in London". I shall act on his advice, and if you want any particulars suppose you call on the Major. I will let him talk this time.'

'I presume you are in sympathy with the men who caused the explosions?' queried the reporter. 'Of course I am. I am heartily in favor of using any weapons we can against the English.' 'Do you know anything about this explosion?' Mr Rossa refused to state the exact knowledge he possessed, but he looked wise enough to have planned the entire scheme in his own fertile brain: and Mr O'Brien, who had been quiet thus far, remarked, testily: 'Don't ask us what we know about it: we don't want to talk on that subject'. 'The Irish patriots of a sanguinary turn of mind seem to think you are responsible for the explosions', suggested the reporter to Mr Rossa. 'Well, I have advocated a warlike course from the very first, and the *United Irishman* is the only journal which openly avows that plan.' 'And we are the only party who will carry it out,' remarked the loquacious young man in a threatening tone. 'I have', resumed Mr Rossa, 'received considerable correspondence to-day from different parts of the country and about twenty congratulatory dispatches, and better than all, some money; not as much as we ought to have though; only about $100.'

Rossa also complained that the Trustees of the National or Skirmishing Fund had refused to allow him to 'use this money in inciting warfare against England in the peculiar manner for which he is so famous'. Thus $5,000 had been raised by Rossa for a new skirmishing fund. When asked by the reporter if any of this money had been expended on the recent explosions 'Mr Rossa was as dumb as the deep. The same mysterious muteness was also noticeable in the other members of the party'. John Devoy was also interviewed, saying 'we are not ready to begin an attack on England now. I have not heard of the explosion, except through the newspapers, and it may be an accident for all I know. Rossa may know something about it, but I don't believe he does. I certainly do not.'[13]

That same day E. G. Jenkinson ventured the opinion that the bombers were members of O'Donovan Rossa's 'Missioners' or 'Skirmishers'. Reminding the Home Secretary that he had given warning of possible reprisals, Jenkinson suggested that the Albert Memorial was an obvious target for future attacks and thus demanded close protection. The Dublin 'spymaster' was also concerned with the measures being taken to protect both Harcourt and Hartington from assassination. *The Times'* editor saw the explosions as a reply to Gladstone's speech of the previous Wednesday; a speech in which Parnell had been warned by the prime minister that the government would not reopen the land question and promising that renewed Land League agitation would not change his mind. Jenkinson, however, rejected this interpretation, seeing the explosions not as a simple reaction to a given pronouncement by Gladstone, but as 'part of a plan which we may see still further developed'. But how to deal with the developing plans of the Irish-American terrorists? The Home Secretary had no hope of either catching the bombers or preventing further explosions lacking any effective English counter-terrorist organisation.

At that very moment, within the Criminal Investigation Division of the Metropolitan Police, a new bureau was being organised, the Special Irish Branch. Harcourt viewed this Special Branch as *the* anti-Fenian organisation outside of Ireland; the Metropolitan Police under Henderson was to be solely responsible for the safety of London and thus must run the show with the aid of others, e.g. 'Anderson and some stray Irish Constables with no-one over them to control and direct them, in communication with Dublin . . . when these two forces hunt the same game they spoil all the sport'. Therefore he proposed that all sources of information would in the future

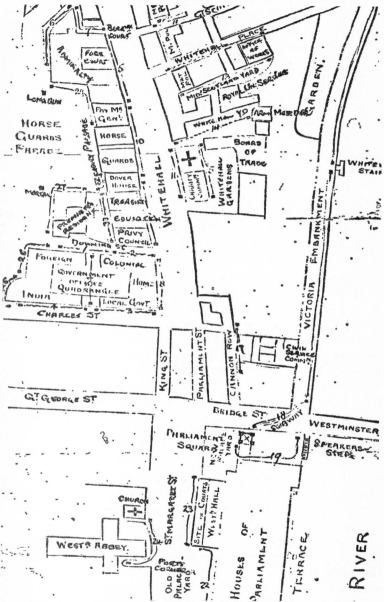

Plan showing the public buildings situated in 'A' Division of the Metropolitan Police and the special posts for their protection.

communicate with Special Branch's Chief Inspector 'Dolly' Williamson. He directed that Jenkinson communicate directly with Williamson; Spencer agreed to this.[14]

Vincent as head of the CID arranged for Williamson 'to be relieved of the greater portion of his regular duty and to devote his time entirely to Fenianism'. Williamson was also given full responsibility for the selection of Special Branch's personnel. Vincent instructed Williamson to report all matters of importance directly to the Home Secretary.[15] Offices for the Special Branch were provided on the first floor of a small two-storied building situated in the centre of Great Scotland Yard, across from the Rising Sun public house. The building was well known both to pedestrians using Great Scotland Yard and to the frequenters of the pub, for on the ground floor, directly beneath the new detective office, was a public urinal, a fact of some significance, as later developments would dramatically show.

Harcourt and Anderson had met on Thursday of that first week in order to define more clearly the latter's function which, as agreed three years previously, was confined to obtaining and communicating information; his responsibility ended when police action began. Furthermore, all information on Fenians in the London area was to go immediately to the CID and Vincent. Anderson was personally convinced that he had strictly adhered to these limits 'so far as the condition of Scotland Yard has rendered it feasible'. His subsequent memorandum recorded the express sanction of Harcourt for withholding from the police anything that would directly compromise the safety of an informant, although he had complete trust in 'Dolly' Williamson. Anderson had hopes that the 'new departure' would eventually beat the Fenians. Williamson arranged to come to Anderson, as Harcourt's deputy, daily and agreed that while the four RIC policemen in London were to be in daily touch to report and to receive instructions it was undesirable for them to 'be much at Scotland Yard'. The resultant 'new departure' memo was to stress again Anderson's belief that he had been given a large discretion in the forthcoming operations especially in cases of emergency, as well as protecting his informants' names and seeing that they were not required to give evidence in court without their consent.[16]

Harcourt had also written to Spencer on 15 April offering the government's authority to allow the Post Office to intercept and open mail, for in the present emergency he was prepared to do 'anything or everything' which could in any way be an aid to public safety.[17]

Even as these discussions were in progress E. G. Jenkinson was on his way to London from Dublin. By 21 March Williamson's position and authority had still not been finally settled, no fresh orders had been issued to the RIC, and most importantly, no central office had been established for collating and interpreting the information coming from Special Branch and other sources. The RIC strength in Britain was sixteen: four each in London and Glasgow and two each at Birmingham, Manchester, Holyhead and Glasgow. These men had to report to Anderson and to carry out his instructions as Jenkinson's representative at the Home Office, while remaining in direct communication with Jenkinson in Dublin. The four men in London were effectively attached to Special Branch. Jenkinson was still not happy with the 'new departure'. He was convinced that Special Irish Branch (which was apparently the Home Secretary's idea) alone would prove inadequate in combating a 'perfect and powerful Fenian organisation covering the whole of Ireland, and extending into England and Scotland', not to mention the United States. Jenkinson submitted a memorandum which clearly indicated how the Irish political crimes organisation operated under his control. He noted that the Home Secretary could not expect Special Branch to deal with Fenianism in Glasgow, Liverpool, Newcastle-on-Tyne, North Shields and most of the other northern towns, in addition to London and Bristol in the south. The necessity for a 'secret' (crossed out in the original memo) department in England, whose particular duty it should be to collect information patiently and systematically, was stressed. Its head should be in close and constant communication with Jenkinson as the Head of the Criminal Investigation Department in Ireland. This was of course what Jenkinson had spent the last year organising in Ireland and now he was proposing a parallel organisation for England. The need seemed obvious to Jenkinson because although he regularly received information from North America, 'except from the few reports from the constabulary stationed in

England, and from occasional communication from Mr R. Anderson, nothing is known of what is going on in England'. Jenkinson suspected that many of the leaders of the Fenian operations in Ireland resided in England and hatched their conspiracies there. Reminding the Home Secretary that a department such as he suggested took time to organise and that results would come slowly, he recommended that the department's head should be directly responsible to the Home Secretary, as he was to the Irish viceroy.

Jenkinson also stressed that the new Irish Branch must be completely independent of the Yard and controlled by the new Head of a Political Crimes Department (definitely not a policeman) in the Home Office, by-passing Anderson. Harcourt would be well advised, he continued, to avoid offering any precise directions to the London RIC to avoid any 'jealousies or misapprehensions'. All communication between Dublin Castle and the RIC in England under such a system would pass through the hands of the new Head of Department except in cases of great urgency. The Head of Department should be empowered to send at least three carefully selected intelligence agents to recruit local informants such as publicans, manufacturers, tradesmen, and mechanics who 'either already belong to the Fenian organisation or who may be in a position to hear what is going on, and to give reliable information'. These agents must not use their own names, or be known to each other. Only the Head of Department must know who they are and they must appear to be following occupations or professions that will serve to allay suspicions of their real activities. Most important was that before embarking upon such a scheme a commitment must be made to continue the department and its activities with a liberal expenditure of money 'through quiet and uneventful times without any interruption, just in the same way as the Fenians carry on the work of their organisation'. The Head would communicate privately with all police authorities while receiving information on local Fenianism from them. All arrangements were to be made in the quietest possible way thus preventing leaks in the newspapers. Still smarting over the publicity given to his own appointment, Jenkinson recommended that the new English 'spymaster' begin his work in secrecy and carry it on in the same manner.[18]

One of the first moves towards the creation of such an under-cover system had already been made when Jenkinson, chief commissioner Henderson and 'Dolly' Williamson of Special Irish Branch had sent their first agent, a Mr Hogan, under an assumed name to meet Harcourt at his private residence. Chief commissioner Henderson recommended to Harcourt : [Hogan's] 'general instructions will be to make it his business to obtain informants who will put him in possession of the present organisation of the Irish Societies, including the authors of recent outrages. When he had succeeded in establishing a good system of communication within Glasgow he can be sent else-where. He is willing to go for £3 per week with £1 for lodging allowance and travelling and contingent expenses'.[19]

What about public fears of bombers in every city of England and Scotland? Various attempts were made to allay public anxiety and one of the most interesting letters to appear in *The Times* came from George M. Roberts, RCS, the Technical Manager for Nobel's Explosive Co. Ltd :

> I have often by way of experiment, exploded a pound of dynamite suspended from the end of a fishing rod by a string about 6 ft long, holding the rod in my hand the while. As there was no solid matter to project I received no injury, and the end of the fishing rod was not even scratched. About 3 ft of the string at the end of the rod was always left uninjured.[20]

Cold comfort for the public in that. One man who was not so convinced about the harmless effects of dynamite was Henry Cloid who recalled, for the readers of *The Times*, the Bremer-haven blast of 11 December 1875 when a small barrel of gun-powder exploded on the quayside, killing one hundred and severely injuring another thirty people.[21]

The forensic reports of Professor Able and Dr August Dupré, Professor of Chemistry at Westminster Hospital and chemical advisor to the Home Office respectively, indicated that the 'wood dynamite' of *The Times'* bomb contained 30 per cent nitro-glycerine as opposed to only 19.2 per cent (75.4 per cent saw-dust, a little charcoal and 5.4 per cent moisture) nitroglycerine of the Possil Canal Bridge, Glasgow bomb. Sifting through the debris of the Whitehall blast Colonel Majendie had not found any evidence suggesting that a clockwork mechanism had been used in the bomb. Because of this he recommended that the CID release two men then in police custody. At the time of the explosion they had been lodging in a Covent Garden coffee house and had been seen with a japanned ladies' hat box of the type used in the recent explosions. However they possessed an alibi for 8.45 p.m. Majendie, ignorant of the forty-minute delay characteristic of the Rossa-type fuse, reasoned that only clockwork could have provided the time delay which would have allowed the two men to have set off the Whitehall bomb.[22] The two men, who were in fact part of the Rossa team of bombers, were released. One fled to America and the second returned to Glasgow, while a third man was later found to have remained in London.

One of the most serious problems facing the bombers was that of securing the necessary explosives. The attempts in Glasgow and London had been made with home-made explosives, not commercially manufactured slabs of dynamite. The Irish-American press had put great emphasis upon the skills necessary for do-it-yourself explosive manufacturing, exemplified by the famous lectures of Professor Mezzeroff, described as a great Russian chemist.

PROFESSOR MEZZEROFF'S LECTURES

The Professor will be open to engagements during the next three months to deliver lectures within a day's journey of New York, on 'Dynamite and the Resources of Civilization'. Address, as to terms, Patrick Joyce, Secretary, Box 2197, New York.[23]

Carrying explosives about obviously increased the possibility of detection, and few men would knowingly wish to add to their personal risk by travelling long distances with dynamite, however stable and safe it might be, much less nitroglycerine, a fluid which might explode from jarring or even temperature extremes. As it was, the 1875 Explosives Act only provided for a penalty of two years imprisonment for the illegal possession of explosives. The soaking of nitroglycerine in sawdust—lignine dynamite—was a bulky but reasonably effective means of transporting the highly dangerous substance. Bombers, it was assumed, would seek to make their own explosives and most likely their 'factory' would be fairly near their target.

E. G. Jenkinson did not exclude the possibility that the bombers might attempt to purchase explosives under assumed names for a bogus purpose or even take the greater risk of theft, which had been a favourite Fenian means of securing revolvers and guns in times past. In early February 1883 HM Customs agents had discovered and seized three cases of dynamite and dynamite (nitro) glycerine at Queensborough, one of the ports on the Thames estuary, which had been entered on the bills of lading as 'PRINTS'. The consignees were not located.[24] Correspondence with Sir William Harcourt indicated that Jenkinson's bets had been placed upon the next round of Irish-American explosions being produced by home-made lignine dynamite— nitroglycerine soaked sawdust. He sought to convince the Home Secretary that those chemicals used in the manufacture of nitroglycerine should be the object of legislation requiring registration for purchase. This would have meant that the purchaser would have had to declare his name, address, and purpose for the chemicals as was already the case for the purchase of poisons. Clearly it would be easier to have detectives making periodic checks on the registers kept by both chemical manufacturers and dispensing chemists than attempting to watch all of Great Britain's chemical suppliers. Harcourt was sympathetic, although not convinced. He was not prepared to put forward new legislation along these lines, possibly because of political problems but more likely because of the difficulty of enforcement. Having been thus rebuffed Jenkinson asked him whether the government would wait until some terrible explosion happened and then pass the legislation required?

Jenkinson recognised that at the chemical suppliers the bombers risked losing their anonymity and he would be waiting, not to pounce, but to mark and watch until he was able to roll up the entire team of bombers. Patience was his watchword. The chemicals that would point to the explosives' manufacturers were nitric acid, glycerine, sulphuric acid and sulphuric arsenic—common ingredients associated with the manufacture of nitroglycerine.

The first break came in Cork on Easter Monday 1883, when a man, later identified as Henry Morgan, a drayman at Lavitt's Quay, purchased quantities of powdered chloride of potash and powdered sugar from T. R. Lester, chemists, of 107 St Patrick

Street. These were not nitroglycerine components, but commonly associated with 'Fenian fire' which was a combustible substance that would be far more effective in setting fires than the boxes of matches often referred to in the Irish-American press. A government explosives expert said that if 'a mixture of chlorate of potash and sugar is acted upon by sulphuric acid, it produces brisk inflammation almost amounting to detonation. By inflammation I mean ignition. If red orpiment (realgar) is added to it, it makes the inflammation more brisk. . . .' Contact had been made with a group of Rossa's bombers and the purchase at Lester's was for the detonators used in conjunction with the lignine dynamite; Jenkinson had been right. He now made a connection, at least the hypothesis of a connection, between the Cork group and the reports of RIC detectives in Liverpool, that one of O'Donovan Rossa's agents was operating at Sutton, a village south of St Helens along the London and North Western Railway.

At the end of February, Jenkinson had advised Captain Nott-Bower, Liverpool's chief constable, to keep Patsy Flanagan, a guard for the railway at St Helens' Junction under surveillance. Jenkinson's RIC detectives then established a connection between Henry Morgan and several other men in Cork: Edmund O'Brien Kennedy, a resident of Philadelphia posing as 'Timothy Featherstone', newspaper correspondent; Timothy Carmody, slater; Daniel O'Herlihy, stationer and newsagent, and a railway porter, Denis Deasy. O'Herlihy had been under surveillance for several months because as the Crime Department report put it, 'He is a bad class of Fenian'. His mail had not been intercepted because the Cork City postmaster demanded that the writing on suspected envelopes had to be similar to known Fenian conspirators and that Dublin Castle had also issued an order that the contents of such letters should be likely to provide information 'relating to a treasonable conspiracy'.[25]

Jenkinson had identified the bombers none too soon for Deasy had already purchased a boat ticket. When he was finally missed the RIC detectives found that he was bound for Liverpool on the City of Cork Steam Packet Company's *Upupa* with a large deal box. As Jenkinson told Harcourt later: 'I only just had time to send a telegram warning them to expect Deasy, and the steamer which reached Liverpool a few hours later'.

The detectives who had allowed Deasy to slip away were under no illusions as to how Jenkinson felt about this lapse. Jenkinson had to depend upon the Liverpool police, and although anxious lest they should fumble the affair, he had no choice but to telegraph Captain Nott-Bower that Denis Deasy would be arriving from Cork with explosives that probably were to be used to blow up the Town Hall of St Helens. He was to be searched carefully for a letter of introduction to someone near Liverpool—most likely Patsy Flanagan, who had then been under surveillance for the better part of a month. Jenkinson, who had only been back in Dublin for three days before the storm broke, having been involved in the investigations surrounding the London bombs, continued the watch on Featherstone and his associates in Cork.[26]

The *Upupa* docked at Prince's Landing Stage at about 7 p.m. that Wednesday (28 March). Detective Inspector George Marsh and several Liverpool detectives, as well as RIC detectives Canning and Curran met the boat. Ten minutes after the gangway had been run out a thick-set man of about twenty-five came ashore and collected a porter. A few minutes later they disembarked and proceeded along the pierhead towards Waterloo Dock Gate, with the porter carrying a heavy wooden box. Marsh's patience at an end, he stopped Deasy close to the south gate. 'What have you in this box?' he asked. Deasy replied that it was cattle food. Marsh then took Deasy into the police hut and called a cab. Deasy claimed that he had been employed by a commercial traveller, Mr Murphy, to deliver a box of cattle spice to Liverpool. When Deasy was searched detectives found the key to the wooden box and two documents, the first a reminder.

Pat Flanagan
at Mr Brennan's
24 Covent Road, Sutton.
Go to St Helens Junction. Stay at 43 Regent Street, Liverpool. Go to Lime Street Station.

The second was a letter of introduction in the same hand, indicating that Deasy had not met Flanagan. It was addressed to 'Dear Pat' and recommended Deasy as the young man for whom he had asked him to find employment, 'for he is a good

This is a copy of a tracing taken by me from one
of the Exploding Machines — Made of Brass —
weighs 8 or 9 ounces — nearly 6 inches long (1) Small scre
button to give air or vent to the cup   (2) Cover of cup
which unscrews at $\frac{a}{a}$ ——   (3) Cup or hollo
space containing the acid ——   (4) Cock to be

turned like a gas cock so as to let the acid trickle
through . (5) an inner tube into which the acid
flows escaping at _b_ . Round this inner cylinde
which is fixed to 4 & 3, folds of tissue paper a
wrapped, through which the acid soaks & final
drops on a percussion cap at (7) exploding it (6)
an outer cylinder screwed on at $\frac{c}{c}$.

Drawing of a Fenian bomb fuse, made by E. G. Jenkinson.[28]

fellow and will mind his business wherever placed'. It was signed 'Edmund'. At the top of the letter was drawn a shamrock with the number 31 beneath it, which was assumed to mean that St Helens' Town Hall was to be bombed on 31 March. Deasy said that the letter had been given to him by Murphy. Meanwhile RIC detectives Johnston and Canning were on their way to Sutton where they arrested Flanagan on his way home from work at St Helens' Junction. Taking Flanagan back to his lodging house, they discovered a locked box containing a small tin canister filled with powder, a loaded six-chambered revolver, forty cartridges, a bottle of liquid, and a false beard. Under questioning, Flanagan said that the powder was 'tooth powder', and the fluid was for a 'liver complaint'.[27]

At 8.15 that evening Deasy's box was untied and unlocked by Superintendent Williams in Liverpool's Detective Office. James Campbell Brown, Professor of Chemistry at University College, Liverpool, found that the box contained two tin canisters stitched up in canvas filled with lignine dynamite. It proved to be a highly concentrated explosive mixture containing 70 per cent nitroglycerine, sawdust and a little chalk—weighing 28 lbs 8 oz. There were also three brass fuse tubes and packets of chlorate of potash, sugar and a lump of realgar bearing the label 'Lesters' Cork', and two bottles of concentrated sulphuric acid ('oil of vitriol'). The tin canisters contained holes $1\frac{1}{2}$ inches in diameter in their upper half corresponding to openings in the canvas loosely plugged by a piece of paper into which the brass fuses were apparently to be inserted. At first glance Professor Brown saw the fuse as an 'elaborately clumsy method' which was extremely dangerous for the bomber; there were easier and far more effective methods available. Brown soon changed his mind, however, for he reported the next day :

> If the mixture of chlorate of potash and sugar were packed in the space between the outer and inner brass cylinders in the brass tap, and if, closing the tap the upper chamber were partly filled with the oil of vitriol the instrument thus charged might have been placed in the tin cylinder of the nitroglycerine case, then on turning the tap the acid would fall into the inner brass cylinder below, the

E

paper which is tied over the holes in the inner brass cylinder would prevent the acid from immediately touching chlorate and sugar and so allow the operator time to escape.

In a short time the paper was destroyed, the acid reacted with the sugar and chlorate of potash, and the fire and flame was driven partly downward into the lignine dynamite through the opening in the end of the tube producing detonation. In a report filed on 30 March, referring to the previous report, Campbell Brown found that the detonator could be managed by a 'very slightly skilled' person much more easily and more safely than he could have believed without actually trying the experiment. He later admitted that when he first attempted to make the fuse work he charged it, and then when nothing had happened after ten minutes he took it apart to look! On his first attempt it took twenty minutes to work and he found that the time could be varied according to the number of layers of porous paper (like newsprint) coiled 'on the orifices which have to be penetrated'.[29]

Following the arrests there was a flurry of telegrams between Dublin, Liverpool and London as Jenkinson, Chief Constable Nott-Bower of Liverpool, and the Home Office worked to produce a common policy for dealing with the dynamite teams. Jenkinson, while deferring to Harcourt for final decisions, manoeuvered for the right to supervise future operations. What concerned Jenkinson was that it was almost impossible to convict bombers outside of Ireland except when they were caught in the very act itself. If they were caught without 'fuse in hand' they could only be imprisoned for the illegal possession of explosives or, say, of a revolver. The situation was, however, entirely different in Ireland where the coercion legislation did not allow such loopholes. The arrests in Liverpool had to be played down lest 'the birds will fly from Glasgow, London and other places if too much stir is made'. Jenkinson wanted all the bombers—not just some of them. Jenkinson also chided Harcourt about his apparent reluctance to take seriously the warnings about the possible bombing of the Albert Memorial; Jenkinson said 'these men are just now more active than ever'.

Jenkinson waited until 30 March before moving against the Cork suspects. Sending a cypher telegram to Harcourt via the

Irish Office, effectively bypassing Anderson at the Home Office, he notified London that the RIC had arrested Morgan, 'Featherstone', Carmody, O'Herlihy and Deasy in Cork, but pleaded for the deferment of action at Liverpool and elsewhere until his recommendation could arrive by post on the next day.[30]

With the arrest of 'Timothy Featherstone' in Cork, Jenkinson had the answer as to the source of the chemicals: Featherstone had purchased them in Glasgow from J. Montague and Company, using Daniel O'Herlihy's name. Further investigations would indicate that at least £20 of the money was traceable to O'Donovan Rossa, and that two carboys of acid were still waiting for collection on the Cork quayside. Having the name of the retailer/wholesaler was an important lead for it was possible that it was the same source used for the Glasgow explosives, especially if this was part of the same operation. Jenkinson stressed the need to get a competent man to Glasgow, who could carry on an investigation without disturbing Featherstone's associates. Further, he recommended that Deasy, assumed to be the weaker of the three men, be kept in solitary confinement and encouraged to inform on his associates. The picture had dramatically enlarged, linking Cork with Liverpool and Glasgow. Information had also arrived that one of Rossa's men was on the way to London via France with a considerable sum of money for an agent already in London. Again Jenkinson stressed the need for a chemical register with heavy punishment for illegal purchases *'both in England and Ireland'*. Jenkinson sent one of his Crime Department detectives to Liverpool on the evening of 31 March to take a statement from Deasy, complaining to Harcourt that Deasy had been arrested too soon. The Liverpool police were very lucky not to have alerted Flanagan for they had ignored his instructions to *follow* Deasy to see where the box was being taken. Harcourt was also told of a cypher telegram just received at Dublin Castle: 'Notify Bank of England to be cautious in receiving boxes for safe custody'. The implications were clear: bombs were not to be safely stored in the Old Lady of Threadneedle Street. On 1 April Jenkinson wanted to be put in direct contact with the Home Office agent in Glasgow (Hogan?), since he possessed information locating Featherstone in Glasgow in February. 'Dolly' Williamson was given the name and description of the Rossa

courier, a small dark man named John O'Connor. Special
Branch was waiting for the Skirmisher operations to begin.
Jenkinson stressed to Harcourt, as he had to Williamson, that
the police must not be in a hurry. They must give him rope,
watch patiently and bide their time! By 24 March John
O'Connor was under police surveillance. The Dublin 'spymaster' stressed that it was critical that Inspector Williamson
tell *no one* at Scotland Yard, obviously including Howard
Vincent of the CID or Chief Commissioner Henderson. If the
Rossa agents concerned knew that they were being watched
they 'will be off and the whole game will be up'. Harcourt told
Spencer that 'Jenks' had done splendidly as a marvellous
resource and first rate informant, and altogether 'we are
indebted to him for what security we possess against these
fiends'.[31]

Special Branch kept a close watch on O'Connor, a former
blacksmith who had emigrated to the United States in 1873.
Currently visiting his parents, he lodged next door to them in
Eden Place. He was often at Bowles American Reading Room,
14 The Strand (in addition to the pubs, according to the police
report), looking for a man named 'McCarthy'. Later, in the
company of a 'stout fair man' he had visited the Clock Tower,
Houses of Parliament, and 24 March had been observed gestur-
ing 'as if illustrating the blowing up of the structure'. A report
of Special Branch on 4 April showed that O'Connor was continuing his sightseeing, somewhat unusual activity for a former
resident of London. He also seemed to be taking notes concerning various points of interest. The 'stout fair man', referred to
by Williamson as the 'lesser important man', was also looking
for McCarthy. Who was McCarthy and was he the Rossa
courier, or were these men part of not the Skirmishers, but
Clan na Gael? Only time would answer that question and
neither Williamson nor Jenkinson knew how much time they
had.[32]

5

The Gallagher Team

. . . a victim of an unfortunate combination of circumstances.
Petition of Thomas Gallagher,
26 June 1883, to the Home Secretary.

ROBERT ANDERSON had been warned by Major Le Caron that Clan na Gael was planning a dynamite campaign and that the selection and training of candidates had been underway since the previous summer of 1882. The Clan made no secret about its objective being the dynamiting of England's cities, but thus far had deferred to the inept attempts of O'Donovan Rossa's Skirmishers. Although that summer Alexander Sullivan had told Le Caron that Dr Thomas Gallagher had already made a visit to England, this was anticipation rather than realisation. Gallagher did not in fact set out for England from New York until 15 October 1882 to do the necessary groundwork preliminary to a series of bombings planned for the spring of the following year.

Using poor health as a pretext for the trip, Gallagher had left New York on the SS *Alaska* bound for Liverpool. As befitting such a tour, the Glasgow-born doctor visited relatives in Scotland before travelling by rail to London, remaining for a month at Rayment's Hotel, 18 London Wall, E.C., a short walk from St Paul's Cathedral. Carefully selecting potential targets, he played the role of the American tourist with style, looking very much the professional man with carefully trimmed beard and gold headed cane. He apparently visited the House of Commons on 16 and 17 November. During question time on the sixteenth, Harcourt was asked if he was aware that 300 tons of dynamite was stored in one room at Bury Port, Carmarthenshire within a short distance of shipping and works with hundreds of employees? And even more important had there been an explosion of waste dynamite there on last Saturday? The

Home Secretary said that there had been a detailed investigation of the incident and he would be happy to show its results
to the questioner. At the conclusion of question time the visitor
in the gallery would have been well advised to continue his
sightseeing in Westminster for the House then proceeded to
debate its New Rules of Procedure until 1 a.m. Gallagher left
London for Dublin where he stayed at the Gresham Hotel,
made a short visit to Donegal to visit relatives and then met the
SS *Bosnia* at Queenstown on 10 December, arriving home just
before Christmas 1882. Gallagher returned to the United States
with increased confidence that he and his team of Clan na Gael
dynamiters could avoid the security measures taken to stop such
attacks. When he had the opportunity to speak to Le Caron
at the Clan convention in Chicago that next month he was filled
with optimism and spoke endlessly about 'dynamite, its production, its effectiveness, and the great weapon it was soon to
prove against the British government'.

And yet, as events were to prove, Le Caron had nothing
substantial about the attacks' details, nor did he have details
on the targets, dates, method of securing explosives, or the
names of the dynamite team members. Even more significantly
Le Caron, in common with the other leaders of the Clan, did
not know that Gallagher had reached a secret agreement with
O'Donovan Rossa and was for all intents no longer under the
control of the Revolutionary Directory. The bombers would come
to Britain and the big questions were how many groups of them,
when would they arrive, and most significantly what were their
targets.

The Revolutionary Directory meeting in secret session heard
his report and gave final clearance for his proposed attacks
on England. The dates set for the explosions, probably
known only to Gallagher, lay in the second week of April
1883.[1]

The operation was planned, the money allocated, men trained
but not finally selected; what remained was the major problem
of securing an adequate amount of explosive material. Although
the security arrangements of the English and Irish police
authorities appear in retrospect to be far from efficient, there
was sufficient security to make Gallagher hesitate about any
attempt to smuggle the explosives into Liverpool or any other

port. It was probably not in his nature to rely upon commercially made dynamite when so much of his time in recent years had been occupied with its manufacture and its use in the fabrication of various types of bombs.

Gallagher had been born in Glasgow in 1851, starting work as a child in a local foundry. His family, which comprised a widowed mother, six sons and two daughters, emigrated to the United States when Thomas was about fifteen or sixteen. He found work in an iron foundry in the New York area, but in his spare time he studied medicine, showing such a talent for it that his employer encouraged him to take it up seriously. Gallagher eventually left the foundry, where he had doubtless had ample opportunity to practice his healing arts on fellow workers, to set a practice in Greenpoint, Brooklyn out on Long Island. Here he served the local Irish population while taking an active part in Clan na Gael. His status as a professional man in the Irish community and his intelligence made him a natural leader in the efforts being made to free Ireland from the English yoke. His familiarity with chemistry as a side product of his practice of medicine made him aware of his own talents in the manufacturing of explosives, a natural outgrowth of his hatred of England. Coming to the conclusion that the best way to secure the necessary explosives for the campaign was to manufacture them in England, he sought a major city with a large Irish population into which one could 'melt'. He chose Birmingham, 111 miles to the northwest of London and only two hours journey on the train to Euston Station. The man sent to prepare the explosives, 'Jemmy' or James Murphy, travelled under the alias 'Alfred George Whitehead', which may have been an intentional pun upon Robert W. Whitehead's self-propelled torpedo, invented in 1866 and the prototype of that weapon.

'Whitehead' sailed from the United States in the last fortnight of January, appearing in Birmingham on 6 February 1883. How long he had been in the city looking for a shop in the Irish districts cannot be determined, but on that particular date he decided to rent a shop at 128 Ledsam Street, Ladywood, south of the city centre. Whitehead told John Dibble, the agent, that he was in business in Devonport but wanted to open a shop for mixing oils and colours while selling the usual line of paints, brushes, and wall papers. He left a deposit of £1, asked for the town gas to be connected and rented a room next door in which to live, preferring not to live above the shop. It had been decided that the best cover for Whitehead's activity would be for him to pose as a retail merchant which would allow him to purchase chemicals without drawing too much attention to his real activities. He put his name over the door and stocked the shop with about £10 worth of merchandise—eventually selling five sheets of paper, two paint brushes and 3d worth of paint. He purchased earthenware pans for chemicals from John Clewlow, manager for Moulton's China dealer, mentioning that he had come from America, possibly in response to a comment from Clewlow concerning his accent. The first lot of chemicals was ordered from Thomas Canning, an apprentice at William Canning and Co., Great Hampton St; it amounted to 160 lbs of nitric acid, 300 lbs of sulphuric acid, and fifty lbs of glycerine to be delivered the next day. Whitehead installed a funnel in the back kitchen connected with the chimney, to carry the fumes off. He hired a thirteen-year old boy, James Crowder, as a shop assistant after advertising in the shop window at the beginning of March, when he was possibly too preoccupied with the chemical processes to tend the store. About a week after the boy had begun work in the 'paint' shop there was an explosion in the back kitchen that broke a pane of glass. When asked what had happened, Whitehead claimed that his pistol had gone off accidentally; this apparent error might well have terminated the entire operation if the production had been further advanced. Such an explosion would have involved over 400 lbs of nitroglycerine, the amount decided upon by Gallagher, and would have levelled a large part of the neighbourhood.

He continued to purchase chemicals from Cannings as well as from Judson and Sons, Liverpool St. The reason that such purchases did not immediately arouse suspicion was that the three chemicals were often sold together in very large amounts because of their use by the many gilders and jewellers in Birmingham. Whitehead nevertheless seems to have questioned his own wisdom in buying the three chemicals together. Thus while continuing to purchase the acids from one set of retailers, he looked for another source of chemically pure glycerine. This he located in Philip Harris & Co., Bull Ring, and he made his first purchase there on 23 February. He ordered four 56-pound tins of the chemical with a specific gravity of 1.250. In order to further allay suspicion he also purchased two gallons of linseed oil and turpentine. One storeman did however, think it somewhat unusual for a paint and paper retailer to require £27 worth of pure glycerine, but was partially satisfied when Whitehead explained that he sold the chemical to hairdressers and chemists for hair preparations. The storeman, George Pritchard, perhaps noticing an Irish accent, tinged with Americanisms, or vice versa, remarked to his mates that Whitehead might just as well be making nitroglycerine.

Pritchard later asked the company's carter, Charles Hinson, who had delivered the glycerine, if he had noticed any large bottles or carboys at the Ledsam Street shop. Hinson recalled that he had seen nothing but a little stock but had been interested in Whitehead's chemical stained fingernails and his obviously acid-eaten clothing. On 20 March Whitehead returned to the supplier to complain that a second delivery of glycerine was not of the correct specific gravity. It was found that a lower grade had been sent but the correct price charged. Pritchard, prepared to exchange the glycerine for the chemically pure variety, asked Whitehead to write out an order for the correct glycerine so that 'no dispute could arise'. Whitehead agreed to pay the extra 2d per pound but refused to write out an order explaining that he could not write because of a bad hand, concealed by oversized gloves. Pritchard's suspicions were confirmed 'by a few questions' which convinced him that Whitehead was not what he claimed to be. Pritchard then asked Hinson, preparing to go to Ledsam Street to exchange the two orders of glycerine, to take a careful look around the shop. Hinson later reported having seen three or four carboys and that Whitehead had been very keen to prevent his looking over the premises. Pritchard did not report the suspicious paint merchant on Ledsam Street to the police until the 27 March, when he told Detective Sergeant Richard Price.[2] For some unexplained reason the house does not appear to have been put under police surveillance until 31 March. On that day Sergeant Price entered the shop disguised as a painter and purchased a paint brush. On 2 April at 2 a.m., Price, Pritchard and another officer entered the shop using skeleton keys and took samples from the various chemicals in the shop. Having entered in stocking feet they received burns from the chemicals spilled on the floor but their mission was successful. Dr Hill, a city chemist, verified that these were chemicals which could be used in the production of nitroglycerine. By the end of that day the Birmingham authorities were convinced that they had located an Irish-American bomb factory, confirmed in part by a coat in the shop bearing the label of Brookes Brothers, Broadway, New York.[3] But where were the bombers?

William Lynch was a twenty-two year old coach painter at the works of Mr Merry in Brooklyn. Living at home on Bergen St, Brooklyn with his mother and sister, he became drawn into the Fenian Brotherhood by a fellow employee at Merry's. He joined the secret society in 1881 at a meeting of the Emerald Club of the Fenian Brotherhood. 'On the evening I joined the club I was taken to Second St, Bowery, New York, to the Oddfellows' Hall; I entered an anteroom and was taken to the meeting room, where there were about 30 men—strangers to me. I never knew their names. They were known by numbers. I was taken to the presiding officer, Thomas Burns (No. 10), and was given an oath, some of the words of which were "Stand by the watchword, obey the superior officers, and to preserve the funds of the Brotherhood", and I kissed a book. I paid two dollars upon entrance and subsequently ten cents a week for dues. The meetings were weekly, I attended about twice a month.' The watchword 'Providence' was given to gain entrance and was changed once or twice, with notice of this being given at the meeting. There were also supposed to be other clubs in New York with such names as Esperanza, Sarsfield, and Michael Davitt. Meetings of the Emerald Club were in addition to the dynamite classes which were held for those young men like Lynch, committed to 'freedom for Ireland by force alone'. The leader of this wing of the American Fenian movement was O'Donovan Rossa, usually referred to as the 'Old Man'.

On 6 or 7 March, Lynch received a letter from Thomas Burns instructing him to go to 420 Manhattan Avenue in Brooklyn. He did so the next day and found the name Thomas Gallagher, MD over the door. Gallagher subsequently told Lynch that 'You are wanted to go to London'. When asked

why, he was told that he would find out when he got there.
He was warned to say nothing to his family who would be well
taken care of for the two months he would be away. Lynch
was given a total of $150 and instructed to buy a ticket for
Liverpool using the alias 'Norman'. When he arrived in London
he was to leave a letter for Dr Gallagher containing his local
address, at the American Exchange on the Strand. Lynch was
apparently upset about having to leave his job but a chance
meeting with Burns assured him that 'the "Old Man" would
see him righted'. Lynch followed instructions and stayed over-
night in a New York hotel, sailing the next morning, 9 March,
on the SS *Spain*. During the long trip he looked inside the
small brown paper parcel which Gallagher had given him. He
found a wooden box which contained a coil spring with a piece
of lead at the end of it. The box was six or seven inches long
by two inches broad. Afraid that it might be discovered by a
custom's search at Liverpool, he broke the box up and threw
the spring overboard. The ship arrived in Liverpool on the
nineteenth and Norman, rather than going directly to
London, bought a suit of clothes and stayed until the twenty-
second at Mr Cooper's 'Temperance Hotel', not arriving at
Euston Station until the evening of the twenty-second. The
American Exchange had closed for the day. It remained closed
on Good Friday, 23 March, and Norman visited the site of
the explosion at the Local Government Offices to see the extent
of the damage caused by Rossa's bombers on the fifteenth. The
presence of the heavy guards mounted by both police and
infantry at London's public buildings must have been very
obvious even to his inexperienced eye. Norman now waited
for Easter and Thomas Gallagher.[4]

Gallagher was close behind having sailed on the fourteenth
as a saloon passenger on the SS *Parthia*. His twenty-nine year
old brother, Bernard, was on the same ship but travelling in
steerage. He was an alcoholic. It is not clear if Bernard knew
what his brother was involved in. There was another man in
steerage whose relationship to the plot is equally unclear,
William Ansburgh, who was also travelling on to London.
Upon arriving in Liverpool on the evening of Easter Monday,
26 March, Bernard Gallagher was sent off to Glasgow while
Thomas caught the 9.50 train for London. He did not stop at

Birmingham. Arriving at Euston he left two bags and a bundle at the booking office and took a cab to the Charing Cross Hotel. Signing the register in his own name he settled down in room 312. At 9.52 that morning he telegraphed the following to Whitehead from the West Strand Telegraph Office:

> Will see you soon, am feeling all right
> Fletcher.

He then travelled up the Strand to the American Exchange where he identified himself and was given the letter which had been left for him by Norman on Saturday. Gallagher then collected Norman from his ground floor room at Edwardes' Hotel, Euston Square. They went to Westminster together where, walking past the Local Government Offices, Norman asked Gallagher if this was where the explosion was. He replied that this was a 'bad job for us', referring possibly to the slight damage done by the lignine dynamite. Norman then asked 'Is that what we're going to do?' to which the reply was 'Yes, but it won't be child's play'. Continuing down Whitehall they turned and crossed half way over Westminster Bridge and then turned to look at the Houses of Parliament, with Gallagher commenting, 'This will make a great crash when it comes down'. Scotland Yard was later pointed out as the headquarters of the London detective force: 'That will come down too'. Lynch/Norman was assured that they would not want for money because the 'Old Man' would see to it all. He was subsequently given £7 for his personal requirements. That was on 27 March.[5]

E. G. Jenkinson was convinced that the Local Government Offices bombing had all the marks of O'Donovan Rossa's Skirmishers including their use of lignine dynamite packaged in a tin hat box. This was the *modus operandi* in Glasgow and at *The Times* offices in the city. But to which group did Gallagher and his team belong—the Clan or the Skirmishers? This was an important question because Rossa, based in New York, had been expelled from the Clan for failure to accept the discipline of the FC (Clan executive committee). Gallagher was a Rossa agent, as was Norman, working within the Clan for the purpose of getting it to pay for Rossa's operations. Whatever the precise details, Gallagher was funded by the Clan and directed by Rossa.

Tom Clarke had emigrated to the United States from Dungannon on an old cattleboat three or four years earlier. He and a close friend, Billy Kelly, soon became members of New York's Napper Tandy Club (Camp No. 1 of Clan na Gael at 4 Union St). Clarke and Kelly both attended Thomas Gallagher's dynamite classes and Clarke sometimes went with the 'master' to a desolate spot on Long Island where they experimented, blasting rocks with nitroglycerine. Kelly had to give up his 'further dynamite education' when he got a job at the Garden City Hotel, Long Island. In early 1883 Clarke was offered the job of managing the Brighton Beach Hotel on Long Island, but in early March one of the men selected to join Gallagher for the London mission refused to go and Clarke was chosen in his place. The twenty-two year old Clarke was given money, and instructions to report to Whitehead at 128 Ledsam St, Birmingham. Clarke gave up his job and to preserve secrecy embarked at Boston. The ship struck an iceberg and sank but the passengers were fortunately rescued by a passing vessel and landed at Newfoundland. Clarke gave his name as Henry Hammond Wilson, a returning Englishman; he was given clothing, £5, and passage on a Liverpool-bound ship. 'Wilson' arrived in Birmingham by 28 March, but there was a fifth man already in Britain, John Kent.[6]

Kent, aged thirty-four, had emigrated from Ireland in 1872 and took up work as an iron moulder in the New York area. Here he came to know the two Gallagher brothers. Kent had left New York on the SS *Egypt* not long after Whitehead but travelled to Queenstown and then to his parents at Fermoy, County Cork, where his father was a publican. Continuing on to Glasgow, via Liverpool, he carried a letter of introduction from Thomas Gallagher to Denis Kilfeather, Merton Street, in the name of 'John Curtin' (his mother's maiden name).

Kilfeather, who had known Gallagher for at least twenty years had received a visit from him just before Christmas. He was asked to help 'Curtin' find work, which he did at a Clyde shipbuilding yard. That was 3 February. On 2 March, Curtin ostensibly went to Blackburn to visit his sister and returned to Glasgow five days later. He continued to live with Kilfeather and to work in the shipyard until at least the seventeenth, when Kilfeather seems somehow to have lost touch with his

movements. Curtin waited to be called to London : he received
two postal orders for the sum of £5.10s. from Gallagher. Then
the message came, carried by Bernard Gallagher, who spent
most of his time in Glasgow's public houses. On 4 April,
accompanied to the station by Kilfeather Curtin took an evening train for Blackburn, but got into a carriage that went
through to Liverpool. Kilfeather had cause to wonder about that
'mistake'. The final piece had been added to the instrument of
destruction : 'Fletcher' (T. Gallagher), 'Wilson' (T. J. Clarke),
'Whitehead' (James Murphy) 'Curtin' (John Kent) and 'Norman' (W. Lynch).

Gallagher's tour of Westminster on Easter Tuesday (27
March) must have given him genuine cause for concern. The
public buildings were all under heavy guard both day and
night. Unless he chose to strike at unguarded targets, the
chance of getting close enough to a building to plant the
explosives without being seen appeared very slight. He may also
have had some concern about Wilson's whereabouts, and perhaps about just how useful Norman would be in the operation
ahead : at least he himself had trained Whitehead, Wilson and
Curtin. Norman was an unknown, but he had come from the
Rossa ring and to that extent represented the other dimension
of Gallagher's allegiance. He had no financial worries, for, in
addition to over $2,300 which he carried on his person, there
was a £600 letter of credit requiring only his signature to obtain
the money. On the morning of the twenty-eighth, just as
Jenkinson and the Liverpool police were preparing to spring
their trap on the team of bombers preparing to attack St Helens'
Town Hall, Norman received an early morning visit from
Gallagher. The two men went out together and Norman was
told that Gallagher was leaving London for a couple of days,
but that he was to remain at his hotel until contacted.
Gallagher then proceeded to Euston where he took a train for
Birmingham.

That afternoon, young Crowder, Whitehead's shop assistant,
met Mr Fletcher, a man with a long beard, who came into the
shop and asked for the owner. He, being told that Whitehead
was in the back of the shop, rapped on the window in the door
separating the shop from the back premises. When Whitehead

opened the door Fletcher enquired if he sold oils. The answer was 'Yes'. Crowder was then sent on an errand, and when he returned an hour later he was given a half-day holiday, and told to have a long walk around the city. During that absence the two men worked out the difficulties they faced. Wilson then appeared, perhaps having already made contact with White-head, unobserved by Crowder. Gallagher and Wilson travelled back to London together, arriving at Euston at 9.55 on the evening of the next day, the twenty-ninth. About twenty minutes later the two men checked two bags, a bundle and a portmanteau at the cloakroom. Gallagher paid the charges and asked the clerk to keep the portmanteau in a cool place. The next day Gallagher returned to Euston and collected his belongings. Wilson, in the meantime, started looking for lodg-ings. They had decided that the time had come to shift their base of operations to the heavily populated Irish community at the south end of Blackfriars' Bridge.

On the thirty-first, Saturday, Wilson presented himself to Charlotte Matilda Clare at 17 Nelson Square, Blackfriars, between 2 and 3 in the afternoon. He took a garret room for six shillings a week and returned to Euston where he picked up his portmanteau, which the clerk George Dickinson estimated must have weighed close to sixty pounds—an interesting accumu-lation for a man who had so recently lost everything in a ship-wreck. Wilson returned to his room on Nelson Square, while Detective Sergeant Price was making one of the few purchases from Whitehead in his shop in Birmingham. On Monday, 2 April, Wilson borrowed pen and ink from his landlady, explain-ing that he was studying for a medical examination with a tutor at Charing Cross. The uncoded letter was not to his 'tutor' Gallagher, but to Whitehead in Birmingham. The letter carried the Nelson Square address and the signature of Henry Wilson:

My Dear Friend,
If you are not otherwise engaged, I should like to have the pleasure of your company at one of the theatres this evening. I will be at the place to be decided on to meet on such occasions at 6.30.

Wilson was expected on 4 April. This still did not solve the

problem of how to transport 400-500 pounds of highly dangerous nitroglycerine which could be detonated by the slightest
jarring, or even by temperature extremes. The container agreed
upon was the type of rubber bag used for various purposes by
doctors. Gallagher had already sent Norman to Birmingham on
Monday to bring the first consignment of nitro to London.
Norman had spent £5 for a respectable looking trunk into
which to put the explosives. When he arrived at Ledsam Street,
Whitehead was amazed to find that he had not also brought rubber bags, pointing out to Norman that one could not simply pour
it into a trunk ! He then sent Norman to Harris & Co. for rubber
bags with the comment that if they did not have them then no
one in Birmingham would. Harris & Co. could not provide the
rubber bags. This had taken the better part of the day and while
Norman had anticipated returning to London on the evening
train, and had arranged for the 'boots' at Edwardes' Hotel
to meet him at Euston to help with the trunk, he decided instead
to remain the night and wired the hotel of his changed plans.

When he did return to London the next morning, finding
Gallagher was no easy matter. He first went to his own hotel
and left one letter at the American Exchange and another at the
Charing Cross Hotel. Then, returning to Edwardes' Hotel, he
found Gallagher had just left. Finally, he received a telegram
from 'Fletcher' (Gallagher) to come to the Charing Cross Hotel.
After recounting the problems he had experienced in Birmingham, Gallagher gave Norman a large rubber bag and commented that 'The chap I sent there this morning did not have
a rubber bag'. Norman was told to take the bag to Whitehead
first thing in the morning (that would be 4 April) when Wilson
was also expected at Ledsam Street. Wilson had gone to
Gallagher on Tuesday morning to discuss the method of bringing the nitroglycerine down from Birmingham. He had already
purchased one large rubber bag on the thirtieth, the previous
Friday, when he first arrived in London, but it clearly would
not be enough to bring all of the material down, perhaps only
200 pounds. He had decided to use his portmanteau and the
rubber bag he had purchased would certainly not fit into it, and
so Gallagher agreed to go out to William Walkley, 5 Strand,
to see if he could purchase some smaller bags which would fit
into the portmanteau. The owner's son served Gallagher and

regretted that they did not stock the 'gas bags' for which he had asked. Pressed for time, Gallagher, looking round the shop, saw a pair of rubber fishing stockings, and said that they would be 'useful for wading in summer'. He paid 21s for them and asked for them to be sent around to him at the Charing Cross Hotel as quickly as possible, which was done about ten minutes later. Not long after, Wilson came into the shop and asked if the 'gas bags' had been sent to Dr Gallagher. Walkley replied that Gallagher had purchased a pair of rubber fishing stockings instead, and they had already been sent to the hotel. Wilson went back to the hotel to discuss how to use these stockings, which if only partially filled, might fit into the portmanteau. Taking the stockings with him, Wilson returned to Nelson Square that afternoon, emptied the portmanteau, leaving a few items in the room and headed for Euston to catch a train to Birmingham.

That night he stayed at the Midland Hotel, and may well have gone to the theatre that night with Whitehead, a moment of welcome relaxation for the two conspirators. In the meantime, Norman had been given the large rubber bag by Gallagher who told him to return to Birmingham in the morning. When he knew which train he would return on, he was to send a telegram to Gallagher at the Charing Cross Hotel. He would then meet him at Euston Station with further instructions. The next morning Wilson checked out of the Midland Hotel at about 9.10 a.m. and took a twenty-minute cab journey to Ledsam Street. He helped Whitehead to pour between 40–44 lbs of nitroglycerine into each of the fishing stockings, tying them carefully at the knees and packing the two stockings into the portmanteau. In the process he got some of the explosive chemicals on his shirt sleeves. A cab was called. Robert Lanchester, the driver, attempting to carry the portmanteau to the cab, exclaimed to Wilson, 'Good God, have you got sovereigns in here?' Wilson helped him to get the case on to the cab and they were gone by 10.40 a.m., followed in vain by one of the detectives watching the shop. One of the handles of the portmanteau had been broken in the effort to get it to the cab. When George Dee, a New Street station porter, took it from the cab to the 11.30 train for London, he thought it had pig iron in it. Dee was asked to be especially careful of the bag.

Wilson left Birmingham probably unaware that an attempt had been made to follow him.

He arrived back in London at his lodgings about 3 p.m. It must have been a tremendous relief to have completed that part of the operation without mishap. When he entered the boarding house Charlotte Clare commented on the broken handle. Wilson explained 'The railway smashers smashed everything'. Refusing her offer to take the bag upstairs he carried the 80–90 pounds of high explosives to his third-floor room. His work was not done yet, for it was obvious that more bags would be needed to shift the remainder of the explosives. That afternoon he and Gallagher purchased at least four more rubber bags.

By the time the detective, who had tried to follow him, returned to Ledsam Street, another cab had arrived and its occupant, a man, was in the back of the shop with Whitehead. Norman was still having problems, for although he had brought the rubber bag there was nothing to put the bag into after it had been filled with the 'butter-milk' like explosive. Whitehead sent him out to buy a black wooden trunk, which he did, from Henry Avory on Snowhill Street. The two men proceeded to remove its partitions, and then gently lowered the rubber bag filled with 200 pounds of nitroglycerine into the box, snapped the lock and called a cab. The police were only marginally better prepared this time to follow their suspects. The box was set on the top of the cab, and it headed for New Street—the time was about 4 p.m. There were still close to 200 pounds of explosives in Whitehead's kitchen to be picked up on the next trip.

Norman was followed by detectives when he left Whitehead's shop. Constable Grey of the RIC wired Head Constable Ryan that another suspect had left Ledsam Street, apparently heading for New Street Station. Ryan held the 6 p.m. train long enough for the Birmingham detectives to purchase tickets and take the compartment next to that of Norman. Constable Grey also arrived to join the Birmingham detectives. A telegram was sent to Scotland Yard warning them of the situation and requesting assistance. Norman had arrived at the station by 4.30 p.m., which had left him quite enough time to send the telegram to Gallagher advising him of his arrival. It was not a matter of needing help with the explosives, as had been the case on the previous abortive trip when he had arranged for help from the 'boots', from his hotel. Now there would be no 'boots', since Norman had checked out of the Edwardes' Hotel (leaving his luggage there to be collected later) before leaving for Birmingham. Gallagher met him at Euston at 9 p.m. getting into the cab as it was pulling away from the station. He gave Norman the address of his new hotel, £5 and explained his new cover as a medical student. Gallagher slipped out of the cab as it proceeded to the Beaufort Hotel, Southampton Street, Strand, having arranged to meet him the next day.

The train had been met at Euston by Special Irish Branch detectives led by Inspector John Languish. They followed Norman's cab to the hotel, waited until 12.30 a.m. and then climbed to the third floor room and arrested Norman. Accepting the keys he offered, they unlocked the box and were confronted by a large rubber bag containing enough nitroglycerine to reduce the hotel to rubble. Norman was found to be carrying the £5 note which Gallagher had just given him, and a copy of the telegram which Gallagher ('Fletcher') had sent him earlier recalling him to the Charing Cross Hotel. Now they had the first clue to the existence of Gallagher, the man they had just missed arresting when he had slipped out of the cab. As the nitroglycerine was being shipped off to Woolwich Arsenal for disposal, the net began to spread to capture the other conspirators.

Birmingham's chief constable was notified by telegram of the arrest of Norman and he decided that they could not take the risk of Wilson escaping. The chief constable, Chief Inspector James Black, Sergeant Price, and several police officers took Whitehead into custody at 6 a.m. that morning, 5 April. It was Whitehead's carelessness which completed the destruction of the operation. Wilson had got away with enough explosives to bring down Big Ben. Gallagher, the explosives expert, was available to lay the charges and both men, because of police failures, were still at large. In addition to this, Curtin (Kent) had not yet arrived from Glasgow, leaving a diminished but still potentially effective team of dynamiters. The Birmingham police, however, found a pocket book at Whitehead's shop with the name of Wilson on one page written four times in the same handwriting, and most significantly the letter which Wilson had written to Whitehead concerning his impending arrival contained the return address at Nelson Square. Scotland Yard was soon in possession of the address and they moved quickly, establishing a base in the ground floor room of a retired vicar. Wilson was not at home. At 1 p.m. Wilson and Gallagher appeared and went up the stairs with Inspector Littlechild and his Special Irish Branch men right behind. Gallagher, in an effort to cover his tracks, had shaved his long beard and left only a moustache and sideburns. His connection with the Charing Cross Hotel had already been established and there detectives found a letter intended for Gallagher from Curtin giving his address as 12 Upper Woburn Place. Sergeant William Melville was immediately sent to be a 'lodger' and keep watch on Curtin. The detective had breakfast with Curtin the next morning, who said that he was not staying long in London. Curtin went out for a walk, loitered outside the Charing Cross Hotel, and then went to a pawn shop to raise more money, perhaps sensing that something had gone wrong. He was arrested later that day by detectives as he was crossing to Euston, possibly to take a train out of the city. The net was also spread to Glasgow, where a drunken Bernard Gallagher was arrested in a public house, and to Savage's Hotel, Blackfriars, where William Ansburgh was staying, a card with his address having been found in Gallagher's possession. That was the lot.

Six men and close to 500 pounds of the most powerful explosive of the day had been swept up in a combined operation of the Birmingham Police and the newly established Special Irish Branch of the Metropolitan Police's CID.[7]

The arrest of the Gallagher ring also was, however, the end of John O'Connor. He had been under surveillance for the previous two weeks and the Special Branch was not prepared to take the chance that he was ignorant of Gallagher's scheme. He was arrested at Bowles American Reading Room the same day as John Kent (Curtin). O'Connor gave his name as 'Henry Dalton' which proved to be his alias. His interrogators were satisfied that he was not part of the Gallagher team, but as soon as he was released on that charge, he was rearrested and sent to Liverpool under heavy escort. It was apparent that he was connected in some way with Featherstone, Deasy and Flanagan.

The capture of Gallagher and his fellow-bombers dramatically altered the security situation. Up to now, Harcourt and Gladstone had been reluctant to tamper with the 1875 Explosives Act. The carting of over 400 lbs of nitroglycerine on the London and North Western Express moved them to look again. The limitations of the 1875 Act were clear: it had been drawn up not to deal with explosives used for criminal objects, but 'reckless and negligent or careless use of a very dangerous commodity'. The Act allowed every private person to hold 15 lbs of dynamite or 30 lbs of gunpowder and thus in a lodging house of ten persons, 150 lbs of dynamite or 300 lbs of gunpowder could be stored legally. The average person found it hard to understand that, if a citizen chose to apply for a licence (which local authorities could not refuse), he could keep up to 200 lbs of gunpowder, 500 lbs of explosives and 200 lbs of fireworks—or 60 lbs of mixed explosives or of dynamite 'or something still stronger'. What the Home Secretary found even more extraordinary was that Whitehead, if he was for some reason released from prison, could immediately demand and expect to receive a licence to keep 60 lbs of dynamite at his new residence. Faced with the preparation of new legislation, Harcourt convinced the cabinet that the large part of the Home Office's normal business should be transferred to the Local Government Board under Charles Dilke. Dilke was rather amused by Harcourt's zeal for police work and thought that the Home Secretary fancied himself the equal of Fouché, the famous French minister of police under Napoleon I and the restored Bourbons, and thus 'wanted to have the whole police work of the country, and nothing but police'.[8]

This comment was directly related to Harcourt's unyielding opposition to a provision of the proposed Municipalities Bill. This would have removed the Metropolitan Police Authority from the jurisdiction of the Home Secretary to that of the new Greater London Municipal Government. He did so because, as he argued, a 'watch committee' could not respond to the Fenian threats with 'sufficient dispatch'. He was even prepared to resign from the government on the issue if it remained in the bill.

The amended explosives bill which emerged was to be called 'The English Coercive Act' by Robert Anderson. Looking back upon these events thirty years later Anderson felt that whereas sentimental objections are heard regarding crime in Ireland 'no drivel of that kind gets a hearing when crime in England is in question. And so, when the dynamiters began their fiendish work, "ordinary law" was discarded and a most extraordinary statute—Sir William Harcourt's Explosive Substances Act, 1883 (46 Vic.ch.3)—was hurried through parliament, with the result that the crime against which it was aimed was soon stamped out'.[9] The extent to which the provisions of this act made the work of the police easier is still open to question, but Anderson was certainly correct about the bill being hurried through parliament. On Thursday 5 April, the day following the arrest of the Gallagher team, Harcourt wrote to Gladstone outlining his suggested amendment to the 1875 act and promptly received permission to proceed. Four days later, in the Commons, Gladstone moved to postpone the Orders of the Day until after Harcourt had presented the new Explosive Bill. It took the Home Secretary one and a half hours to introduce it, to have it read, passed and sent to the Lords.

Harcourt had used the introduction of the bill in the Commons as an opportunity to reject the recent 'unjust aspersions on the police'. He personally regarded 'The English and Irish police as the best in the world. That they are the best police for the preservation of order, consistently with a due regard to liberty, I believe no man will deny. Criticism has been passed upon their capacity for detection; but you must remember that here they work under great disadvantages for this purpose.' Without expanding on the disadvantages, he made the point, that he thought—sometimes—that the criticism under which they labour 'disarms them of the means they ought to possess, and which they ought to employ for the purpose of putting down secret crime'. He still strongly resisted the Metropolitan Police being put under a 'watch committee', having intimated to Gladstone that because of the problems of dealing with the Fenian menace he could not spare the time to take the proposed Municipalities Bill through the Commons. In order to do justice to the bill he would have to give his whole time to it and he had none to spare: 'I have indeed for the last few weeks had necessarily to be my Chief of Police . . .'— perhaps Dilke was closer to the truth than he imagined. By the end of May, the difficulty over the control of the Metropolitan Police was to kill the Municipalities Bill in its entirety.

Harcourt had had very much his own way in the Commons because he had the support of the former Conservative Home Secretary, R. A. Cross. The main question which was to be raised in the debates was why the new explosive bill was not a temporary one to run for three years as in the case of the Irish Prevention of Crime Act. The answer which Harcourt gave was that although the present crisis was hopefully temporary the problems raised by the new developments in explosives was a permanent one and the nation required permanent protection. Not so easily dismissed was the objection to the possible application of the fourth clause. This made it a felony to make or possess explosives for illegal purposes and carried a sentence of penal servitude not exceeding fourteen years or two years imprisonment, with or without hard labour. What worried MPs was that the suspect had to show that the explosives were for lawful objects. The amount of explosives was not specified and objections were raised that a poacher possessing one ounce or one pound of gunpowder would qualify for fourteen years of penal servitude. Cross, who raised this in the committee stage, was not willing to press it too hard. Finally, Edward Gibson, MP for Dublin University, raised the issue of the registration of the sale of relevant chemicals, a matter close to Jenkinson's heart, but the Home Secretary replied that because of interference in local government prerogatives it would be a laborious, but not impossible task under the Explosive Act of 1875. It was not, however, a priority matter. On that point, he added that he had instructed the Inspectors of Explosives to consider alteration of the Order in Council No. 8 so as to prohibit any private person from possessing more than 15 lbs of dynamite or gunpowder. The bill was passed unanimously and sent to the House of Lords, which had been notified of its existence at about 8 p.m. The bill received rougher treatment at the hands of the Conservative leader in the Lords, the Marquess of Salisbury, who expressed his grave concern not about poachers, but people who risked having to prove that they possessed sulphuric acid for lawful purposes. Salisbury quoted

'Liebig', a distinguished German chemist, who claimed that 'you can know the prosperity of a country by the amount of sulphuric acid that it manufactures'. Salisbury was more scathing about the government's use of a national emergency to pass permanent legislation, accusing them of sharp practices by springing the bill upon the Lords. Surely the government could have given a day's notice of the bill rather than violating the rules of the Lords by suspending the Standing Orders to consider permanent legislation? Salisbury protested against what he saw as a panic-stricken violation of the doctrines of England's criminal law; as well as 'the introduction of this bill by the practice of a manoeuvre which was unworthy of the government'. The bill then passed the Lords without amendment, who then adjourned at 11.30 p.m. It received the Royal Assent the next day.[10]

Harcourt realised that he could not continue for long to have a significant part of the Home Office work done by Dilke's department, nor could he personally carry on as his own chief of police. It was becoming increasingly obvious that he required a deputy who would be able to assume that part of his burden, while Harcourt carried on with the normal responsibilities of a minister of state and a member of parliament. At the end of March, Jenkinson had suggested new arrangements, similar to those which existed between Lord Spencer as viceroy and himself as under secretary for crime in the Irish Government. The recommendation for establishing an English Crime Department was accepted by both Harcourt and Spencer in principle; they were at a loss concerning the choice of a man for the appointment and, as they readily admitted, Jenkinson was a 'happy accident'. Jenkinson thought that the best idea was to abolish the post of Director of CID and in its stead put a new post of 'Head of Criminal Investigation Department for England and Scotland' directly under the Home Secretary, thus providing the basis for a national detective force. Such a move would take time to accomplish and in the interim Spencer was prepared to 'loan' Harcourt a man from Dublin to take charge of collecting and disseminating Fenian intelligence. The man under consideration was Major Blair, who had been mainly responsible for breaking up secret societies in Armagh. There would also be a confidential clerk working at the Home Office to provide the necessary staff for co-ordinating the efforts in England with those in Ireland. Jenkinson was also prepared to pay for part of Blair's salary (£500) if he would be allowed to drop Anderson from the payroll. The Home Secretary was not quite that ready to dump Anderson (he paid £300 of Anderson's salary of £800 for Secret Service work) even though his last memorandum back in March had been devoid of hard information : '. . . of course if Rossa has emissaries here, that is a distinct source of danger, and I have no information on the subject'. Jenkinson received a proposed solution from Harcourt at the beginning of May and after discussing it with Spencer it was decided to send two Resident Magistrates from Ireland of whom the senior officer was to be Major Nicholas Gosselin, Royal Artillery, with Blair, described by Spencer as 'a rough sort of man', in a subordinate role. Gosselin's present pay was £450 per annum which was to continue with the addition of a guinea per night expenses. Jenkinson continued to be unhappy about Anderson's Secret Service function and reminded Harcourt on several occasions how pleased he would be when some other provision could be made for him, but in the meantime he had no other option but to continue paying the larger part of his salary from Dublin Castle funds. Despite the radical suggestions offered on the establishment of a national detective service for Britain the CID remained within the Metropolitan Police as before and Vincent, as its Director, was increasingly excluded from anti-Fenian work.[11]

Jenkinson came to London in early May to sort out the new arrangements which were embodied in yet another memorandum, this one dated 8 May. Anderson was to put all information he possessed into the hands of Major Gosselin. No longer was Anderson to receive reports from either the RIC or Williamson of the Special Branch. Williamson was to be released from the supervision of Scotland Yard and would report only and directly to Gosselin. It was to be tactfully explained to Anderson that the appointment of Gosselin was necessary because the new requirements demanded a full-time person free to travel about Great Britain. The sentence stating that Gosselin was to be in direct communication with Jenkinson was lined out. The changes and appointment were to be kept secret.[12]

The Bank of England continued to be a source of special concern, for Jenkinson now had details concerning an attack by James Moorhead, believed to have engineered the bombing of *The Times* and Local Government Offices in March 1883. The ploy was for an accomplice to be dressed in the livery of a servant and for the two men to put the bomb 'on deposit'. Faced with the guards set on the bank, they apparently gave up the idea. By 18 May Gosselin was preparing to come to London to begin work.[13]

Although Anderson had clearly been relegated to an inferior role in the new arrangements he continued to act out his self-proclaimed role of spymaster. A memo had been circulated concerning Williamson's role particularly in relation to his own, and Anderson assured Harcourt on the 21 May that he and the Special Branch chief saw eye to eye on the matters. He also said : 'I have in view a scheme for getting information of local Fenians in northern towns, and opening communications with the police, but it is not yet matured'.[14] Harcourt was able shortly thereafter to report to Jenkinson that Anderson was also getting along well with Gosselin, who had made a good start. The problem of Glasgow was seen to be at the very top of the security priority list, since the men responsible for the January bombings had not been discovered much less apprehended. Thus Jenkinson, acting most likely on Harcourt's instructions, had sent Gosselin to Glasgow at the end of May. The procedure adopted was for Gosselin to make contact with the members of the RIC in the northern cities and 'find his feet' with local conditions, while recruiting agents. He was not to contact the Glasgow police nor introduce himself to the chief constable. Jenkinson had a great deal of confidence in Gosselin's tact, which he was sure would enable him to get on well with Anderson, despite the latter's being upset about not having been appointed to 'the superintendence of all the work in England'. At the same time, Jenkinson again pressed Harcourt to make other arrangements for Anderson so that the £500 of his salary from the Irish government might be directed to a useful purpose.[15]

Gosselin also was interested in Newcastle. Writing to Harcourt in early June he said that he now had information that there had been a change in the IRB attitude towards the

American Fenian bombers. His information was that the IRB executive of the north of England province had sent the following instructions to its various centres.

That Travellers who may visit them with proper credentials are to be received.

Gosselin added that 'to strip it of a useless cloak, American Dynamite Agents are to be helped in every way'.[16] IRB correspondence was more often than not sent virtually *en clair* through the post, a technique which was quite secure until the Home Secretary issued instructions for the post addressed to suspected IRB members to be intercepted; then the messages were transparently clear. The Supreme Council was composed of eleven members of which seven represented the four Irish provinces, three represented England and Scotland. The other four were honorary members elected by the seven; they were to remain unknown except to the other council members. Gosselin's informer had told him that the acceptance of the American 'visitors' was a complete change in policy and that it was a 'bad job'.[17]

The problem of keeping revolutionaries safely in gaol after capture was especially acute in Ireland, where Earl Spencer had strong doubts as to both the efficiency and loyalty of the prison system. The matter was initially raised on 2 June and followed by Harcourt's reply three days later. He assured Spencer that he should like to help. But he pointed out all the problems of Irish security were to some extent common to England and 'in some respects the watch and ward which your state of siege in Ireland compels and enables you to keep on your gaols is a better security against escape than any we have here'. If the Irish prisoners were to be transferred to English gaols then 'They would be a metal which would attract to our heads all the Irish electricity in the air'. Their removal would hinder access for visits by relatives and the Irish MPs would 'howl'. Yet for all this he still agreed with Spencer's assessment of the Irish Prison Board and was prepared to discuss the matter with Du Cane of the English Prison Board, Robert Anderson's 'boss'. Harcourt reminded Spencer that Jenkinson was not only concerned with the security of the Irish prisons, but saw the transfer of Fenian prisoners as a means of scaring information out of them. The Irish viceroy refused to take comfort even in Jenkinson's feeling that the gaols were in fact secure and over the next few months continued to press Harcourt for help.[18]

The trial of Gallagher and his associates began on Monday 11 June 1883. The defendants stood charged with 'Feloniously and Unlawfully compassing, imagining, and devising and intending (1) To depose the Queen from the Imperial Crown of Great Britain and Ireland; (2) To levy war upon the Queen in order, by force and constraint, to compel her to change the measures and counsels; (3) to intimidate and overawe the Houses of Parliament; and expressing the same by divers overt acts set out in the indictment'. It took three days to hear the evidence. The defence argued that there was no evidence offered on points two and three and that war could not be waged except by regular forces. The three judges decided that the bench had never attempted to say that there was no other way to wage war and that there was no judicial decision on the definition. Lord Chief Justice Coleridge advised the jury that they should find the defendants guilty as charged on the three points if they were convinced that they had intended to destroy property and to destroy or endanger life.[19]

Whitehead however argued that it was the prosecution's responsibility to prove that he intended to use nitroglycerine illegally. Wilson, Whitehead, and Curtin refused to reveal their real names, although Wilson (Thomas Clarke) could not resist giving his occupation as 'clerk'; the *double entendre* went unrecognised.

Five days after his arrest Norman wrote to Inspector Languish offering to give Queen's evidence. What Norman was to say in his statement was not in itself very significant, except to give his real name, William Joseph Lynch, and connect the plot with O'Donovan Rossa. Norman portrayed himself as a dupe of clever and evil men with whom he had no sympathy claiming no personal political connections, much less opinions on Irish independence. The prosecution was willing to accept Norman's self-image for it would be far easier for it to justify trying him for a misdemeanour and then secretly spiriting him out of the country with his freedom and a Crown reward.

Photographs of the accused had been sent via diplomatic

pouch to New York to establish their identities but a secret report, probably from the Pinkerton Agency, did little more than confirm it was Thomas Gallagher. Intensive investigations during the two months following the arrests established a fairly complete narrative of the men's movements since their arrival in Britain. The prosecution was not greatly helped by Norman's testimony because he had been a late recruit to the conspiracy. One interesting aspect of the trial was the exploitation of one of the prison officers from Millbank as a handwriting expert. He 'identified' various telegram forms sent by 'Fletcher' as being in Gallagher's hand. Harcourt told Earl Spencer he hoped the trial would go well, but one could not be sure of the conviction of either Curtin or Ansburgh. The jury went out at 5.45 p.m. on 14 June, returning with its verdict at 7.05 p.m. Thomas Gallagher, Thomas Clarke, John Kent, and 'Alfred George Whitehead' were sentenced to life imprisonment. Ansburgh and Bernard Gallagher were released for lack of evidence.[20] Kent's conviction, according to Harcourt, was a bonus.

The Lord Chief Justice Coleridge, before dismissing the jury, stated the bench's gratitude to the police, 'especially to Price, the policeman of Birmingham, and we wish it to be expressed to the authorities. It is not a case in which I think we can make any order, but we would make an order if it was in our power. That is our united view'. Rewards were given. Inspector James Black and Sergeant Richard Price were promoted to first class inspectors at fifty shillings a week. Sergeant George Rees was promoted to a vacant post of third class inspector. This was 'small beer' in comparison to the Town Council and Watch Committee seeking permission from the Home Secretary to increase the chief constable's salary from £700 to £800 per annum. Approval had to be obtained because one-half of the cost of local constabulary came from the Treasury out of the Exchequer Contribution Account. Opinions were expressed privately within the Home Office that rewarding men for doing their 'ordinary duties was not a good precedent to set', but the increases were approved. Head Constable Ryan and Constable Grey of the RIC also shared in the rewards, but the latter's health had suffered so much from the experience (he claimed) that he had been in hospital since early April.[21]

The development of the Secret Service system was a matter which continued to demand top priority and Major Gosselin pressed ahead in the six weeks following his appointment travelling between Liverpool, Glasgow, and Newcastle. He satisfied Jenkinson that they now had reliable sources of information in Liverpool, but nothing as yet had developed in Glasgow. There was almost no Fenianism amongst the Irish residents of Glasgow because they feared being turned out of work by the Scots, who were 'more loyal than the English'. Jenkinson expressed the opinion that 'This I fear, is too good to be true'. It had become obvious from Gosselin's contacts with the RIC in the various northern cities that there was need for one person to co-ordinate their work and establish an information system. Gosselin had discovered that the Birmingham police were so angered by Scotland Yard's receiving 'too much of the profit' in the Gallagher case that in the future they would keep information on new cases very much to themselves. Jenkinson proposed that Gosselin now introduce himself to the local police authorities as an Irish Resident Magistrate on temporary duty to look after the RIC and co-ordinate Fenian affairs. Working with the local authorities with all their petty jealousy was going to require great tact. It would be valuable to 'drop the name of the Home Secretary' to the chief constables and then meet the detectives. The problem of co-ordination and responsibility was a major one, but perhaps no less important than dealing with the informers who were being relied upon increasingly for the details of conspiracies.[22]

The chief constable of Bristol warned Harcourt on 9 August that George Mottley, a principal witness against one of the Phoenix Park assassins, Timothy Kelly, had been reported in a Dublin newspaper as having been killed in Philadelphia. This turned out to be false but Jenkinson determined that Mottley had left Canada and was on his way to England to settle at Bristol. His passage to Canada had been paid by the government and he had been given a large reward. If Mottley, according to Jenkinson, had kept away from drink and held his tongue he would have remained out of danger.[23]

Denis Deasy, Patrick Flanagan, Daniel O'Herlihy, Edmund O'Brien Kennedy ('Timothy Featherstone'), and John O'Connor ('Henry Dalton'), the Liverpool bombers, had been charged under 24 & 25 Vic. c.97, sec. 54—Treason–Felony. (Of those originally arrested in Cork, Henry Morgan and Timothy Carmody had not been indicted.) Upon the recommendation of the Irish attorney-general they were sent for trial in Liverpool, rather than Dublin. The reason for this move was to enable Deasy to be tried on the more serious charge of conspiracy to murder. Although Jenkinson had recommended back in April trying them as soon as possible while feeling was strongly against them, the case was held back until the beginning of August to allow the Gallagher trial to be dealt with and to tie up the tantalising connections between the Liverpool and Glasgow conspiracies.

William Joseph Lynch ('E. R. Norman') knew nothing of the Liverpool-Glasgow conspiracies and had been deported in early July, but some hopes were raised by Chief Constable Nott-Bower when he reported that Mr Quelch, solicitor to the defendants felt that he could persuade Denis Deasy to turn approver, if the price was right. Quelch wanted £50 for his part and £100 plus a free pardon for Deasy. He was convinced that with such evidence O'Brien Kennedy, O'Herlihy and Flanagan would be clearly implicated, but not 'Dalton'. Nott-Bower had tried several times to 'break' Deasy but without success. The defence solicitor had been in contact with O'Donovan Rossa regarding funds for the defence and the response was the promise that the required money would be available in time for the trial. Rossa also seems to have sent an agent to Cork who was in touch with Quelch. A. Liddell, permanent under secretary at the Home Office, strongly recommended accepting Quelch's offer on the basis of a conversation with the Treasury solicitor, Harry Bodkin Poland. It was suggested that it would be 'very desirable that the handsome manner in which "Norman" was treated should be made known to the Liverpool men with a view to pulling one of them to turn Queen's Evidence', particularly since it was clear that the case against them was 'not strong'. Harcourt accepted the recommendation on 5 July. Deasy rejected the offer nor could any of the others be tempted with their freedom.[24]

The trial began on 2 August and six days later the prosecution rested and Judge Stephen told the jury that there was no evidence against Daniel O'Herlihy, who was acquitted. O'Brien

Kennedy, Flanagan, John O'Connor and Deasy were found guilty of treason-felony on the following day and sentenced to life imprisonment. On the tenth O'Herlihy was cleared of other charges and that was that, except for finally sorting out the Glasgow connection and rewarding those men who had prevented St Helens' Town Hall from being demolished on 31 March. Nott-Bower told of a personal acquaintance on the jury who had informed him that 'when the jury retired, a member of it sitting near to him, whispered: "I am very deaf and didn't hear much of the evidence, but I know you are a gentleman and will decide right, so I shall vote as you do" '. Even more revealing of the jury's mentality was the fact that the jurymen, although clear on the guilt of O'Brien Kennedy, Deasy and Flanagan, could not decide on O'Connor particularly since one of the jury understood the judge to have practically advised his acquittal. The discussion finally ended when one member said 'Why argue, gentlemen? We are *all* satisfied that even if "Dalton" is not proved to be in this particular business, he has been in something quite as bad, or worse. So why not find him guilty and have done with it?' And they did just that.[25]

Following the Gallagher precedent, the police were rewarded for doing their jobs. Chief Superintendent George Williams of Liverpool and his fellow officers, including Inspector Marsh and the RIC officers went to the Home Office on 12 September to receive their rewards only to find shortly thereafter that Liverpool's new collector of taxes was expecting them to pay income tax on the reward money. After a plea to the Home Secretary the zealous official was overruled. Liddell must also have been amused with the letter, dated 29 October, from the Mayor of Manchester requesting that the salary of their chief constable, Charles Malcolm Wood, be increased 'because they had not had any dynamite outrages'. So much for preventive police work, but no increase was allowed. Howard Vincent had forwarded to Harcourt on 11 August a letter that he had just received from Chief Inspector Williams of Liverpool providing more information concerning the role of Mr Quelch. Williams was particularly interested in where the defence money was coming from. He felt that it must have been considerable, for £60 had arrived from the United States only a few days before. The main purpose of the letter was, however, a special plea for Vincent to use his good offices to ensure that when parliament or the Home Secretary passed out the honours he would not be 'left out in the cold', as he put it. Williams concluded with a reference to a trip he was planning to take to New York in three weeks: 'I wish I might bring back O'Donovan Rossa'. Williams was not forgotten, although he could not have felt that £50 was quite the recognition he deserved. He did not produce Rossa upon his return from the United States—it would doubtless have earned him an unsolicited knighthood at the very least.[26]

F

To levy War upon the Queen

By a solemn decision of the highest authority in England, presided over by her Chief Justice, we have compelled her to recognize a new epoch in the art of war.

Secret Memorandum, Clan na Gael,
September, 1883.

CLAN NA GAEL responded to the failure and the tragedy of the Gallagher operation by reducing its executive to three men who issued a secret memorandum to its membership.

We earnestly assure our Brothers that while some disappointments have occurred, we have neither become despondent nor lost faith. Nor are we idle. Other movements are being pushed, both in instructing men and in securing war material. Even our disappointments are not regarded by us as a failure. We believe that while agitation and public organization are necessary these would not have been effective in securing concessions from our enemy, had not the courage, the capacity and the great scientific skill of the secret organization brought terror to the very doors of the oppressor. . . .

Tho' the efforts of your executive have not been fully realized, or rather were marred by the informer's treason, yet those brothers (with one solitary exception) entrusted with the work did nobly, and were at the very threshold of deeds that would have startled the world and put the fear of the organization in the hearts of the enemy. These Brothers, with heroic faith have carried your secrets to the dungeon, under a fate and fortune worse than death. They did nobly. It was by no fault of theirs they failed. . . . They have settled the legal status of a new mode of warfare. By a solemn decision of the highest authority in England, presided over by her Chief Justice, we have compelled her to recognize a new epoch in the art of war.

We cannot see our way to an armed insurrection in Ireland this side of some great Foreign War with England. But in the meantime we shall carry on an incessant and perpetual warfare with the power of England in public and in secret. . . .

(signed) X, Y, Z of the FC, VC

The 'signatures' were those of the Clan's Triangle of president, secretary and treasurer; X, Alexander Sullivan, Y, James Reynolds, Treasurer, and Z, John D. Carroll, Secretary. Major Le Caron was the source of the extract. In a marginal note Robert Anderson, as the Home Office advisor on the Fenians, explained the reference to 'they have settled the legal status of a new mode of warfare'. 'This', he said, 'refers to the passage in the charge of the Chief Justice (much noticed in the Fenian newspapers) explaining that a dynamite explosion was 'levying war upon the Queen'.[1]

The cry of treachery continued to echo throughout the Irish-American organisations. Michael Davitt associated the betrayal of the Gallagher team with 'Sinclair', alleged to have 'convoyed' them to London where 'they were arrested and sent to penal servitude for life'. Davitt claimed that 'Sinclair' was in the pay of Major Nicholas Gosselin, (code name 'Norton'), which is impossible since he had not been recruited to the Secret Service until 12 May, almost a month after the arrests. Another of Davitt's candidates for betraying the dynamiters, as well as acting as an *agent provocateur*, was the shadowy figure of 'Red Jim' McDermott whom he described as being forty-five years old, middle height, well built, respectable in appearance in dress and bearing.

McDermott had been born in Dublin in 1843 and was educated at Clonliffe College, joining the Papal Brigade at seventeen. Fighting in the wars of Italian unification he earned the Order of St Sylvester before emigrating to the United States in the 1870s. He then became deeply involved with O'Mahony's Fenian Brotherhood, Irish-American affairs in general, and may well have been part of the various plots which sought to capture Canada. Whether or not McDermott had been an informer in the 1870s is not so important as E. G. Jenkinson's continued interest in his welfare.[2]

The Home Secretary was already aware of both the existence

and the importance of McDermott, Jenkinson having mentioned him in a letter back in early June 1883. Inexplicably Jenkinson explained that he had unsuccessfully tried to address letters to McDermott in London. If McDermott was in the pay of Jenkinson, such an open reference to an informer is quite out of character for the 'spymaster' who placed such deserved emphasis upon secrecy. Jenkinson said that McDermott, acting as a Rossa courier, had recently been in Paris with two men named Casey (Kaisey) and Eugene Davis. In getting money to the Liverpool bomber 'Featherstone' in Cork he was supposed to have communicated with 'Dalton' in London as well as with the Rossa men operating in the Glasgow area. After the arrest of 'Featherstone' and his associates, McDermott escaped through Belgium and France, leaving his luggage in Dublin lodgings. On 17 June Jenkinson received a cypher telegram locating McDermott in Montreal, at St Lawrence Hall. The news was alarming because the Canadian informant also claimed that death sentence had been placed upon McDermott by the Rossa organisation for having turned informer to the British Secret Service. Jenkinson warned the Home Secretary that if McDermott went into the '[United] States his life will not be worth a day's purchase'. According to Jenkinson, McDermott had brought suspicion upon himself by his indiscreet conduct when he had first arrived in Dublin. As the correspondent of an American newspaper, sometime in late 1882 or early 1883, he had interviewed Jenkinson, returning several times to see his private secretary for information. Jenkinson was certain that McDermott had boasted of being in constant communication with Dublin Castle and that when the Liverpool-Cork ('Featherstone', Deasy, and Flanagan) arrests occurred Fenians thought that it was a case of two and two equalling four.[3]

While in Dublin during May 1883 Michael Davitt had received a letter from the proprietor of the Montreal *Evening Post* to the effect that a 'McDermott of Brooklyn' was trying to organise dynamite operations while freely using Davitt's name. Would Davitt vouch for him? He immediately cabled Montreal.

I believe the reported dynamite plot in your city to be the

work of one Red Jim McDermott, who is credited by many
over here with having been the organiser of the bogus dynamite outrages in Cork, Liverpool, and London.

DAVITT

The cable was printed in the *Evening Post* and McDermott
subsequently left for New York. Three or four days later a
recently arrived Cork Fenian narrowly failed in an attempt to
shoot McDermott.[4]

Following the discovery of McDermott in Montreal, Jenkinson tried unsuccessfully to have the Canadian government
arrest and extradite him; they refused to do so lacking a proper
warrant and sufficient evidence. Jenkinson then took the extraordinary step of sending McDermott a telegram warning him
that the Cork IRB had sent 'Short the butcher' to O'Donovan
Rossa to have him killed for having betrayed 'Featherstone'.
Jenkinson went so far as to tell Harcourt that if McDermott
were killed 'it would be a most disastrous thing for me. I should
get no informers, and the sources of my information would be
dried up'. On 7 August McDermott, using the alias Quigley,
was unexpectedly arrested at Liverpool on board the *City of
Montreal* by Head Constable Ryan of the RIC. Hidden in the
collar of his dress coat was a press card in the name of
McDermott, Brooklyn, New York. On the reverse of the card
was written :

Henry Dalton, care of James O'Connor, 2 Eden Place,
Fulham Road, Chelsea introducing McDermott.
Featherstone

Originally Jenkinson had hoped that McDermott might have
been extradited from Canada in time to stand trial in Liverpool
with the intention that he would be found 'not guilty' for lack
of evidence. A tantalising correspondence developed between
Spencer, Harcourt, Jenkinson, Liddell and Gosselin. Jenkinson
obviously still wanted a prosecution of McDermott which was
not 'bona fide'; the matter was so secret that the details were
to be only communicated orally to Spencer by Jenkinson. By
17 September, the object had been accomplished; McDermott
had been legally freed after he had doubtless been suborned.
Major Gosselin was given responsibility for the 'disposal of

James McDermott after his discharge next Tuesday'. McDermott was freed and there is nothing to suggest that he met his end in retributive violence.[5]

Events continued to move rapidly towards a climax in Glasgow where the bombers of the previous January had not as yet been arrested. The chief constable was prepared to arrest a group of local men whose names had emerged out of investigations, which had taken a positive turn after 4 April. On that date a Glasgow fruit hawker in his mid-fifties, George Hughes, complained to Constable William Porter of assault by one of a group of men that had regularly gathered in the city's Saltmarket–Jail Square area. Porter had been taking a special interest in them since November. Hughes told the police that he knew the names of the bombers. Three men, the core of the Rossa team which had carried out the bombings in the previous March in London at *The Times* and Whitehall, had recruited and trained ten Glasgow Ribbonmen. Of the three key men, 'Featherstone' and 'Dalton' were already in gaol serving life sentences but another man remained at large.

This third man had escaped to the United States via Hull and the continent, leaving his family behind in Glasgow. He was ordered back to Glasgow by O'Donovan Rossa where he found that his wife and child had died. Remaining in Scotland for a time he retraced his earlier route, travelling through Rotterdam to Antwerp. There he came under the surveillance of Jenkinson's agents on station there. Finding himself being watched and feeling trapped he 'volunteered' his help as money ran low. Special Branch Chief Inspector 'Dolly' Williamson went to Antwerp to interview the man about the Glasgow bombings; his name was John Francis Kearney.[6]

Kearney, an employee of the railway, had been in the signal box only one hundred yards from the disused coal shed demolished by one of the three bombs. He remained at his employment until 31 March when he had heard of the Liverpool arrests. Only then did he run.

According to Secret Service agent Major Gosselin, Chief Constable McCall of Glasgow was only interested in keeping his district clear of dynamite allowing others to 'look out for themselves'.[7] On 31 August McCall ordered the arrests of the Ribbonmen: Terence McDermott, Thomas Devany, Peter

Callaghan or Kellochan, Henry McCann, James McCullagh or McCulloch, James Donnelly, James Kelly, Patrick McCabe, Patrick Drum, and Denis Casey. Jenkinson was furious because John Francis Kearney had not produced a full confession and the evidence against his ten accomplices was inadequate to guarantee a conviction. Jenkinson strongly recommended to Harcourt that the discretion of local police authorities be curbed and no arrests of this variety be allowed without the specific approval of the Home Secretary, which included himself by implication. Gosselin, caught in the crossfire, took a more optimistic view. He had found that the so-called 'Scotch system' bore a close resemblance to the Irish emergency legislation in the manner in which suspects might be detained. Thus he felt that McCall might well be able to 'screw' the necessary evidence out of the suspects. Williamson of Special Branch was also going over the details of the Local Government Building bombing trying to locate where Moorhead (reportedly on his way back to England for more attacks) and his associates had stayed in London at the time of the explosions. Williamson came to the conclusion that the two men (Moorhead and Terence McDermott) held briefly at the New Street, Covent Garden coffee house immediately after the explosions had in fact been the bombers! Special Branch detectives took a girl from the Covent Garden coffee house where they had stayed to Glasgow where she identified Terence McDermott as one of the two men.[8]

The Glasgow Ribbonmen stood trial in Edinburgh between 17 and 21 December 1883 for the bombing of the Tradeston Gas works and the Caledonian Railway. Terence McDermott, Devany, Callaghan, McCann, and McCullagh were sentenced to life imprisonment. The others received seven-year sentences, having been 'duped into becoming accomplices by clever men'. Kearney, the last of the Ribbonmen, satisfied Jenkinson that he had told him all that he knew and was given money and passage to the United States. Melting into the Irish-American background, he carried both the guilt of his having betrayed long-time friends and the relief of not having to spend the remainder of his life in a Scottish gaol.[9] The Edinburgh trial finally brought to an end the complicated operations of the Rossa team led by 'Featherstone', in much the same way the earlier trial of the summer had closed the chapter on Gallagher's explosive schemes.

Only limited solace could be gained from these victories in the dynamite war, for by then the Clan na Gael had already made two successful attacks against London's underground railways.

The Metropolitan and District Railways circled London in a series of deep cuts and tunnels. The District Line had fifty-four dull green painted 4–4–0 tank locomotives pulling strings of carriages including two first class, three second class and three third (coupled together in that order)—some four hundred seats in all. This service ran from Mansion House to Gloucester Road, with trains running at five-minute intervals. The first-class carriages were roomy and well upholstered, while in the third class the upholstery was confined to a strip of carpet on the seat and a padded back strip at shoulder height. On the evening of 30 October 1883 a Clan na Gael bomber boarded a train bound for Gloucester Road. At 8.03 p.m. the bomb was dropped from the moving train two hundred and seven yards out of Charing Cross station between the downline and the riverside wall of the tunnel. The bomb exploded upon impact just behind the last carriage. The Irish-American bomber escaped in the inevitable confusion which reigned when the train pulled into Westminster Bridge station. The Westminster Bridge end of the tunnel had been under observation from its signal box and no-one had been seen entering the tunnel. The police found no indication that access had been gained to the tunnel via either the ventilator in the roadway or the one in the Victoria Embankment Ornamental Gardens : they deduced that the bomber had to have been on the train. Damage was limited, some broken glass at both stations, a hole in the road and one hundred yards of telegraph and signal wires torn up. There were no injuries.[10]

At 7.57 p.m., only minutes before the explosion on the District Line another explosion had occurred at the Praed Street end of the tunnels connecting that part of the Metropolitan Line with Edgware Road. The distance between the two explosions was twenty-nine minutes by underground train. The Metropolitan train had left Mansion House at 7.10 p.m. arriving at Praed Street, the Great Western's Paddington Station, about 7.50 p.m. The rear guard, William Smith, described what had happened.

Just after re-entering the tunnel on leaving Praed Street Station, I was looking out of the off-side window to see if the signals were right. I noticed a small white light about halfway along the train, and at that moment an explosion took place. I was knocked down and knew nothing more till we arrived at the junction. When we got to Edgware Station I ascertained that several of the carriages were wrecked; I noticed no smell of gas or gunpowder.

Praed Street's signalman said that the only person he had seen go into the tunnel was Chief Inspector Gosden of Scotland Yard's 'D' Division. He had checked the mouth of the tunnel and then taken the next train south to Gloucester Road ten minutes before the explosion. Stephen Harris, the engine driver, recalled that the explosion sounded to him to be 'that of an ordinary fog signal', which was how the lignine dynamite explosion at *The Times* in March had sounded to Sergeant Mears of the City of London police. The train's gas lights were blown out, the track signals went out and the driver slowly took the wrecked train with its shattered coaches, through the darkness to the Edgware Road Station. Amazingly, it had not been derailed by the explosion.

Seriously injured passengers from the third-class coaches were taken to nearby St Mary's Hospital suffering from shock and injuries, caused primarily by flying glass and splinters from the wooden carriages. Colonel V. D. Majendie, Inspector of Explosives, was immediately recalled from Ireland and he and Dr Dupré, the Home Office advisor on explosives, spent four days looking for evidence in the tunnels, and the debris of damaged coaches. The lack of damage to the District train suggested that the bomb had been dropped from the last coach or had been timed for later detonation or might even have been dropped from an earlier train. The bomb dropped at Praed Street from the middle of the train badly damaged the three rear third-class coaches in addition to shattering a large gas main in the tunnel. The carriages had their left-hand sides driven in with the force of the blast, so much so that some right-hand panels had been forced outwards. If the bomber(s) had wished to destroy the trains and their occupants, they might well have left bombs on the trains and disembarked at a station, allowing the explosion to take place several minutes later. Police and railway surveillance deterred the bombers from simply planting the bombs in the tunnel arches hoping to collapse them.[11]

Harcourt instructed his son to 'tell Mr Gladstone that we are all of the opinion that things were never worse than they are now in the respect of the anticipation of outrage and crime. . . . I went with Lily to the hospital today to see the sufferers. . . . It is amazing how the carriages could be (as they were) blown to pieces with so little injury to the passengers.'[12]

The safety of the Queen's rail travel preoccupied Harcourt who wrote to Ponsonby:

HOME OFFICE, 21 November—. . . . I was very glad to get news this morning of Her Majesty's safe arrival. I had one of the usual scares last night about your journey. Williamson at 12.30 a.m. came in with a letter fresh from the United States describing the machine with which and the manner in which you were to be blown up on the way to Balmoral. As Hartington and the Attorney-General were sitting with me we consulted what to do on this agreeable [*sic*] intelligence, but as you were already supposed to be half-way through your journey it was not easy to know what course to take. However, I sent Williamson to Euston and Paddington to direct that an additional pilot engine should be run at a longer interval in front of you as soon as possible, as the intelligence pointed to bombs to be deposited *after the passage* of the ordinary pilot engine. I presume that this was done but I dare say you were not conscious of it. I thought that if there was any danger at all it would be in the neighbourhood of Preston and Birmingham. I had police at Euston and Birmingham to report to me all night how you were getting on, and was proportionately relieved when I heard you were safe and sound in Windsor. . . .[13]

The Metropolitan Railway listed a total of seventy-two persons injured in the Praed Street explosion. Public philanthropy responded to the needs of the third-class victims of the blast with contributions totalling £233.1s.11d. Howard Vincent, Director of the CID and well known for his philanthropic work, reported to Harcourt (on Boxing Day 1883) that he had paid out £203 to forty-seven people. The District Line offered a reward of £250 which was matched by the Metropolitan Line, with another £500 being supplied by the government. This reward was added to the uncollected £1,000 still on offer for the apprehension and conviction of the Local Government Building bombers.[14] Jenkinson reminded Harcourt that he had warned him in the spring of the danger to the underground railways. There was no discounting the fact that securing the miles of cuttings and tunnels of the underground was an impossible job, especially in comparison with the job of protecting the Albert Memorial. Finally in response to Jenkinson's plea Scotland Yard's 'A' Division began a day and night watch of two constables and three patrols to walk around it beginning on 6 November. The guard was to be constantly visited by the Inspectors on duty in Hyde Park and occasionally by Divisional Superintendent Gernon. These arrangements satisfied Jenkinson but he continued to press Harcourt for tougher legislation which included unspecified new powers to deal 'much more summarily with scoundrels'. In his view it would prove easier to achieve their own salvation than depend on Harcourt's hopes for a 'private understanding with the American government'.[15]

Such hopes were no nearer fulfilment at Christmas 1883 than two years earlier when Her Majesty's government had begun to seek such assistance. Back in March 1883 Granville had been on the verge of making additional representations to the Secretary of State but after the explosions in London he decided to hold back temporarily. On the other hand Sackville West, the British minister, had personally delivered a message to Frelinghuysen in March calling his attention to the publication of 'incitements to the commission of outrages against the government and people of this country by persons who do not in all cases attempt even to conceal their names in the dynamite press'. A copy sent to the Foreign Office was not acknowledged by Granville until 12 May when he delivered a gentle chiding for West's acting without instructions in the matters.

It will have been obvious from the face of your letter that it was written without previous instructions from Her Majesty's government, under the influence of the feelings naturally excited in you by the circumstances occurring in this country and in the United States.[16]

Granville held back in March because the American Minister in London, James Russell Lowell, had written to him on 16 March expressing his horror of the attack on the Local Government building. Granville told Lowell that the State Department could expect further representations on the matter. Hopes that the shock of the bombings in London would produce a change in policy by the American Government proved to be unfounded. Frelinghuysen's refusal either to take the dynamite press seriously, or to accept any responsibility for the freedom afforded by the American safehouse for the dynamiters, forced Granville to take up his diplomatic weapons again in early May.

The despatch of 12 May sought to dismantle the arguments behind which the American government hid, rather than dealing with their Irish-American Fenians. Granville said that the British government was not complaining about the bitter anglophobia to be found in the dynamite press; the object of complaint was 'the open and direct incitement to the assassination of individuals, to personal outrage, to the destruction by fire and explosion of cities and ships, to the sacrifice of lives and property of private citizens; and the collection and advertisement of public subscriptions for these infamous objects'. Dynamite money was not being sent secretly from America, as the Americans claimed, but so openly that it was a matter of public notoriety. Adopting the 'if the shoe was on the other foot' stance, Granville assured his Washington counterpart that if in the United Kingdom there was a public subscription to murder the American President, or burn down New York City, Her Majesty's government would stop it. Granville also recalled that James G. Blaine, a former Secretary of State, had promised in 1881 that if he was to discover such attacks were being planned in the United States 'they would take the most energetic measures to frustrate such schemes'. Granville summed up :

> That the toleration of an open traffic in crime directed against the subjects of a friendly state cannot conduce to the wellbeing of the society of nations, is a view which Her Majesty's government feel confident will not fail to commend itself to the judgement of the government and the people of the United States.[17]

Lord Chief Justice Coleridge had also caused the Foreign

Office grave concern when he chose to visit North America immediately after the close of the Gallagher trial, arriving in New York on 24 August. The State Department answered the Foreign Office's plea for his personal protection by assigning Lt John McClellan of the Fifth Artillery Regiment as Coleridge's bodyguard. There may also have been the less obvious presence of the United States' own Secret Service. There is no evidence that either Special Branch or Pinkerton detectives were part of the Chief Justice's party.

Coleridge travelled extensively on the eastern seaboard making speeches at local Bar associations and at the University of Pennsylvania, Haverford College and Yale University. He dined with one of the great American 'robber barons', William H. Vanderbilt, in addition to being entertained by Frelinghuysen and President Arthur. The high point of the visit was sitting *in banc* with the United States Supreme Court on 19 October, the first instance of the court admitting another justice to the bench. The Irish-American menace was always present. The consul-general in New York received a telegram from London two days before Coleridge's arrival.

> Private. Tell the Chief Justice we are of opinion that he should avoid if possible going to Canada; if there is any risk, we think it greater there than in the United States.
> GRANVILLE[18]

Coleridge was prepared to accept such a request, but it meant forgoing his trip to visit old friends in Toronto, the Goldwin Smiths. He wrote to Smith, whom he had known since their days together at Eton, ' . . . all I have done is to try these wretched dynamite conspirators, I am very sure, in no fierce or hostile spirit, with Brett on one side and Grove on the other, and pass a sentence on them as the law and not I dictated'.[19] Announcements appeared in the New York press warning that the 'Irish Brotherhood' had sentenced him to death for his part in the Gallagher trials. He met Goldwin Smith at Buffalo, New York and then travelled on to see Niagara Falls, but from the Canadian side. Jenkinson and Harcourt, not to mention Granville, were greatly relieved when Coleridge finally left New York for the return trip to London on the *Britanic* on 27 October 1883.

Despite the fears that Coleridge might be murdered in North America, or on the journey, neither Rossa nor the Triangle of the Clan were prepared to give the United States' government any cause to regret the degree of sanctuary which had thus far been accorded to the Irish-American revolutionary activity. Granville was later to thank Frelinghuysen for Coleridge's protection. Frelinghuysen replied that they had seen no real need for it and had simply complied with the Foreign Office's request to provide security. However, the Secretary of State was to add that the President was 'gratified that the efforts made in a spirit of friendship [met] with so cordial appreciation'.[20]

'Poison pen' postcards and letters continued to be sent to various British officials in the United States. The Washington legation sent the following example to the Foreign Office as a fair sample of the post-bag for July 1883.

English Consul, Washington, Brooklyn, N.Y. (Postmark)
July 4, 1883, 10.30 a.m.
Sir a friendly note to the English govt, tell them to kiss our arse we want war with them you will be poisoned or shot and your place blown up your fate will strike terror into Europe.

Threatening postcards from Brooklyn's poorly-educated Irishmen did not overly concern the British government; the continued use of the Irish-American press to raise support and money for dynamite adventures was a real worry. The Foreign Office vainly continued its efforts to get Washington to close down the Dynamite Press but not even a convinced anglophile like the American Minister in London, James Russell Lowell, could offer any hope of success, at least in 1883.[21] Harcourt had written to Earl Spencer :

HOME OFFICE, June 14—.... All the information that reaches me is that the neck of the business is broken so far as violence is concerned in Ireland and Great Britain. But the perpetual reserve of crime in America and the sally-port they have there prevent our eradicating the roots of the mischief, and I do not feel as if things were ever really safe so long as these horrid ruffians can safely come to and fro....[22]

Spencer had his own unique problems and Irish prison security continued to be high on his list of priorities. In November Harcourt reminded Spencer that England's prisons had no military force like the RIC to call upon for security. Recently he had had to refit Newgate prison to take care of Patrick O'Donnell, the murderer of James Carey, because he could not risk him at Millbank Prison. The reorganisation of the English prison system to take charge of twenty Irish prisoners could not be justified, particularly when the fault lay in the 'very feeble folks' of the Irish prison authority. Spencer asked Harcourt to simply mix the twenty Irish prisoners into the main prisons, but he refused to do so. A disappointed Spencer wrote to Harcourt on 19 December that he would say no more about the matter. Although he would try to avert a catastrophe in the Irish prisons, Harcourt would have to share the responsibility with the Irish government if one occurred. Spencer added : 'I shall owe Sir C. Du Cane [of the Prison Board] a great grudge and morally blow him up with dynamite'. Two days before Christmas, Harcourt assured Spencer that if the situation became impossible then they (including Du Cane) would agree the transfer of the Irish prisoners. That letter included the grim news that Harcourt was desperately trying to patch up the government split produced by Hartington's rejection of Chamberlain's advocacy of 'one man, one vote'. He predicted that if the government fell together the party would survive, but if it split then only the Radical section, not Hartington's Whigs, would have resurrection at a later date.

Spencer did not keep his word about saying no more, but continued to moan, particularly about the Invincible prisoners in Dublin convict prisons. Harcourt's resolve finally broke and on 10 January, 1884, he wrote to Spencer :

I can refuse you nothing which you tell me is absolutely necessary so I yield with great reluctance about the prisons. I have told Du Cane and we must settle the matter as best we can. I have seen Jenkinson and spoken to him of it. You will understand that it shall be *temporary* and not longer than the necessity demanded ! !

Du Cane, in the meantime, discovered that a number of Irish

prisons were practically empty and he submitted a memo recommending the reorganisation of Enniskillen or Carrick-on-Shannon as a top security prison. Spencer still wanted Harcourt to keep the twenty men for six months, convinced that in that period of time, he could get English warders, make a clean sweep of the totally incompetent prison board, and make proper prison arrangements for Ireland. At the end of January Harcourt notified Dublin that the arrangements were ready for transfer to the English prisons. He asked that the Irish prisoners be allowed visitors before leaving Dublin but Spencer refused. Harcourt was furious, for such a refusal would lead to an outcry about having denied the relatives visiting privileges before their transfer. 'As it is', moaned Harcourt, 'not being able to make a proper system of drainage themselves they sewage [*sic*] in its most noxious form upon us.' He stressed that the Home Office would make public that the arrangement was only for six months. The upshot of the affair was a Royal Commission on the reform of the Irish prisons and on 3 August 1884, Spencer, doubtless deeply relieved that at least that problem lay behind him, wrote a letter of profuse thanks to the former Conservative Home Secretary, R. A. Cross, for his having played such an important role in the Irish prison commissioners' unanimous report.[23]

Problems of a more serious nature remained. The independence of action afforded the Fenians in the United States provided a safe house from which they could sally forth to knot the lion's tail. Yet Irish-Americans could derive little real comfort from this protection. O'Donovan Rossa's bombers had been wiped out almost to a man. Gallagher and his secretly combined Rossa-Clan operation lay in ruins and its members in gaol. Clan na Gael came under steadily mounting criticism because all of the explosions up to the underground attacks were attributable to Rossa's United Irishmen. Meanwhile, Dr Denis Dowling Mulcahy, who had led the Fenian deputation at the Dublin funeral of John O'Mahony, was still trying to recover his expenses from Clan na Gael. Thus he had sought a legal injunction in the New York State Supreme Court to prevent the National Funds' Trustees from using its assets without the supervision of the Court. The Clan was also acutely embarrassed by the *Fenian Ram* since its launching in the summer of 1881. Holland's failure to put the boat on a fighting basis strained the goodwill of the Clan supporters.

For the past two years he had carried out tests and modifications on the submarine in New York harbour. The boat was operational to the extent that it went up and down and could travel submerged, but he had not been able to find the weapons to make it a fighting ship. Furthermore, lacking even a rudimentary periscope he had not solved the problem of underwater navigation. On one occasion his engineer took the boat out on his own without securing the engine department hatch. The wash from passing boats flooded the compartment, the engineer was blown out of the hatch by the escaping air and the boat settled to the bottom. It cost the National Fund $3,000 to raise her. A very persuasive Holland persuaded the trustees to finance the construction of an experimental, all metal, sixteen-foot, one-ton replica of the 'Fenian Ram', incorporating major improvements.[24] Breslin, now business manager for John Devoy's *Irish Nation*, continued to play a part in the boat's development. He wrote to Devoy 14 April 1883 : 'The Ram has been the excitement of the week in the papers here in New York. We simply moved her to a place more convenient to paint her and make a few experiments. The impression has got afloat that she is gone to sea.'[25] To complicate matters Holland was preparing to sue the builder of the Ram's engine for charging more than initially agreed. Breslin was furious about this open wrangling and criticised Holland, who turned to James Reynolds, the senior trustee and member of the Clan's executive Triangle for advice. Reynolds wrote to Breslin on 8 October 1883 : 'Mr Holland spent the whole of yesterday with me and after a very long explanation I think I find the difference between you is in the main imaginary'.[26] Reynolds was prepared, after a meeting with the trustees, to patch things up with Holland.

Over the next eight weeks the legal situation regarding Mulcahy seriously worsened. Then in late November, in order to prevent the application of a possible seizure order by the courts, Breslin and some associates, carrying a forged pass in Holland's name, entered the docks at the Morris and Cummings pier with a tugboat. They towed the Ram and its small sister-ship astern into New York harbour, rounding Manhattan Island and proceeding up the East River. The new boat's turret had not been fully battened down after having been launched from its blocks by the pier edge. In the choppy waters she floundered and sank in one hundred and ten feet of water. The tug with only the Ram astern sailed on into Long Island Sound, reaching her destination, New Haven, Connecticut the next day. The Fenian 'pirates' lacked the expertise to operate the boat and the harbourmaster at New Haven soon prohibited its use in his jurisdiction. The Ram eventually was placed in a lumber shed and the engine was removed to operate a forge at Reynold's foundry. The seizure had been more than an attempt to simply get the boat out of New York jurisdiction for the New York Supreme Court could not have touched it so long as it remained in New Jersey waters. Holland noted, however, that he 'never bothered again with my backers, nor they with me'. Despite Reynolds' earlier effort to heal the breach between Breslin and Holland, he must have been party to the planned piracy since the destination of the two boats was his foundry at New Haven. The implication is that the fund's trustees had been convinced that Holland was not going to *produce* the weapon for which they had paid several times over. This realisation, compounded by the deep embarrassment of the Mulcahy lawsuit, led to the drastic action of taking the submarines without consulting Holland. The trustees doubtless anticipated that if Holland knew of their plans to take possession of the boats he would have initiated legal action to retain them. That was one law suit that they wished to avoid but they realised that after 'stealing' their boats Holland might still go to the courts. The boat did as Holland suggested it might, 'rot on their hands'.[27] Rumours of the Ram fiasco ruined what reputation the Clan had left amongst the revolutionary Irish-Americans. Nor could the Revolutionary Directory break secrecy and announce to the world that Captain William Mackey Lomasney was in fact operating in London and had just caused two explosions in the underground, with a series of further explosions in the offing, in an attempt to recoup their reputation.

O'Donovan Rossa's United Irishmen were no better off despite having a series of explosions to their credit. In the process they had lost virtually all of their men, with the possible exception of James Moorhead, alias 'T. J. Mooney', to either English gaols, or to treason as in the cases of Lynch and Kearney. 'Black Jim' McDermott (not to be confused with the informer 'Red Jim') wrote to Devoy from his home in Philadelphia : 'The Dynamiters are completely demoralised, but I heard trying to start something new. Their lecture was a terrible fizzle. I don't think they received the rent of the hall and could not get a decent man to introduce [Patrick] Sheridan. . . .'[28] Thus it was with a note of urgency that Patrick Ford, editor of the *Irish World*, sounded a new call to arms out of the depths of revolutionary despondency on Christmas Day 1883 :

> The English have no right whatever to be in Ireland. To drive them out of the country poison, knives, fire, with all other destructive agencies that are available, ought to be called into service and mercilessly used. If rose water or sugared comfits will do as well let them be employed instead.

Other Irish organisations were given Ford's blessing including 'PARNELL and his band of Parliamentarians', the National League, Davitt, Archbishop Croke and T. D. Sullivan. However Ford stressed that all these methods of warfare, 'without the physical forces, will never make Ireland a nation. *But every man can do service in his own way.* . . . I enter this war in the spirit of a crusader. It is in my eyes a holy war. God save Ireland !' So concluded his appeal for the creation of an Emergency Fund to aid the 'active forces on the other side in every practical mode of warfare for the recovery of Irish national independence, to stimulate to deeds of heroism, to punish informers, reward heroes whilst living, and honor their memories when they have passed from the scene of action, and to look after the dependents of men who may fall for Ireland, but who before they have fallen shall have struck SUCCESSFUL BLOWS against the Common Enemy'. Subscription circulars were sent out to newsagents and subscribers to the newspaper.[29] For whom was the money to be collected? It is likely that the Clan's National Fund Trustees were to administer this Emergency Fund, having squandered the resources of the National Skirmishing Fund on Holland's follies and Mulcahy's legal proceedings.

In retrospect one can see that by the end of 1883 both sides of the conflict had slipped into deepest despair over the lack of success of their respective efforts. The Clan could take some secret comfort from the relative success of Lomasney in London but publicly they, like O'Donovan Rossa, had taken a serious beating. From the standpoint of the British government things were equally bleak. Granville could not get the co-operation of the American government, Jenkinson was convinced that it was impossible to penetrate the secrecy of the teams of bombers which were operating more and more in isolation from their central organisation. Harcourt, watching the expense of the counter-terrorist organisation mounting, could see no way out of the dilemma. Explosions in the underground meant that the bombs could be anywhere in London; there was simply no way to stop them. Jenkinson's health had deteriorated to the extent that in September, Harcourt commented upon it to Spencer. Nothing was more indicative of how the Home Secretary, England's 'police chief', felt about the situation than a comment to Spencer concerning a cruise off Scotland's west coast. He said, 'When I once get on board my yacht I think I shall steam away into space and not come back again'.[30]

7

The American Connection, 1884

No other civilised country in the world would tolerate the open advocacy of assassination and murder....
                                    W. V. Harcourt to the Queen,
                                    29 February 1884

BIRMINGHAM remained convinced that it was the object of the next Irish-American attack; despite his success in the Gallagher conspiracy no one was more edgy than its chief constable. On the day before Christmas, 1883 Farndale wrote to the Home Secretary: 'Major Gosselin has not written to me for a long time. I suppose he has no further information of importance. The watching is becoming very tedious and difficult.' Farndale knew that there was a new series of outrages being planned in his city and the Secret Service was not taking the threat seriously enough.[1]

Since October a team of Birmingham detectives had kept an Irish-American by the name of John Daly under close surveillance. Jenkinson was satisfied to let the Birmingham police, assisted by the RIC detachment, do the watching and waiting. Daly had proved to be a fascinating man to watch. He had auditioned for a job at the Birmingham Concert Hall in Coleshill St as a 'story teller'. A senior detective persuaded one of the theatre's proprietors, a personal friend, to give him a 'turn' despite his lack of previous stage experience. Daly was on the bottom of a fifteen-act bill at Leybourne's Benefit performance on 20 December. He appeared as D. O'Brien, 'The famous Irish Story Teller from Hooley's Combination, America, for this night only'. That night Detective Inspector James Black brought several of his men for the performance of a most unusual identity parade. Inspector Black, who owed his reputation to the recent capture of Alfred Whitehead of the Gallagher bombers, reported that the performance was a 'very dry affair'. Daly's act included singing two songs with a 'bad voice' and recounting the story of his life. He told a very unsympathetic audience that he and his family had lost their home in Ireland when his sister had refused to become the land agent's mistress. His parents became ill and died, while his sister, honour preserved, went mad. The Land League also came into the monologue and 'whilst speaking seemed to put his whole heart in what he said'. The audience was less impressed than the police; the act had already run twenty-five minutes and Daly was obviously not finished. The stage manager, unable to get him off the stage, finally dropped the curtain on him. The bill had promised that Daly was on for 'this night only' and his stage career came to an end. His was now the best known face in Birmingham where its detectives were concerned.

Daly continued to lead what appeared to be an uneventful life in a lodging house owned by James F. Egan and his wife. The police suggested that Daly was remaining in the house because he had an illicit relationship with Mrs Egan. Gosselin told the Home Secretary on 7 January that Daly had been more active over the holidays with numbers of Irish visitors to the house and trips to the pubs. Despairingly he added that on the previous Saturday the suspect had become aware that he was being followed by 'two detectives and three boys'. If Daly was aware of the police surveillance he remained calm and did not panic. Speculation continued about what he was up to and whether he knew he was being watched or not. The chief constable was sure that he was plotting explosions in Birmingham but the Secret Service assured him that he was only hatching plans in the Midlands for execution in Dublin. There was even the possibility that Daly was in Birmingham to draw attention away from an attack on Dublin Castle. By 11 January RIC Head Constable Ryan was convinced that Daly was not aware of the police presence because he continued to meet leading Fenians. The Home Secretary gave his approval to Secret Service proposals to continue the watching and waiting despite Farnham's apprehension that Daly might disobey his orders from New York and plant the bombs locally. Nor had Farndale much confidence in one of the sources upon whom Jenkinson depended. This was the informer who had assured the Secret Service that nothing was going to happen in England two or three days before the explosions in the underground. The waiting finally got too much for the patience of the detectives on the case and Farnham authorised them to recruit a woman lodger in the Egan house as an informer.

Jenkinson advised Farnham that Daly must not be allowed to become suspicious, for he might shift his headquarters and not be subsequently located. He also flattered Farndale saying : '. . . it would be exceedingly difficult to find in any other town in England a Police Officer who would know how to deal with such a delicate matter so well as yourself, or who would co-operate with me so heartily and so efficiently as you would'. Farndale was cautioned not to allow the RIC men to be too zealous. All information of a top-secret nature could be safely forwarded to him via Gosselin.[2]

Jenkinson planned to recruit several agents in the United States, who would be controlled by a very senior man with the sort of authority that Gosselin had in England. Operating at a great distance it was contemplated giving him much wider discretion. Lt Col. J. D. H. Stewart had been recommended for this job. Spencer recommended that Stewart be given a six weeks trial. He would accompany Sir John Macdonald, who had directed the Canadian Secret Service during the invasions of the 1860s, to Ottawa and New York. If Harcourt agreed and if Stewart was prepared to take instructions initially from Macdonald, then Jenkinson would provide the full briefing required. Stewart accepted the post and it was understood that the new arrangement, if successful, would replace the very unsatisfactory situation existing at present under Hoare at the New York Consulate. Spencer was quite clear that they need not be 'permanently saddled with Mr Hoare'. Harcourt agreed and added that '. . . . it is quite idle to locate the person whom you desire to collect information in America in the British Consulate. It is the last place where he ought to be seen or known. You will be wasting your money and relying on a broken reed'. The proposed arrangement collapsed when, not unexpectedly, Col. Stewart joined General Gordon on his expedition to the Sudan.

Hoare remained at the head of American intelligence although Spencer was prepared to send him to New York. American intelligence remained a 'broken reed' and for the moment Jenkinson remained at Dublin Castle.[3]

Daly may well have been a decoy but it is far more likely that he was co-ordinating the development of a bombing offensive. Quite separately, another Clan na Gael operation was developing in London itself. In early February a thirty-year old Irish-American cabinet maker called Harry Burton arrived on the German steamer *Donau*. He then purchased two used portmanteaus after having one of the locks repaired. Travelling up to London he took lodgings and employment as a cabinet maker. He and at least one more bomber had brought almost 100 pounds of a commercial lignine dynamite known as Atlas Powder 'A' through customs undetected. They proceeded to assemble four bombs intended for main line railway stations in the metropolis. The detonating mechanism was an alarm clock modified so that when the striker arm was activated it did not ring a bell but fired a small calibre pistol into a cake of dynamite studded with detonator caps. The mechanism was set for twelve hours, wound, and the pistol loaded and cocked. This was fitted into a small tin box and placed in a portmanteau filled with twenty-one pounds of dynamite (about forty-five cakes or slabs of explosives), some old clothing, and newspapers to disguise the contents even if the locks were forced. Into one of the bags went Burton's old trousers and the coat he had worn on the crossing; it was an unusual coat having buttons of 'imitation quartz of a peculiar character'.[4]

On 26 February the portmanteau which had been placed in the luggage room at Victoria Station the previous day exploded. The Queen cabled Harcourt that day:

'Shocked to see account of fresh explosion. Trust it was accidental and no lives lost?'[5]

The Queen was told that the explosion was hardly accidental but there were fortunately no lives lost. Searches at other stations discovered similar bags had been left also at Charing Cross, Paddington and Ludgate Hill stations. The detonating device found at Ludgate Hill was clockwork of the *'Ansonia Clock Co. N.Y. pat. 27 March 1877'*. The alarm was set for 2.30 on 'Silent Alarm', but the clock had stopped at one minute to five. The clock's alarm mechanism was linked to a 22-calibre bore pistol with grips removed and wired to the back of the clock. The portmanteau left at Charing Cross contained a mechanism based on a 'Peep O'Day' alarm clock but it was not the clock which had failed. The cartridge had failed to explode although the hammer had fallen. At Paddington the hammer had also fallen but had caught in the mechanism and thus failed to strike the cartridge in the chamber of the pistol. The police also found a coat with 'peculiar quartz buttons' in the bag at Charing Cross.

Harcourt told the Queen on 29 February that

> the origin of these devilish schemes is certain. They are planned, subsidised and executed by the assassination societies of American Fenians, who announce their intentions and advertise them openly in newspapers published without the smallest restraint in the United States.
>
> Your Majesty will remember that the government addressed to the government of the United States a strong remonstrance on this subject in the spring of last year. To this no reply was made at the time, but at the end of last month a reply of a most unfriendly character was sent through Mr Lowell, to which it is now proposed at once to send an energetic rejoinder in particular relative to the recent transactions. No other civilised country in the world does or would tolerate the open advocacy of assassination and murder . . .

Writing to his son in Madeira the same day, he said 'I have sunk now into a mere Head Detective and go nowhere and see nothing'.[6]

A reward of £1,000 for the bombers was promptly circulated on handbills through the city, but there was little hope that the bombers were within reach—the use of clockwork mechanisms, unreliable though they were, provided ample time of up to eleven hours for the men to effect their escape. The man that the Secret Service connected with the bombings was John B. King who had been seen at Charing Cross Station at the end of January apparently bound for France. Williamson had been provided with his description but he managed to evade the police watch at the ports and in London. The assumption was that the bombs had been manufactured in France from American components and carried over as hand baggage, deposited in the respective cloakrooms with the dynamitards promptly

returning to France either via Southampton–Le Havre or Dover
–Calais. Harry Burton in fact had returned to his lodgings in
London where he remained until September. He then returned
to the United States for 'the presidential election', at least so he
said. The consul general in New York was alerted on the chance
that the men might return to New York. The question immediately raised was whether or not this was an 'overt act' which
would make the American government take action? Even so,
one could not count on that co-operation and the next step had
to be greatly increased vigilance at Britain's ports.[7]

It was imperative to stop the importation of explosives and
severely restrict the Irish American bombers' freedom of movement without going to the unacceptable extremes of closing
all the ports. On Harcourt's instructions Commissioner Henderson issued orders to the 'port police' (mostly probationer detectives from London's divisions), that 'Passengers who from their
appearance are either Irish or Irish-American should be carefully observed'; information on suspects was to be immediately
telegraphed to Scotland Yard. Local police chiefs were required
to aid the 'port police' and the Customs Officers in their work.
Letters went out to the police and mayors of the various ports
on 7 March followed by a similar letter to their Scottish counterparts a week later. Cargo and luggage from Ireland were to be
subjected to greater customs restriction and search. Harcourt
increasingly relied upon E. G. Jenkinson. Jenkinson drew up an
overall port protection scheme. Put into effect almost immediately, it provided for a port police force staffed with a total of
seventy-nine men of whom forty-nine would be detached from
Scotland Yard and thirty from the RIC. 'Dolly' Williamson
began to co-ordinate work from Special Irish Branch offices at
Scotland Yard. His staff was increased by the addition of extra
detectives and a clerk to attend to the telegrams and to reports
received from the port detachments. Supervision of the detachments was shared by Gosselin and Williamson. Gosselin covered
northern and western ports and Williamson controlled the east
coast from Grimsby south to London and along the south
coast as far west as Weymouth. Bristol and other southwest ports
such as Plymouth and Falmouth initially were not allocated to
either man, awaiting consultation with the Inspector-General of
the RIC. Thirty-three ports, in addition to the Port of London,

Gravesend and Tilbury were co-ordinated in Jenkinson's plan. Sixteen of the seventy-nine men assigned to port protection were detailed to the Thames Estuary. Plain-clothes policemen were stationed, one man each at Le Havre, Rotterdam and Antwerp. Two men were sent to Bremerhaven and Hamburg, one of whom was to be from the RIC. Later two men were added to the Secret Service team in Paris, making a total of seven Scotland Yard detectives on the continent. Commissioner Henderson was allowed to augment the Metropolitan police force with fifty-four men in early May to make up for those withdrawn for duty in the ports.[8]

One of Gosselin's major responsibilities was to carefully explain the new procedures to the local police authorities. A high priority was placed upon careful co-operation between the port police and the local police authorities because the local police would be required to watch and follow up suspected persons. The procedures agreed upon were based upon the Secretary of State's instructions that port detectives were to be present at all searches made by Customs House officers. Telegrams and reports of importance were to be sent immediately to Jenkinson at the Home Office. Telegrams were also to be repeated from Scotland Yard to Gosselin when they came from ports under his control. If explosives were found in the possession of travellers they were to be handed over to the local police and the Yard was to be immediately telegraphed. Suspects were to be dealt with in the same fashion. Where someone was under suspicion but there was insufficient reason to hold him, he was to be followed while the police at his destination were to be altered; they were 'not to lose sight of him'. All telegrams were to be followed by explanatory reports by the next post. Ports under Gosselin's control should send two copies of reports, one of which would then be forwarded to Gosselin whose responsibilities kept him moving from town to town.[9]

The next move was Harcourt's. He requested Spencer to send Jenkinson to London to oversee the anti-bomber campaign. Spencer agreed, mindful of the *quid pro quo* being unexpectedly exacted by the Home Secretary. If Harcourt was going to have the Irish political prisoners in English gaols he was also going to have the benefit of Jenkinson's talents. Jenkinson arrived in London on the evening of 7 March personally fearful that Harcourt would be disappointed in the results he would be able to obtain. The next day he and Harcourt agreed upon the details of the new working arrangement which were essentially what Jenkinson asked for. Jenkinson thus 'took charge at the H.O.' on 17 March 1884. On 17 March he received £500 followed by £600 more two weeks later. On 12 May a further £1,000 was directed into making undercover payoffs to various agents and informers. Robert Anderson was relieved of all responsibilities and duties relative to Fenianism in London; he had been passed over for promotion again. The London-based RIC men would now take orders direct from Jenkinson.[10]

The watch on John Daly continued. At 7.45 a.m. on Wednesday, 9 April he was spotted on Wolverhampton station by a detective of the Great Western Railway. Daly had left Birmingham without being detected by the twenty-four hour surveillance of which he was doubtless aware. Fortunately for Gosselin his forethought in bringing railway detectives and ticket inspectors into the police operation prevented a clean escape. Detective James Sefton watched him book a ticket for Birkenhead and took the same train. When the train arrived at Merseyside, Daly got out, spoke to a man on the platform and the two went into the station's refreshment rooms. Daly emerged alone and took the boat to Liverpool with Sefton close behind. Disembarking on the other side of the river, Daly went towards Chapel Street but was obviously suspicious of Sefton for he kept looking over his shoulder. When he reached a corner he broke into a run and managed to shake Sefton off. The situation was now serious. Sefton got a telegram off to the Birmingham police and they telegraphed the warning to the head constable in Liverpool. The information must have reached him too late to have men at either the rail station or landing stage. All that could be done was sweep the city in hopes of finding Daly. Would he be found trying to leave for Ireland or the United States? Gosselin was convinced that he would return to Birmingham. Two days later, on the morning of Good Friday (11 April), Daly entered Birkenhead station at 8.30 and bought a ticket for Wolverhampton. The RIC, Gosselin and Liverpool detectives were waiting. Daly appeared to have some heavy objects in his coat pockets and he also was extremely nervous, sensing the presence of the plain-clothes policemen. He was in a 'funk' and Gosselin, fearful that he might throw the bombs in his pockets out of the carriage window if allowed to proceed, ordered his arrest. Daly gave his name as John Denman; a search revealed £9 or so in his pockets and four parcels, one of which was rather lighter than the others. Three of the parcels contained brass cylinder grenades $4'' \times 2\frac{1}{2}''$ filled with dynamite of 73 per cent nitroglycerine. The other parcel contained the chemicals and glass tubes, corks and leads of the detonator. Detonation was by means of a sulphuric acid-filled glass tube inserted into the bomb shortly before it was to be thrown. Within the tube was a lead pellet which would shatter the tube upon impact; the sulphuric acid, realgar and dynamite would explode with tremendous force and fragmentation from the brass case. Jenkinson's opinion was that they were 'perfectly made and are most terrible weapons'. They were a very sophisticated version of the bombs used in Glasgow and London over the previous two years. Harcourt arranged for an experiment at Woolwich arsenal. A room was set up approximating to the room where the cabinet met with twelve wooden dummies; 'the bomb only had a drop of two feet but there were wounds in every figure, the smallest being seventeen and the largest forty-nine'.[11]

It was clear that Daly had been betrayed. The informer, who remained anonymous, is assumed to be a Liverpool Irishman, 'Big Dan' O'Neill, who had attended Charles J. Kickham's funeral with Daly in 1882. The informer had told Gosselin that the bombs were to be thrown from the Stranger's Gallery in the Commons down onto the government bench. On the Saturday after the arrest Jenkinson told Harcourt that 'the difficulty was to get Daly with the things on him without causing suspicion to rest on our informant'. Daly wrote to John Devoy from Birmingham's Windsor Green Prison : 'That I have been cruelly betrayed is enough for the present and that I could have accomplished what I proposed but for that'. He also told Devoy that he had written to his 'D' [Camp?] about the circumstances of the betrayal. If Clan na Gael would take care of the informer 'I will keep my mouth shut'—otherwise Daly would 'give him to the world at the trial and let him take his chance of an O'Donnell'. (Patrick O'Donnell had shot the informer James Carey in 1883). Daly also regretted having had to pawn

Devoy's watch to the ruffian (O'Neill?) when he was hard up :
'I suppose the chances of getting it now are, to say the least
blue.'[12] The Limerick-born Daly had been stopped but the
question did arise : had the bombs been planted on him by the
police to ensure his conviction? Although John Daly was
accused of preparing to assassinate the government by throw-
ing bombs onto the Treasury bench while the Commons was in
session, there is nothing in Jenkinson's reports for the remainder
of the year to suggest that he took threats of assassinations very
seriously. Nor for that matter did Gladstone. In the aftermath
of Daly's arrest (24 May) he threatened to close Hawarden's
gates to police protection, because he was 'ashamed of the
expense he had already been the cause of inflicting on his
fellow ratepayers'. He did, however, back down on the matter.
The Queen on the other hand was said by Ponsonby on the one
hand to be 'rather sour' at her carriage being followed when
it left Windsor grounds and on the other hand (13 July) complaining that the terrace above the departure station at Paddington had been unguarded the previous day.

James F. Egan had also been arrested in Birmingham as was
another man associated with Daly, William McDonnell. When
the Birmingham police dug up Egan's back garden they found a
bottle of nitroglycerine. Daly claimed to have buried it without Egan's knowledge. Egan was not to escape because 'com-
promising correspondence', some Fenian documents and a copy
of the constitution of the proposed Irish Republic, were discovered amongst his belongings. The trial of the three men
opened at the Warwick Assizes 30 July 1884. It took three
days to hear the evidence. Daly conducted his own defence
with what *The Times* described as 'great fluency and in a highly
declamatory manner'. Daly closed his defence :

> I love Ireland. I presume you, gentlemen of the jury love
> your country. What is a virtue to you is a crime to me. If I
> must be sent to a dungeon it is the destiny of my race. Within
> a dungeon I would love my country. In my memory I would
> visit the spot where my dead father lies and where still my
> widowed mother sorrows for her son. Her last words to me
> were : 'Be just and fear not'. Gentlemen, I am no assassin. There
> is a mystery. God give me fortitude and preserve that mystery.

He did not name the informer probably in the assurance that he would be dealt with by the 'D'. Egan and Daly were found guilty on all counts: Daly received a sentence of life imprisonment, Egan twenty years. McDonnell received a short sentence on a lesser charge of a crime admitted in 1874.[13]

Throughout May the watch on the ports had continued. Problems were most severe at Hull. It was the port through which immigrants from the continent passed on their way to Liverpool and embarkation for America. To expect three detectives to screen vast numbers of people was not only impossible but security presented a major bottleneck for immigration agents such as Messrs T. Wilson and Sons and Co. They applied to the Home Office for permission to send the people in sealed and locked railway vans to Liverpool rather than submitting them to the search procedures. On one Monday in the first week of May 1,537 emigrants with 3,691 pieces of baggage passed through the port with the customs checking only hand baggage. It had even proved to be impossible to require the landing and examination at a central point in the port. Problems had also arisen on the west coast of Britain because of the searching of Irish MPs luggage at Holyhead by Customs' Officers. The detectives on duty were made responsible for which bags were to be searched by Customs and the implication was that they should avoid the luggage of Parnell and his associates.[14]

One of the most interesting although unsubstantiated stories about the Irish-American efforts during this period comes from Michael Davitt's recollections of a 'Major Yellow' who proposed to rescue Daly at the Warwick Assizes. Accompanied by Casey (associated with a leading Parisian Fenian, Eugene Davis) Yellow left Calais for Dover where they deposited an old can, wrapped as a parcel, against one of the walls of the railway station with a fuse attached. They were delighted when the papers announced the following morning that a diabolical plot to blow up the Dover railway station was frustrated by a timely discovery. The two adventurers then proceeded to London where they tried to meet T. P. O'Connor and one or two of the Irish members in the lobby of the House of Commons. Having failed to interest anyone in the rescue of Daly, Yellow took Casey to Scotland Yard followed by a wild drive to an address at Kensington supposedly pursued by detectives, and a narrow escape from arrest while fleeing back to Paris. The point of Davitt's tale was that Yellow was in the pay of the Secret Service but this connection came to an end as a result of this trip.[15]

The problem of secret agents continued to be on the top of Jenkinson's agenda and he wrote to Harcourt saying that he was prepared to take one M. Hydroix on trial, a man recommended by the Prince of Wales.[16]

Jenkinson warned Chief Inspector Williamson of Special Irish Branch to expect explosions before the end of May and that 'the police should be especially vigilant'. Sir E. Henderson maintained the Metropolitan Police's guard over London's public buildings and monuments warning his Divisional Superintendents that he held them 'strictly responsible that every possible precaution [was] taken to this end'. The arrangements proved inadequate.

On the night of 30 May London was once again shaken by the report of explosions. One blast occurred outside the front of the house of Sir Watkin Wynn, a second at the rear of the Junior Carlton Club and the third at the Special Irish Branch office in Great Scotland Yard. The first blast was less serious than that at the Junior Carlton Club where five people were injured and most of the window glass of the club and surrounding houses was destroyed. Witnesses—two cabmen—said that they had seen two men, who were assumed to have thrown the bomb down the steps leading to the club's basement kitchen. But these two explosions near St James were of little consequence in comparison to the penetration of Scotland Yard's security allowing the bombing of Special Irish Branch itself.

The Special Branch office was situated in a first-floor set of rooms in a small building in the centre of Great Scotland Yard, a public thoroughfare—immediately across from a large public house, The Rising Sun. It was not enough that hundreds of people crossed through the yard day and night; in the north-east corner of the ground floor of the police office there was a public urinal. That was where the bomb was placed, exploding with devastating effect at 7.20 p.m. The police constable placed at (× in the diagram facing) the front of the office had 'observed nothing suspicious in any persons who entered the urinal'. He

Diagram of the Scotland Yard explosion, made by E. G. Jenkinson.

was unable to be questioned further because, although not seriously injured, he was in a state of shock. Special patrols on the south side of the yard and on the Whitehall front had seen nothing suspicious. Jenkinson said: 'If the Constables had been properly posted I do not see how men could have approached and put anything in the urinal unobserved. . .'. Nor was he aware, apparently never having visited Williamson at his office, that there was a urinal '*under* the room in which the detectives sit! Fancy them allowing the public to go there at night, or indeed at any time after the warnings they had received'.[17]

In addition to the minor injuries suffered by the duty constable, four other people were taken to Charing Cross hospital. Casualties were light but the damage to the Special Branch building was extensive, blowing down a large portion of wall and destroying a significant part of the records held then on Fenian affairs. Guards at the Albert Memorial were armed, but they were only to shoot in self-defence and not as one bit of advice suggested: 'shoot down the men before they could get up the steps'.

When dawn of the thirty-first had arrived, after a long night of work by Jenkinson, Williamson, Special Branch detectives and the explosives expert, Majendie, another bomb was found near one of the lions in Trafalgar Square; it had not detonated and Nelson was still on his column.

This bomb was contained in a bag similar to the ones left in the railway station cloakrooms. The pieces of fuse found in the bag were American, as were the slabs of Atlas-type dynamite which filled the bag. Jenkinson advised Harcourt that these facts should be brought to the attention of the American government. He had reliable information that these outrages had their origins in America and that they were planned by the same men who were concerned in the explosions of 25 February at the cloakrooms of the Victoria Railway Station. Jenkinson's theory was that the bombers had remained in London and that the remainder of the dynamite, about 250 lbs of it, was still stored somewhere in the metropolis: he was right but still could not find the men led by Harry Burton. Jenkinson hoped that Harcourt would not allow this business to interfere with his holiday since there was really nothing that the Home Secretary could do. 'If it were not that a scare is created, and other lives

are endangered by such explosions one would feel inclined to
laugh at the whole thing. It is so childish and contemptible'.[18]
With Jenkinson in London, CID Director Howard Vincent lost
what control he had over the anti-Fenian effort. Disillusioned
about this and concurrent Scotland Yard re-organisation (Metropolitan Police Act, 1884) he had decided to retire that summer
and take a world cruise. Vincent was succeeded by James
Monroe, formerly the inspector-general of Police in Bengal.
Monroe was a professional policeman and he took over the
CID as an assistant commissioner, something that had been
denied to Vincent when CID had been created in March
1878.

The details of Jenkinson's salary had not been sorted out
when he moved to London in March. The matter was complicated by his having been paid previously from Irish revenues.
Spencer was unwilling to debit the Irish vote beyond that which
Jenkinson normally received as assistant under secretary for
Police and Crime at Dublin Castle. Now that he had to live
in England Jenkinson felt he was entitled to £1,000 salary and
£300 house allowance. Harcourt's suggestion that the Irish
government should increase Jenkinson's stipend was rejected by
Spencer.

At the end of August Jenkinson wrote what he hoped was
a comforting letter to Harcourt opening with 'You will see from
the memorandum which I enclose that you are not quite so
poor as you thought you were'. The sum set aside for the work
in 1884–5 had been £5,000 which after deducting the £1,300
for Jenkinson, £1,183. 5s. for Gosselin, £683. 5s. for Major
Blair, £200 for Jenkinson's private secretary, £100 for his clerk
and £180 for two constable messengers, and £1,000 for
'obtaining information' left about £1,000 in hand, over £600
having been carried forward from the previous financial year.
Gosselin had not drawn as much from Liddell (permanent
secretary at the Home Office) because Jenkinson had been paying out the informant money. Unhappily Sir Robert Hamilton
had notified him that at the end of October the Irish government would stop paying the salary of Gosselin's assistant, Major
Blair, another Irish Resident Magistrate. If he could not be
paid, as in Gosselin's case, by the Home Office he must return
to Ireland. There was no additional money available and he

would return. Jenkinson's total estimated expenditure for England and Ireland for the current year (1884–5) was £23,700, which included agents operating in America, Paris, and elsewhere. Hopefully less would be actually spent. The Home Office was expected to pay £4,800, including £800 spent by Jenkinson at the close of the previous financial year 1883–4, while the chief secretary for Ireland was responsible for the balance of £18,900. The one virtue of the arrangement was that Jenkinson was responsible for the allocation of the funds from both the Irish government and the Home Office, avoiding the complications of having to mediate the allocation of funds for the various requirements. Apparently Robert Anderson's stipend was cut from £500 to £162 per annum; Birmingham's police authority received £60 1. 10. for watching Daly. Gosselin was out of pocket by some £200 for the previous year because of the expenses associated with his travelling from town to town. Jenkinson stressed that Blair and Gosselin had to have an allowance of £1 15s. a night, which was the usual arrangement in Ireland.

The cost to the British government was £24,000 in Secret Service money alone. Scotland Yard estimates show that it had expended £4,338 on providing police for the ports. The cost of augmenting the Metropolitan Police from 1 April to August of that year was £19,199, of which half had been applied for but not authorised. It looked like port protection would cost a total of £12,000 per annum, not including RIC costs which were possibly one-fifth of that figure. The cost of repairing the Special Branch's office was £445, rather less than the original surveyor's estimates, in part because the urinal had not been reconstructed! All of the requests for compensation were refused, ranging from the owner of the Rising Sun to the owner of the carriage which had been wrecked in front of the pub. The Rising Sun despite its damage did a tremendous business in the following days from those members of the public who wished to have a pint while visiting the scene of the crime. At the end of June, the Mayor of Windsor, in response to a government 'suggestion', announced that the urinal at the base of the Curfew Tower, Windsor Castle was to be closed.[19]

By late September Jenkinson was increasingly worried about a situation developing in Paris where the movements of various

Irish exiles were currently being watched by five agents. Considering it as the only place from which danger might be reasonably expected, he was sure that the dynamitards were becoming increasingly active. Because of a fresh influx of American money, he expected to hear an explosion any day. Some consolation could be derived from the feeling that it would not be a big one; public buildings were now so well watched as to make it almost impossible to get a bomb next to them.

> They will be told that the explosions must be simultaneous and that they must watch [for their] opportunity, and if they cannot injure public building(s) they must attack private houses and places of business.[20]

Bombers still had to be caught in the act or recognised on the spot, for there was no possibility of convicting them otherwise. If they escaped to France or America there was insufficient evidence to support a case for extradition. The bombers were on a very good wicket because no precautions could stop them; there was no means of guarding all the potential targets and little opportunity for discovering their plans beforehand. The limited successes of the Secret Service operation, based upon informers, had made the bombers of both Clan na Gael and Rossa's Skirmishers anxious. 'I know for a fact', said Jenkinson, 'that men who came over to Paris very hot for an active work from America hanging back when they came face to face with what they have to do, and that their leaders find it very difficult to bring them up to scratch.' No man could now be sure that his most intimate friend was not in the pay of the British Secret Service and this, despite plenty of dynamite money, meant that sympathisers were 'loathe to act'. Despite the bravado associated with the dynamite organisers Jenkinson was sure that terror was the object and not any desire to destroy property on a large scale or to take human life.

Turning to current political assessments he suggested that Parnell was against dynamite. He assumed he was playing a winning hand and that any serious outrage would check and injure the cause. And yet Jenkinson feared an out-and-out break with Clan na Gael would not happen because of Parnellite dependence upon American Fenian money. There might also be the assumption that having a 'party of force' in the wings would strengthen their own position both in parliament and the country. 'They do not object to dynamite and outrages on principle, but on grounds of expediency.' The middle course being pursued by the Irish Parliamentary Party could not succeed in the long run and thus Irish agitation had to be crushed. An end had to be made of concessions or the British 'government must avow the principle of Home Rule, and steadily work up to it'. The present course was leading to a drift into Home Rule. Jenkinson was sure that Harcourt would not agree with that particular appraisal.

Turning to transatlantic matters, Jenkinson was convinced that the National Land League convention in Boston during August was only a cover for Clan na Gael. All of the new officers, including its president Patrick Egan, were Clan members. It had been arranged beforehand that Alexander Sullivan (leader of the Clan Triangle) should retire from the presidency. He was replaced by Egan because of the discontent concerning Sullivan's leadership, particularly because of charges of his using its organisation and funds for political purposes. The Irish Parliamentary Party would continue to receive financial aid and if the constitutional agitation were to fail, 'more active measures' were to be taken by the Triangle and Revolutionary Directory. Jenkinson could not believe that John Redmond and Thomas Sexton, both members of parliament in attendance at the Convention, were unaware of what was going on. Jenkinson had it on 'good authority' that Redmond was on intimate terms with the Clan na Gael men. Egan, while supporting the parliamentary group, was 'heart and soul' in the dynamite movement and was undoubtedly the source of the £5,000 drawn out of Land League funds for the organisation of the Dublin Invincibles in 1881–2.[21]

Prominent London Fenians continued to be watched and information about their associates continued to be collected. Additional information, Jenkinson warned, would not come in until the Special Branch and RIC detectives learnt to work more secretly and get reliable informants in their pay. The man (still unidentified) who had informed on John Daly had been tried by a jury of five Manchester Fenians 'last Sunday week' (letter dated 19 September 1884) and acquitted : 'I had a man on the jury. They were unanimous in saying there was no evidence against him. But they recommended his expulsion from the IRB because he gave shelter to a dynamiter [Daly?] without the permission of the Supreme Council'.

Jenkinson continued to worry about various dynamiters reportedly in Paris. He added another agent, making a total of six, to improve the level of surveillance. Theirs was not an easy task, for by his own admission the Fenians were 'secret and cunning' in their movements and could easily leave Paris without trace. Four of them had recently done so and Jenkinson feared that, despite port vigilance, they were possibly in London. All that could be done was to provide Scotland Yard with their descriptions. If such men kept quiet and avoided observation there was no chance of finding them in London. Realising that there was no effective way to deal with the headquarters of the conspiracy in Paris added weight to his renewed plea for the introduction of a passport system. Hotel keepers would have been required to provide information to the police on strangers; 'if we do not take such precautions we must make up our mind to have explosions'. But with an easily discernible note of sarcasm, Jenkinson added that the public may prefer explosions than the 'annoyance of a passport system, and of other precautionary measures'. Jenkinson was pleased with the progress that Assistant Commissioner Monroe was making in improving the efficiency of the CID. A minute to Monroe from Jenkinson dated 29 September reiterated the seriousness of the developing situation in Paris, which seemed destined to produce a spate of terrorist bombings within metropolitan London before long. The control of the ports had to improve and *all* handbags and such parcels should be examined, and the *'persons'* of all suspicious looking Irish or Irish-Americans should be searched'. Personal searches were essential for he had been told of dynamite being smuggled in in small quantities in pockets and body belts. In addition to Harwich and Ramsgate, special care had to be taken with steamers coming up the Thames to London, where the Bologne-London steamer touched. The United States government continued to ignore the Foreign Office pleas, and it appeared that the French government were equally unwilling to be helpful; 'afraid [we] can't expect much, if any, assistance from France at present'. Jenkinson was prepared to discuss the

French matter with Pauncefote at the Foreign Office in early October, but he remained very pessimistic about any success. The least effective of his secret agents in Paris, M. Hyroix, was fired. Furious, he demanded £300 separation pay and threatened if Jenkinson refused to pay *'revendications scandaleuse'*— so much for the friends of the Prince of Wales.[22]

Jenkinson's position in London, and his prolonged absences from Dublin, produced noticeable irritation in the chief secretary's office at Dublin Castle. At the end of November, Sir Robert Hamilton (KCB, January 1884), the permanent under secretary of the Irish government, began to press for either Jenkinson's return to Dublin or the shifting of the cost of his salary to the Home Office vote. Harcourt, writing to Spencer on the twenty-third, intimated that he held a low opinion of Hamilton, for Jenkinson was owed a great deal and was still most useful; Hamilton was not to be made 'monarch of all he surveys'. Any suggestion of raising a question in parliament concerning Jenkinson's official position or salary was to be steadfastly resisted. Harcourt was willing to compromise to the extent of allowing Jenkinson back to Dublin more frequently and for longer periods. Whether this satisfied Hamilton is doubtful.[23]

During the previous spring and summer, Dublin had been the scene of an amusing set of incidents, almost unique in those otherwise depressing years of the dynamitards. Sometime in April of 1884 a 'Mrs Tyler', the twenty-seven year old daughter of a noted, but anonymous, chief inspector at Scotland Yard took a set of rooms at the Gresham Hotel in Dublin. This 'exceedingly pretty woman' proclaimed her support for the Irish republic while she received potential conspirators from what Michael Davitt described as Dublin's standing corps of practical jokers. Some of those who enjoyed playing upon her credulity plotted to unmask her as a spy of the English Secret Service. The plan went into effect at one of her revolutionary dinner parties. While the meal was in progress a man dashed in to announce that Inspector Mallon and a force of Dublin detectives were in the lobby. Mrs Tyler told her guests that they had nothing to fear and went down to the lobby. In her absence the men searched the bedroom and found fragments of a telegram in the dustbin. Upon her return she was induced to contribute £20 to aid in the escape of dynamiters captured by

Scotland Yard. The 'boys' returned in high spirits to the Imperial Hotel, where they pieced together the bits of torn telegram addressed to her from the Home Office and then wrote a letter to the chief secretary for Ireland, Sir Charles Trevelyan, enclosing the £20 they had extracted from Mrs Tyler and charging the Home Office with using a female *agent provocateur*. The 'practical jokers' led by Fred Gallagher, the son of J. B. Gallagher, editor of the *Freeman's Journal*, told the story to T. M. Healy, one of the Irish MPs. He raised the matter in the House on Friday, 25 July. Hansard's Parliamentary Debates, under the heading 'Ireland'—Money returned through the Post', recorded the exchange :

> '*Mr. Healy* asked the Chief Secretary to the Lord Lieutenant of Ireland, what disposition was made by him of the money recently returned to him through the Post; and will it be refunded to the Secret Service Department?
> *Mr. Trevelyan* : Sometime ago I received £15 in notes in a letter without address. Knowing nothing of the matter, I followed the course I always follow with regard to anonymous communications which appear to require notice, and handed the letter and its contents to the police authorities'.
> *Mr. Healy* : I beg to inform the Right Hon. Gentleman that the money belongs to Mrs Tyler, of the Secret Service Department'.

Healy had made his point and in so doing had doubtless brought a bank of smiles from the Irish benches, for had not the woman promised that if someone would bomb the House of Commons she would personally take him to Italy for safety?[24] This episode brought relations between Hamilton and Jenkinson to the breaking point. Hamilton, in particular, felt that escapades of this kind jeopardised his hopes of reconciling Irish opinion to the government.

The railway station attacks failed to convince the American government that they were in part responsible for the bombs because of their refusal to stop the open collection of funds in the dynamite press. On 13 March the next of the Foreign Office's letters went to Washington asking Secretary of State Frelinghuysen to do his duty. It followed the established form of addressing the dispatch to West, the British minister, who was to read it to Frel-inghuysen and 'give him a copy of it'. Granville's letter went over very familiar ground. Frelinghuysen had not replied to Gran-ville's letter of May 1883 until 4 December and then Lowell did not communicate its contents to Lord Granville until 21 January. This was the letter referred to by Harcourt in his letter to the Queen on 29 February as being 'a reply of a most unfriendly character'. What Granville responded with was another letter in an effort to clear up the 'misapprehensions' to be found in the Secretary of State's belated reply to his letter of the spring.

The point was that Her Majesty's government had not com-plained that the dynamite money publicly collected in the United States was openly forwarded to Britain, for in that case it would have been intercepted on its arrival and 'arrested in its employment'. Rather the complaint was that the money was publicly collected 'to pay for murder and outrage, and [was] openly advertised as having been employed for those objects'. Furthermore it was not enough to say that since, as the Secre-tary of State suggested, these papers belonged to a 'low class', that they were without influence or significance. One did not need to take 'official notice' of them to make them potent for they already were, as the explosions thus far detonated in Great Britain testified. Granville suggested that the American govern-ment would never tolerate a situation in which 'persons of a vile and degraded reputation were to publish lists of particular houses to be broken into and their proprietors murdered in New York, and if subscription lists were opened to provide the invest-ments of burglary and assassination . . .', yet so long as the target was London, the Americans do nothing. The dynamite press demonstrated 'a continuous and flagrant incitement to, and collection of funds in the United States for, the promotion of murder and outrage upon the subjects of the Queen, not only in a general form but frequently with relation to particular individuals designated by name, such as judges, public officials, and others'. Even if, as Frelinghuysen states, one cannot estab-lish a causal relationship between the incitement and the acts of outrage, a civilised nation had the right to expect that, at the very least, the incitement be stopped by a friendly power, such as the United States.

The only place where Granville exceeded the evidence was where he claimed that 'in most instances the material employed has been shown to be an exclusively American manufacture and not available in Britain for normal usage'. The hand of Harcourt appeared in one reference to the systematic assassinations carried out by the 'Molly Maguires' in Pennsylvania. The suggestion was that it would not have been permitted that journals in the United States should have openly advocated and collected subscriptions for the promotion of these murders. Why cannot the Queen's subjects expect the same? Granville concluded that British government had complete confidence in Frelinghuysen's assurance that his government would not 'fail to place its hand on any known or proven overt act of which Great Britain may complain'. The answer, however, would not be available until the end of November of that year. So much for the delaying tactics of American diplomacy; Britain's defence was in her own hands.[25]

At the end of November, following the national elections the American Secretary of State finally allowed himself the luxury of a reply to Lord Granville's despatch. It had been read to him by West of 27 March, a fortnight after transmission from London by diplomatic pouch. The fact that the messages had to suffer the delay involved in the transatlantic steam packet service was an indication both of the difficulty of transmitting a message of that length accurately and safely by telegraph and that the Foreign Office was not prepared to accept a sense of urgency in the affair; possibly because they had so little hope of success. Frelinghuysen's answer was transmitted through James Russell Lowell, who was a close personal friend of Granville. The reply gave no indication of any American inclination to take seriously the British 'suggestions' for positive immediate action against the dynamite press. The *New York Tribune* (14 March 1884), echoed by the *Irish World* (28 March), had reported that the United States attorney-general, Benjamin Brewster, had sent a circular to all district attorneys and federal marshals ordering men to increase efforts to prevent the illegal exportation of explosives. This was the result of a directive of President Arthur's to see that the statute making it a penal offence to export explosives, unless done openly and according to specific rules, was enforced. To that end the Justice

Department had 'employed special means for the prevention and discovery of any such acts'.[26]

The existence of the correspondence remained secret by request of the American State Department. It was the British minister Sackville West who had suggested to Granville the necessity of humouring the Americans, saying (15 April 1884) that if Congress got hold of the correspondence, particularly the despatch of 13 March, the Irish-American members 'would make political capital out of it and force Mr Frelinghuysen to make a disagreeable answer'. Clearly the Secretary of State would not follow any course of action that could be demonstrated to have been requested or demanded in an election year by the Foreign Office. He could not risk being accused of being a 'tool of British imperialism'. The British legation in Washington had followed up the first American letter by seeking legal advice, which confirmed (12 April 1884) that nothing could be done about the dynamite press under existing state or federal legislation. Furthermore, the President, a Republican, and his executive wing of the government had its hands tied because there was no hope of the Democratic-controlled Congress providing the required legislation even if the President was to press the issue. West continued :

> It may be asked—Why is this the case? Especially when the feelings between the two countries never perhaps was so cordial. The answer is to be found in the fact that a large portion of the members of Congress depend for their seats upon the Irish vote in their constituencies, and that, although they scorn, with some exceptions, to be associated with Irish agitation, they nevertheless dare not appear in the House [of Representatives] as its opponents. . . .'

West also appraised Granville of the significance of the approaching Presidential election that autumn, in which the Irish vote would play an important part and for which therefore both the Democratic and Republican parties were bidding. This was a particularly important point to take into consideration for although Clan na Gael was not supposed to engage in politics, in practice it did, for nearly all of its leaders were professional politicians. Their involvement in the Democratic Tammany Hall 'machine' in New York and the Republican 'machine' in Chicago for example, increased their influence by producing votes in American urban areas. The Republican's power had been severely curtailed by their loss of their governing majority in the House of Representatives in the election of 1882 and now it looked quite possible that they might lose the presidency. Arthur was unexpectedly rejected for renomination and instead the Republican standard-bearer was to be James G. Blaine. He was perhaps the outstanding Republican of his time, and well known to the Foreign Office as Secretary of State during Garfield's brief administration. The Democrats on the other hand, nominated the reform governor of New York State, Grover Cleveland, a man despised and feared by Tammany Hall. His private life, however, proved to be a problem and his refusal to deny the charge that he was the father of an illegitimate child seriously narrowed the extent of his popular victory, which was cut to only 23,000 out of a total of 9,726,967 votes cast.

Sackville West (10 June 1884) had predicted that relations with Britain would take a turn for the worse if Blaine were elected, for he would not hesitate to pander to the New York Irish vote to carry this state; as it was, Cleveland carried New York. West added:

> It must always be borne in mind that the object of the Irish Party here is to create ill feelings between the two countries, and they are delighted therefore at the announcements in the London papers that you are sending out a strong despatch on dynamite conspiracies.[27]

To illustrate his views on Blaine and the Irish vote (parenthetically noting that he preferred him nonetheless to Cleveland), he enclosed a clipping from a newspaper concerning the Joe Brady Club (a Clan na Gael camp) that met at Kessel's Hall, 475 Pearl Street, New York.

> 'There will be no meeting of the Joe Brady Emergency Club to-night. All dynamiters who favour the election of James G. Blaine for President of the United States will meet here on next Tuesday night. Blaine is the true friend of the Irish'.[28]

The significance of Frelinghuysen's despatch of 24 November

was that it was the answer of a rejected President, Arthur, and a defeated Republican administration which as in the case of a 'lame duck' (the American term for this situation) would limp along until Cleveland and the Democrats took over the White House in March of 1885. Still, the text was interesting because of the ease with which the British arguments were dismissed, despite the tremendous care which William Vernon Harcourt had taken in developing them. Frelinghuysen's legal advisors had been beavering away at the British statute books and come to the conclusion that not even Her Majesty's government could have prosecuted the dynamite press if it was publishing in England. The matter of Ireland was carefully avoided and the despatch again refused to take seriously the veracity or influence of the dynamite press, although in an empty gesture the 'lame duck' administration offered the possibility of a reciprocal arrangement with Great Britain on trans-national incitement to violence. One of the distinctive marks of Harcourt's hand in the despatch of 13 March had been a reference to the 'Molly Maguires' : '. . . it is not supposed that it would have been permitted that journals in the United States should have openly advocated and collected subscriptions for the promotion of these murders'. Frelinghuysen simply noted that his government had not complained to Her Majesty's government of the time because most of the members of this terrorist group in Pennsylvania's coalfields were British subjects! He rejected any responsibility for the American-manufactured dynamite nor did he accept it as evidence of an American-Irish plot; his government had not complained to Her Majesty's government about murders committed in the United States with Sheffield knives or pistols made in Birmingham. It was also made quite clear that the despatch which James Russell Lowell was reading to Lord Granville had been prepared not for the purpose of continuing the correspondence, but to set the record straight from the standpoint of Washington. Frederick Frelinghuysen concluded :

> Alike jealous of the national birthright of political liberty and asylum from oppression, we are also alike concerned in seeing to it that such liberty shall be restrained within due forms and guarantees of law.

Lowell read the despatch on 10 December.[29]

Sir Edward Watkin, a well known railway promoter and MP for Hythe, forwarded an extract from a personal letter to Harcourt, (eventually seen by both Jenkinson and Spencer), which had been written to him by Mr J. S. Moore, a prominent and longtime member of the Democratic Party. Moore, a personal acquaintance of Watkin, was concerned that Her Majesty's government should be aware that it was generally agreed amongst his political associates in Washington, that if evidence would be obtained on the dynamiters, the new administration would take the required action. This was indicative of a material change which had been going on in the Democratic Party, which controlled the House of Representatives in relationship to the Irish vote. Blaine, they were convinced, had pandered to the Irish vote and had succeeded in syphoning it off the Democratic totals. This could have been disastrous for Cleveland, except for his appeal to the independent voters. This situation was accentuated by the defeat of two of the most violent anglophobes, Congressmen Finnerty of Chicago and Robinson of Brooklyn. 'Now then', said Moore, 'the feeling of the Democratic leaders (especially as we gained the victory) is to let the Irish element understand that the Democratic Party henceforth is their master and not their slave.' The party had demonstrated its ability to survive without the Irish vote and would not shirk from administering stern justice. Cleveland could be depended upon, and so could his newly nominated Secretary of State, Thomas F. Bayard. Moore claimed to know the sentiments of Bayard on the subject of Clan na Gael and the Skirmishers; sentiments which would enhearten the British government. 'Show beyond a doubt that the Conspiracy is hatching *here*. You can no more expect that the government here will hound these fiends with detectives, than you could expect England should be hounding the Socialist fiends.' Jenkinson could but thank Harcourt for a copy of the letter and express his hopes that Mr Moore was right.[30]

8

London Bridge is falling down, falling down . . .

Our enemies are making rapid progress in the arts of attack —we none in those of defence.

Harcourt to Spencer, 25 January 1885

THROUGH the long black December nights of 1884 London sheltered desperately behind Scotland Yard's inadequate shield. Citizens imagined bombs carried by every shadow projected by the pools of gaslight. The bombers, however, remained safely beyond the shafts of light stabbing from the bulls-eye lanterns of the police. London waited nervously for the next explosion: it finally came on the evening of 13 December, seventeen years to the day after the horrifying Clerkenwell explosion. The blast occurred at 6 p.m. under the south-west end of London Bridge. The waiting was over: Captain William Mackey Lomasney and his Clan na Gael bombers had launched their final assault of the dynamite war.

At dusk Lomasney, his brother-in-law (Peter Malon?) and John Fleming rented a boat near the bridge. The three men rowed to the bridge, and attached a bomb to the iron grating which was fixed over the drain holes to protect the bridge arches at low water against just such an attack. The fuse was set; the bomb exploded prematurely and the three men died instantly. The wreckage of the boat and what remained of the bombers was carried through the dark to the sea on the ebb tide.

Windows in the neighbourhood were shattered, pedestrians on the bridge shaken but uninjured, the bridge buttress's wooden baulks were shattered. Despite the large hole blown in the granite buttress itself the blast did no major structural damage to the bridge. Lomasney had been aware of the limited damage that the blast would produce but according to his old friend John Devoy, he had not intended to destroy the bridge but sought only to frighten Her Majesty's government and England's ruling class. Devoy continued: 'And that it did frighten them as all the other dynamite operations did, there can be no doubt'.[1] The price of fear came high.

E. G. Jenkinson correctly connected the May explosions at Scotland Yard and in St James's area with London Bridge, as the work of the same man. Even more worrying was that Jenkinson's *very reliable source*, who warned him about the bridges, now predicted an attack on the House of Commons. Colonel Majendie improved the protection of the bridges while Scotland Yard was asked to take special precautions on the Westminster riverside and about Westminster Bridge. Jenkinson warned CID director James Monroe that the increased security had to be mounted quickly and quietly to protect his informant. The London Bridge blast provided the excuse for more vigilance, especially in the use of river patrol boats. On the riverside of the House of Commons, one police boat was stationed from 4 p.m. until dawn, while two Wapping district boats worked their way along the Victoria embankment.[2]

Unaware of the bombers' self-destruction, the City of London offered a reward of £5,000 for information leading to their conviction. The City hoped that the Home Secretary would also offer a free pardon to any involved, so long as they had not actually committed the offence. Harcourt took the position, shared by Spencer, that rewards did not work. Besides being ineffectual they were actually 'mischievous'. Their only virtue was providing an illusion for the public that something was being done. Almost three years' experience, said Harcourt, showed that money was best spent on obtaining secret information and to exclude bombers from the promise of pardon was wrong for 'evidence of this kind is often the most conclusive'. The Lord Mayor told the Fruiterers Company that the Home Secretary had treated them disrespectfully. Harcourt, according to the Lord Mayor, was to offer nothing, and he got nothing in return. The reward money, which was to come from the City 'cash' and not the rates, remained on offer but was given no further publicity.

Secret intelligence and discreet activity was the only way forward. Large rewards encouraged false information, making the police's job more difficult in separating truth from fiction.

Rewards also encouraged the police to chase that sort of crime. The government had shown that it was prepared to reward the police when the time came, since it was advantageous to their discipline. Six months before, Harcourt had told the Queen that rewards had to cease in favour of increased reliance upon informers. Informers knew that they would be rewarded without reminding them.[3]

Harcourt was deeply depressed about the situation. His despondency had been quite evident to E. G. Jenkinson. The 'spymaster' was so deeply affected that he wrote to Harcourt to share his own worries. Jenkinson told Harcourt that all his energies had been invested in the work. It was necessary to appreciate that the information his organisation had collected for use 'now and in the future' had prevented additional outrages in Ireland and Great Britain: 'no doubt that the Fenian movement is kept in check by the system which I have organised'. The security forces simply were not going to win all the battles in such a war. Improvement was going to be doubly necessary because recent experience had taught the dynamiters not to trust anyone other than three or four men immediately involved and 'not one of them can be got at'. Furthermore Fenian informers were becoming scarce as anti-English feeling steadily grew along with nationalist and Fenian certainty of eventual success. Men previously tempted by Jenkinson's money 'now keep on what they think is the winning side'. A major hindrance to improving security was the local fragmentation of police authority in England. In Ireland the anti-Fenian system was operated solely by Jenkinson: 'Here in England there is the greatest jealousy of me and my Irish staff. The English detectives are utterly useless in their particular kind of work, and it is quite impossible to establish any system because [of] no central authority over police...'. Jenkinson had frequently watched valuable information wasted by the 'stupidity of some so-called detective'. Hampered by his inability to do more than give advice, Jenkinson had to satisfy himself with influencing the decisions of the various chief constables. Lacking tact and management, virtues which Jenkinson felt he and Gosselin possessed, the Home Secretary would have had a 'hornets' nest of police' about his ears. Under the present decentralised police authority the British government had no more hope of beating the Fenians than 'the Czar versus the Nihilists'. The need for American co-operation and a passport system still had the highest priority. In a reflective mood Jenkinson questioned whether they should continue to expend so much time and money on work which could not possibly be successful without major reforms in the current system. The Home Secretary could not force American compliance on either the dynamite press or passports, nor was he prepared to face the daunting, if not impossible, task of centralising the English police. Jenkinson retained Harcourt's confidence. As Home Secretary Harcourt had been able to do little more than provide Major Gosselin with a letter, 11 December, authorising him to call on any of the chief constables in the United Kingdom with his request that 'they will assist you in the enquiries I have authorised you to make on behalf of the government'.[4]

On 8 January Jenkinson submitted an official minute on the security problems of Westminster Bridge and the Palace of Westminster to Commissioner Henderson, with a copy to Harcourt. The document was particularly concerned about possible access to the House of Commons through underground passages, sewers, and approaches from the river. What Jenkinson failed to recognise was that the greatest danger lay at the main entrance to the Palace of Westminster.

Eighteen inspectors, forty-one sergeants and 971 constables were assigned to protection duties : twenty-three men at Buckingham Palace and sixty-three at the other royal palaces; ninety-three men on personal protection duty including seven for Gladstone and fourteen for Harcourt. Eighty-seven men protected the homes of members of parliament, and there were fifty-three on bridge duty, forty-nine at prisons, eighty on plain-clothes patrols. Of some 13,000 members of the Metropolitan force almost 1,100 men were immobilised by anti-Fenian duties in addition to the fifty members of the RIC on loan from Dublin Castle. The expense of police and secret service was staggering by Victorian standards. The Chancellor of the Exchequer, H. C. E. Childers, raised the question of how much money would be required to continue the security operation in the fiscal year 1885–6. Jenkinson estimated that things would go on very much as they had before, thus £17,500 should be the sum allocated to the Secret Service allowance. Harcourt recommended to Spencer (6 January 1885) that he ask for as much as he could get while the Home Office would ask for the usual £5,000. He added sadly:

> I wish I thought we got more for our money. If we did I should not hesitate to ask for more but the recent events in London are very discouraging.[5]

Such discouragement was based upon the nagging fear that the Clan and Rossa tactics would change. If the bombers chose to make indiscriminate attacks there was very little that could be done to protect London's population from tremendous suffering and loss of life.

Informers had thus far proved to be the only effective way of dealing with the problem; only they could provide the element of anticipation that allowed the security forces, lacking modern police techniques, to stop the bombs. One of Jenkinson's most valued agents, Thomas Phelan, became a *cause célèbre* in late 1884. The American press reported that Phelan had been stabbed to death in a fight with Richard Short in O'Donovan Rossa's New York offices. Phelan had first come to England in 1883 to work for Jenkinson on the Glasgow bombings. Although he had a large family, he asked for little more than his expenses. Jenkinson felt that this 'quiet little man' had little interest in money but was deeply committed to stopping dynamite attacks. In the autumn of 1884 Jenkinson, aware that Phelan was in danger of exposure, sent him money to get him out of the way, but to no avail. Phelan had been 'shopped' by John Francis Kearney, the Glasgow bomber who remained on the Secret Service payroll, at least that was Jenkinson's assumption. Shortly after the attempt on Phelan's life, Kearney wrote to Williamson of Special Irish Branch attributing the affair to a statement in the *Kansas City Journal* disclosing Rossa-dynamiter secrets. Phelan, suspected of being the leak, was summoned to meet Rossa in New York City. Much to Jenkinson's surprise, he went, although Jenkinson's 'agent' in New York should have stopped him. Phelan in fact survived the attack; Short was arrested and tried for attempted murder but was acquitted.[6]

Even as Lomasney finalised the details for what was to be

his final dynamite attack—London Bridge—a second team of Clan na Gael bombers was crossing the Atlantic. Twenty-three year old James Gilbert Cunningham sailed from New York on the steamship *Adriatic* on 10 December 1884, arriving ten days later in Liverpool. He passed undetected through customs with a large brown Saratoga trunk containing close to sixty pounds of Atlas Powder 'A' dynamite, fuses and detonators of the variety made popular by the Rossa dynamiters. The Philadelphia-manufactured explosive was a powerful variety of commercial lignine dynamite which could be moulded to required shape. The second bomber, thirty-year old Henry Burton, had used this same explosive in his attacks on the London railway stations in February of that year. Burton arrived in Liverpool from New York on the day before Christmas. There was at least one other if not two men in the carefully planned operation, one of whom was doubtless Luke Dillon. Burton was responsible for co-ordinating the effort of mounting two major attacks simultaneously.

Cunningham's first attack took place on 2 January 1885. He boarded the Hammersmith train out of the Metropolitan Line's Aldgate station at 8.57 with the bomb concealed in a workman's tool basket. It exploded at 9.14 in a forward carriage as the train approached Gower Street station. Cunningham escaped and although the train was heavily damaged there were few casualties.

The main targets in the campaign were among the most prominent symbols of English power, starting with the Tower of London, which had originally been built to protect the city from attacks up the Thames and to overawe the local inhabitants. The second target was the Palace of Westminster. The plan was to attack in broad daylight (if that was the right expression granted London's normal weather) counting on the element of surprise. They guessed that since all previous attacks on buildings had come at night their audacity of daylight bombings would be rewarded with success. They were right, for it had never occurred to the senior Scotland Yard officer responsible for the security of the Houses of Parliament that 'an outrage would be attempted in broad daylight by carrying explosives in the pocket'. He had given even less thought to the possibility of a bomb suspended under a 'lady's' skirts! Burton allocated the attack on the Tower of London to Cunningham, who bought a very large overcoat with short sleeves so as not to look too peculiar. He was to wear the overcoat with the bomb strapped around his waist.

The attack on the House of Commons posed a problem because the target was the Chamber of the House, where there was a constable on duty at the Bar of the House when Westminster Palace was open to visitors. On occasions, as many as 10,000 tourists had visited the building, putting a tremendous strain on the police responsible for security. There were policemen stationed at the gates, in addition to two constables in the Crypt, one at the top of the steps at Westminster Hall, one at St Stephen's Hall, one in the Central Hall, one in the members' lobby and the man at the entrance to the Chamber of the House itself. The Royal Irish Constabulary was conspicuous by its absence. No detectives were on duty but another six constables were in the building. Since all hand bags were searched upon entry it was necessary for the explosives to be carried into the building concealed under personal garments, one of which might have been those of a woman. The plan was a simple one. In order to draw the constable away from his post at the Chamber of the House a diversionary explosion would take place in the Crypt. This meant that the attack had to take place on a Saturday which was when the Crypt was open to the public. As soon as the Crypt bomb exploded, the second bomber, having positioned himself near the Bar of the House, would deposit his bomb under the Peers' Gallery as the constable sprinted in the direction of the first blast. His escape would be the most difficult for the other bomb would be fused to detonate at 2 p.m. allowing the Crypt bomber adequate time to clear the building.

Upon his arrival in London, Burton had taken rooms at 5 Mitre Square (not far from Cunningham on Great Prescott Street) without realising that the boarding house was also the residence of a City of London policeman. When Constable H. Wilson, wearing his uniform coat, opened the door of the house to admit Burton he had a fright. Burton unfortunately decided that he had better move and this served to heighten Wilson's natural suspicion of the Irish-American cabinet maker who seemed to do very little work. He searched Burton's room and reported his suspicion to an inspector, who detailed Detective

Thomas Roper to watch Burton. Burton moved his lodgings 'closer to his work' but Roper stayed with his man, observing his movements. On 10 January he saw Burton with a man he later identified as Cunningham.

The date of the co-ordinated attacks was set for Saturday, 24 January. Cunningham, a short dark man, wearing his bomb under his large overcoat, headed for the Tower of London. Meanwhile the 'Dillon' team, probably dressed as man and wife, he with a bomb under his large coat and she with it under her skirts, took the underground railway to Westminster. The three bombs were specially designed to be worn under the large coats or skirts. At least two of them were parcels $1\frac{1}{4} - 1\frac{1}{2}$ inches thick, 14–15 inches in breadth and two feet in length, covered with 'American cloth' and strapped with India rubber webbing. They were filled with slabs of Atlas Powder 'A'. Just after dinner Cunningham entered the Tower of London with a few other tourists and proceeded through the courtyards to the White Tower at the centre of the Norman fortifications. He made his way up the steps to the Banqueting Room. As the Tower Warder moved on into the chapel, Cunningham slipped the parcel secretly out of its straps, set the fuse and deposited it behind a gun carriage. He then left the room without arousing suspicion. The bomb exploded at 2 p.m. Somehow he had mis-judged the amount of time required to make his exit or the fuse prematurely detonated. He was stopped at the gates; he gave his name as Dalton but his Irish-American accent and an uncon-vincing alibi singled him out as the prime suspect. He was held. The gun carriage had absorbed much of the blast, which nevertheless seriously injured two young women and two boys.

The other two bombers mingled with the sightseers at West-minster Hall, some 2,000 of whom had entered already that day, passing through the police inspection at the gates. Once inside, the bombers headed their separate ways, one man for the Crypt and the other, possibly disguised as a 'woman', to the Bar of the House. At about 2.10 p.m. a woman in the Crypt cried out, 'I think one of your mats is on fire'. Constable Cole, seeing that it was in fact a smoking parcel, grabbed it and made a dash up the stairs for Westminster Hall but it exploded before he reached the top. At the sound of the blast the constable

208   *The Dynamite War*

in the Chamber of the House left his post, and the second bomb
was dropped into the Chamber with a short fuse; minutes later
it exploded causing extensive damage. The clock on the chamber
wall stopped at 2.13 p.m. The two bombers escaped in the
confusion; miraculously injuries were limited to the constable at
the top of the Crypt stairs and the unfortunate Constable Cole.
Both men suffered shock although the latter had four ribs broken
in addition. His survival was possible only because of the small
charge of dynamite in the diversionary device. If he had
charge of the large bomb in the House he would have died
instantly. One of the two men was probably Luke Dillon and
he might have been seconded by Henry Burton although Burton
was never identified as having been in Westminster that morning. Burton was arrested because when Detective Roper saw
Cunningham after his capture, he recognised him as having
been with Burton on the tenth. Careful police work was to
establish the latter's responsibility for the attacks on Charing
Cross station and possibly Victoria, Paddington, and Ludgate
Hill twelve months before.[7]

London was under seige. Harcourt ordered plain clothes
officers to be immediately placed at Westminster Abbey, St
Paul's Cathedral, the British Museum, National Gallery, Kensington Museum. The newspapers were full of the precautions
being taken around London to prevent a recurrence of the
attacks. Even Dean R. W. Church of St Paul's was moved to
write a letter in *The Times* defending the steps taken to protect
the Empire's parish church. Sir E. Henderson was given permission to call up 200 men from Scotland Yard's waiting list with
Harcourt's promise of more if required. Jenkinson was appalled
at the absence of detectives at the House of Commons after
he put out his Boxing Day warning of an impending attack
on the House of Commons. Any confidence he had in Scotland
Yard was shattered; the apparent incompetence was beyond his
understanding.[8]

Harcourt had cause for additional concern because of the
almost complete breakdown of communication between the
Metropolitan Police and the Secret Service resulting from
Jenkinson's accusations of incompetence. The background to
the argument which slowly emerged centred on the use of an
informant. Police Constable McIntyre had made the contact

with a man who had been involved with New York dynamite groups a year before. He was reported to have specific information concerning the former Dublin Invincible Frank Byrne. Jenkinson wanted to 'use' McIntyre but Monroe refused. The 'spymaster' told Harcourt that if this sort of thing continued then he could not be responsible for repeated failures. Monroe could not use the informant properly. Jenkinson explained he had been to the Yard almost daily and was on most friendly terms with the CID director. He had not asked Monroe to come to him at the Home Office 'because I knew he did not like coming'.[9] Jenkinson's offer of assistance following the attacks produced the following reply from Monroe:

30 January 1885

Mr Jenkinson,
I am glad to be assured that you do not differ with me in holding that all communications with my subordinates should be through me.
   Many thanks for your offer of assistance in this case—I think however that, so far as I can see at present, I am able to work it myself. Should I in this or any other instance, find a case beyond me, I shall be most happy to ask you for aid.
   Monroe

Jenkinson told Harcourt that 'offensive as the letter was he was not intending to take any notice of it and would go on just as before'. His anger had been further fanned when he found that the informant, a man named Quinn, had made a statement on 24 January; it had not been communicated to either the Home Secretary or himself for seventy-two hours. The statement apparently contained an accurate description of the bomb which was to be used at either Westminster Palace or the Tower of London.[10] The battle raged amongst the security establishments while, in addition to promotion and a reward of £200, Police Sergeant Cole received the Albert Medal. The presentation was made on the very spot where the explosion occurred, on the landing 'midway on the steps leading alike to St Stephens Hall and to the crypt beneath'.

The Times (26 January 1885) asked: why the attacks? The editor answered:

To strike terror into the souls of Englishmen, whether by the indiscriminate slaughter of holiday makers and working people, or by the destruction of precious historical monuments, is the avowed object of the dynamite party in the United States.

The trial of Burton and Cunningham finally began on Monday, 11 May 1885. It took a week to hear the evidence and the pleas of innocence from both. On Monday the eighteenth the jury retired at 2.45 p.m.; fifteen minutes later it returned with a verdict of guilty for both men. Cunningham was sentenced to life imprisonment for the bombing of the Tower of London and the explosion on the Metropolitan Line at Gower Street on 2 January 1885. The same sentence was passed on Burton for having planted the bomb-laden portmanteaus at Charing Cross Station and probably Paddington in February 1884.

January had also found the government at the brink of a severe political crisis based in part on Joseph Chamberlain's concerted Radical attack in the country with an 'Unauthorised Programme' including manhood suffrage, wide-ranging land reform, and graduated taxation. Although Chamberlain's bid for the Liberal leadership had panicked the Whigs, it was his demand for an end to coercion in Ireland that caused greatest concern from the security viewpoint. The cabinet's right wing, determined to renew the Crimes Act, was however prepared to be conciliatory to the extent of also providing for a Land Purchase Act and limited extension of local government. Chamberlain and his fellow radicals rejected the Land Purchase scheme and saw the local government proposals as too limited. On this occasion Harcourt and Spencer found themselves at opposite poles with the Home Secretary, believing that the only alternatives were separation or more force, wanting an even more drastic Crimes Act; Spencer however argued for a mild act and strong self-government. He had even proposed that the lord lieutenancy be replaced with a secretary of state and, to encourage Irish loyalty to the Queen, the establishment of royal residency with periodic royal occupation. Harcourt, in return for support leading to the passage of a satisfactory Crimes Act, offered to support Spencer's position on local government and some reforms which might help to separate the lord lieutenancy's connection between crown and party politics. He was quite convinced that it was too late, however, for an 'Irish Balmoral'. At the other extreme of the Liberal Party, Hartington and his Whigs were firmly opposed to any measure of Irish local government. Gladstone did not agree with Harcourt's belief in force and, siding with Spencer, felt that a significant measure of Irish self-government was the only choice other than being overwhelmed or surrendering to national independence. Harcourt (18 January 1885) had told Spencer that Jenkinson felt that the Crimes Bill was going to be whittled away in what was a 'fatal old game'. Prepared to promise full support to a new Tory government if they retained the bill in its entirety, Harcourt warned that he would not help if they changed a 'jot or tittle'. Spencer could not be swung away from his old desire for moderation. He might well have smiled at Harcourt's warning not to appear 'shaky' on any points in the Crimes Act because Gladstone would emasculate it and there would be no hope of 'repairing the mischief'.[11] If Harcourt was worried about Spencer's support for the 'force' course in Ireland, it gave him not half the concern that other members of the cabinet gave him. His son found on 4 January that Harcourt was furious because despite the 'present mess' certain ministers could think of nothing but getting down to their places in the country or being in time for their dinner. Gladstone left in the middle of the last cabinet to catch the 2.45 to Hawarden. Trevelyan ditto the 3.30; Chamberlain ditto the 4 o'clock; then Selbourne tried the excuse of 'people staying in country but W.V.H. refused to let him leave'.[12]

The Irish population in Great Britain continued to be a source of concern. An IRB report sent to Clan na Gael in 1884 gave its strength as follows:

IRELAND

Ulster	...	10,000
Munster	...	12,000
Leinster	...	9,000
Connaught	...	5,000
		36,000

GREAT BRITAIN
North of England		6,000
South of England		2,500
Scotland	...	3,000
		11,500
Total	... ...	47,500

Commenting on the report Jenkinson suggested that in the event of an armed rising in Ireland, 'which might take place if England was engaged in a war with any European Power, these numbers would no doubt be largely increased'. It was important to deprive the IRB of access to the radical Fenian press encouraging dynamite and assassination.[13] Jenkinson finally received an opinion from the Home Office Law officer (10 February) that Patrick Ford's *Irish World* (sponsor of the Emergency Fund) could now be seized in the United Kingdom with reference to the Crimes Act. Its copies had first to be intercepted by HM Customs or the Police.[14] At the end of February a store of dynamite manufactured by the Safety Nitro Powder Company, San Francisco, was found in a house in Harrow Road, apparently all that remained of Captain William Mackey Lomasney's store of explosives.

Sir Stafford Northcote, Conservative leader in the Commons, had approached Harcourt personally on behalf of Captain Stuart Stephens. Stephens, one of Jenkinson's secret agents in Paris, had been dismissed because of heavy drinking and indiscretion. Jenkinson advised the Home Secretary that the man had behaved so badly that if he returned to Paris his life would be in danger. There was enough trouble in Paris without Jenkinson being pressured into reinstating men of demonstrated incompetence. Paris was aptly described by Michael Davitt as 'a general emporium for plots, secrets, revolutionary designs and treasonable documents'.[15]

The Times (30 January 1885) reported that its Parisian correspondent had learned of a forthcoming meeting of 'dynamite delegates' in Paris, on an island in the Seine. Its object was to unite the various Fenian societies, an idea originally proposed by James Stephens, who had lived in Paris. A subsequent report followed, describing the convention and giving details of an inspired speech by Stephens. The whole episode was in fact a hoax perpetrated by Eugene Davis, Paris correspondent for the *Irish World*. The French government's attitude underwent a dramatic change in the face of the attacks on Westminster Palace and the Tower of London, to be closely followed by the reports of a convention of dynamitards. M. Ferry, the prime minister, in the words of *The Times*, came to the conclusion that 'the presence of men advocating and applauding, if not concocting dynamite outrages, is not altogether innocuous, even for France'! The French police moved against the resident Fenians in the early hours of 12 March, entering a lodging house in Rue St Honoré and arresting Eugene Davis, 'who was recently mentioned as likely to become the head of the European section of the dynamite party', according to *The Times* of the following day. At 10 a.m. they arrested the sixty-one year old James Stephens, 'the former Head Centre', who, as *The Times* recognised, while advocating rebellion, had always condemned 'dynamite outrages'. The French police also arrested and deported three other Irish-Americans. Stephens blamed his misfortune on Scotland Yard : the 'lying and libellous reports of Scotland Yard detectives caused an infamous and diabolical injustice. M. Ferry's government broke up my little home in Paris, compelled me to herd with the scum of scoundralism in the city bridewell, and eventually hustled me out of the country, as if tainted with political leprosy'. Stephens claimed that he had no connection—directly or indirectly—with the so-called Irish extremists. Expelled to Mons, he subsequently settled in Brussels. Davis was escorted across the Swiss border where he continued his exile at Lausanne. Cypher telegrams were rapidly exchanged between the Foreign Office and Lord Lyons, the Ambassador to France. Granville and Harcourt were very much interested in whether the French police might co-operate with the British government, particularly if any fresh information had emerged as a result of the arrests. Would Lord Lyons diplomatically enquire? He apparently was received with a diplomatic silence.[16]

John Devoy finally laid the blame upon the correspondent of the London *Standard*, 'a very gullible man, who gave

Davis £5 for reports of meetings which never took place.[17]

The Foreign Office's hopes had been slightly raised by news from the United States related to proposed federal and state legislation. Of special interest was an explosives bill before the New York State legislature, which contained a section making it a felony to raise money for the purpose of explosive attacks. Another bill had been introduced into the United States Senate on 24 January by Senator Edmunds. Its intention was to prevent American citizens from involving themselves in Britain's troubles. British minister Sackville West had spoken to the Speaker of the House of Representatives (the leader of the Democratic Party in the lower house) who suggested that the bill could not get through the various stages required for passage by 4 March, the end of the session. That being the case, it would have to be reintroduced into the next Congress. In an editorial entitled 'The Protection against Dynamite', the *New York Tribune* of 27 January 1885 suggested that Edmunds' Bill before the Senate would not help London because it believed that dynamite itself did not cross the Atlantic Ocean while money did. Thus the *Irish World*'s solicitation for its Emergency Fund had to be ended. The *Tribune* also made the valid point that the problem was part of a much larger issue of extradition in general. It recommended combined international action, which in addition to the United States and Great Britain, required the efforts and co-operation of Germany and Russia. An international treaty for extradition and punishment of *dynamiteurs* was clearly needed and English statesmen had to be prepared to discriminate clearly between political offences and dynamite outrages. The skeleton in the English cupboard was that Orsini's famous grenades had been manufactured in Birmingham; in this instance it had been England that had provided the base for the bombers' operation. Three of these grenades had been used in the unsuccessful attempt on the life of Emperor Louis Napoleon in Paris on 14 January 1858.

The Foreign Office was also interested in a statement on American neutrality legislation made by outgoing President Arthur. He recommended legislation to increase the punishment of men making preparations for the commission of criminal acts, such as dynamite attacks, whether they were to be committed in the United States or in a foreign country with whom they were at peace. Clearly recognising that there was little hope that the federal government would or could give substance to this declaration, the British government used it as an excuse to re-open the correspondence which Frelinghuysen had sought to conclude on 24 November. The first draft was circulated to the cabinet at the beginning of February not long after the West-minster Palace explosions. Harcourt's heavily edited copy of the draft showed the extent of his influence upon the final shape of the message. The despatch was to point out that Patrick Ford had claimed in the *Irish World* on 31 January 1885 that he had thus far raised in excess of $16,000 for the Emergency Fund 'for the commission of murder and outrage in the United Kingdom'. How could the United States government ignore such a blatant claim? The despatch repeated the claim that the majority of bombs exploded in England were of American manufacture and that John Daly's bombs had been delivered to him 'by an emissary from the United States immediately before his arrest'. Harcourt's interest in the 'Molly Maguires' remained keen, pointing out once again that the laws of the United States had been effective in dealing with its Secret Society crimes. The British government hoped that these laws might operate as effectively against persons organising crimes against British subjects.

The message broke new ground in two important respects. Firstly, it had been recognised that the case of Johanne Most, the anarchist editor of *Freiheit*, sentenced by Lord Coleridge on 29 June 1881 to sixteen months hard labour, might be used as an example of how British justice dealt with politically subver-sive newspaper editors. Upon his release, Johanne Most emi-grated to the United States, where his German-language news-paper *Freiheit* found new readers. The edition of 24 January 1885 provided full instructions with diagrams to illustrate the use of dynamite for 'the purposes advocated in that paper'. This case then became a reply to Frelinghuysen's claim that English law could not deal with the newspaper incitement to violence. The main point was that the prosecution of Most had proceeded not only on the English statute but 'also upon an indictment under the Common Law, which it is believed is in force in the United States as in Great Britain'. The argument continued: 'Nor was it deemed necessary in the case of Most to show that any particular crime had resulted from his wicked instigations, the fact of the incitement being itself the gist of the offence'.

The second new point in the projected despatch concerned an offer by one Shaun O'Neill of a reward of $10,000 for the body of the Prince of Wales, dead or alive! The advertisement had appeared in O'Donovan Rossa's *United Irishman* of 11 February 1885 and was immediately telegraphed in cypher to the Foreign Office by vice-consul Hoare in New York. Was this not enough of an incitement to warrant prosecution of Rossa?

The Foreign Office was also aware that the Committee on Foreign Affairs of the House of Representatives had requested the Secretary of State on 3 February to provide it with copies of all verbal and written requests from Her Majesty's government concerning London dynamite attacks. The matter of the correspondence and all the arguments put forth, and presumably Frelinghuysen and Blaine's replies, were about to become public knowledge. Harcourt was not, however, going to depend on the correspondence appearing in *The Congressional Record*—the American equivalent of Hansard. He personally sent twenty copies of the three series or reprinted extracts from the American dynamite press to Sackville West for private distribution. Harcourt was prepared to believe that the influential citizens in the United States were ignorant of the threat. That would explain why they were so incredulous; Harcourt added, 'I am myself taking measures privately to have them made known in the United States'. The person used by Harcourt was a friendly American correspondent in London who was urged particularly to press home to the American public the significance of the Johanne Most case.[18]

Having well-informed influential American friends was important and that was one of the reasons that the British government was unhappy about the recall of the American minister to London, James Russell Lowell, in early March. Lowell wrote personally to his friend Granville announcing his impending departure; he concluded, *Moritatus te saluto*! His successor, Edward J. Phelps, appointed by the Democratic successor to Arthur, Grover Cleveland, was known as one of the ablest lawyers in the United States. Although Phelps had no previous diplomatic experience, Lowell was sure that this outstanding

Vermont politician, would be *persona grata* to the British government. *The Times*'s editorial tribute to Lowell on 24 March 1885 was typical of how many people regarded this extraordinary American poet/diplomat:

> If ... he decides to make his permanent home in the country, which has never treated him as a stranger, we must ask America to console herself for her loss. ...

Harcourt kept Spencer in touch with the inner workings of the cabinet. The gist of his letter of 19 May was that the Liberal government was resolved on suicide; the cabinet was like a 'man afflicted with epilepsy and one foot succeeds and then—each worse than the last'. The Liberal Party on the other hand was like a first-rate man-of-war 'just going into action, the ship sound, the crew eager to fight and win and the captain looked up to with enthusiasm. Only the gentlemen in the gun-room insist on blowing out their own and each others' brains just before going into action, and so the ship is captured'. Harcourt was convinced that Gladstone was ready to resign and the government would fall within a month. There was doubt as to whether he or Hartington should try to form another government, but none as to Salisbury's refusal if he had a grain of sense. Writing again on the 31 May, Harcourt announced the resignation of Charles Dilke and Joseph Chamberlain as the government moved closer to collapse; he remained convinced that he was the only sensible man in the government.[19]

Although the American government refused to take seriously the offering of a reward for the Prince of Wales, dead or alive, and would not prosecute the newspaper, the *United Irishman*, since it was an advertisement, rather than an 'editorial comment', the government was rightly concerned about his safety. The royal family and all leading members of the government had long been under police protection. But were there Irishmen with access to the *United Irishman*, despite efforts to intercept it, who were prepared to collect the reward? The Prince's subsequent visit to Dublin passed without incident. The Lord Mayor was, however, seriously embarrassed when the city's flag could not be flown in honour of the visit, because it had been stolen by a patriot. It was later returned in the post.

H

The *United Irishman* of 4 April 1885 carried the report of a Fenian Brotherhood meeting at Chickering Hall in New York at the end of March, during which a resolution was read demanding the execution of the Prince of Wales.

> Resolved—That the landing of Albert Edward Guelph, commonly called the 'Prince of Wales', on the shores of Ireland, must be and is regarded as an act of invasion, and that said Albert Edward Guelph is entitled only to that reception which a liberty-loving people should extend to an invader of their country; and that by all laws of war he merits that death which the world, by unanimous consent, has decreed to be the desert of the hostile spy in the time of war.

This meeting of the reorganised Fenian Brotherhood was indicative of O'Donovan Rossa's new bid for prestige and power in the Irish-American ranks. At the beginning of February, Rossa had an 'almost miraculous escape from the bullets of an hired assassin' which did his popularity no harm. A most unlikely assassin, 'a little English woman, with a pleasant intellectual face' had lured Rossa to Philadelphia with an offer of dynamite money whereupon she fired five bullets at him but fortunately (or unfortunately depending on the viewpoint) only one struck him and that not seriously. Mrs Yseult Dudley would not be forgotten in her chosen role of Charlotte Corday. Even if Rossa had been in a bath tub it would have been difficult to imagine him as an Irish-American Jean-Paul Marat. This meeting at Chickering Hall had interesting speeches from both Professor Mezzeroff and the sometime leading Clan na Gael figure General F. F. Millen, the latter regularly drawing a British Secret Service salary. The shadowy Professor Mezzeroff was introduced as 'England's invisible enemy'. He not only dared congress to pass laws preventing Irishmen from making dynamite but offered to send a batch to help El Mahdi in the Sudan and the Russians 'if help they needed'. Professor Mezzeroff or Mezzerhoff (alias 'Wilson') was almost a required feature at such meetings. The *New York Sun* of 20 March 1882 had described him as a '... sharp-faced man of some fifty or sixty years with the accent of an educated Irishman'. On 4 September 1883 the same paper added that he was 'very tall, dressed in sombre black, curly dark hair rolled back from the top of his forehead, grizzly moustache and wearing plain steel-bowed spectacles'. At a meeting held at New York's Clarendon Hall he had told his audience that :

> I was born in New York. My mother was a Highlander, my father was a Russian, and I am an American citizen. I have diplomas from three colleges, and have devoted my life to the study of medicine. When I was a boy, I fought in the Crimean War, and I bear the scars of five wounds.

He also provided that night, as he did each night upon the dynamite platform, an exciting presentation on the joys of dynamite, promising that he had recipes for forty-two explosives safely away in a burglar-proof safe. That assertion notwithstanding, Robert Anderson secured a copy of one of Mezzeroff's 'Prescriptions to students'. Submitted to Home Office chemists, they said he was an impostor who traded with a very moderate knowledge of chemistry; Anderson added 'to make his living at the expense of his dupes'. And yet it would seem a 'moderate knowledge of chemistry' was all that the dynamiter required.[20]

General Millen's speech at Chickering Hall was no less fascinating, as he proceeded to convince his audience that George Washington was a naturalised Irishman! He also condemned New York's Democratic political machine's refusal to let the Fenians use Tammany Hall for their meeting that evening. This might have been indicative of the shift of Democratic support following the Irish defection in the autumn's presidential election.

The *United Irishman* of 4 April 1885 also touched the British government's raw nerve concerning Irishmen serving in the British army. Rossa said 'if there is one thing more than another that paralyses the arm of England and inspires her statesmen with dread, it is the fear of disaffection among her soldiers of the Irish race'. This particular article was an excellent example of why the newspaper had to be kept out of Irish hands wherever they might be, for it recommended the establishment of Fenian organisations, desertion, and the murder of their officers 'in the heart of the battle'. The Anglo-Irish soldier was encouraged to help El Mahdi and his gallant Arab warriors. While Fenian dynamiters served in London, the Irish soldier in Sudan 'should avail himself of every opportunity to assist the swarthy warriors of the desert, who, to maintain their freedom, are fighting gallantly against the cruel, hypocritical, blood thirsty nation that for so many centuries has held Ireland in bondage'. Free copies of the *United Irishman* were offered postpaid to Irish soldiers in the 'English' army anywhere in the world.

Little had happened on the dynamite front since the explosions of January. The only notable event was an explosion at the Admiralty on the first of June and Jenkinson and Monroe agreed that the outrage had no connection whatever with Fenianism. On the other hand, Jenkinson was pleased to see that O'Donovan Rossa had taken credit for the explosion: 'This may I hope be thoroughly disproved'. Relations between himself and Monroe of the CID remained strained. That summer a situation developed which illustrated that not even Jenkinson was infallible. An American named Burkham had been recommended to Jenkinson by Mr Stanley of San Francisco, whose reputation in such matters seemed above question. Burkham then presented Jenkinson with a plot and plotters; a group of eleven men, considered to be as important a catch as the Gallagher team. The story was that the group had been sent out by John Desmond of the San Francisco Clan na Gael and by early June were preparing to begin operations in London. The surveillance and arrest of the men was the responsibility of Scotland Yard. Whereupon Special Branch detectives discovered that Jenkinson had been humbugged! Humiliated by this revelation, he claimed that it was the *first time*. He also reminded Harcourt that it was impossible to go on with this work without being deceived some time. What he could not fathom was why Burkham had done it? The man associated with him, Nicoles, had been paid nothing for the information and Burkham only received his salary of £200 a month for April and May—no mean sum. Was it a deliberate Clan na Gael effort to embarrass the Secret Service or simply an agent on trial producing something to ensure continued employment? If it was the latter then the question immediately arose as to how he thought he could get away with it unless he held the Scotland Yard detectives in even lower esteem than Jenkinson. The 'spymaster' knew that the incident would give the Yard the 'pleasure of laughing at him'. Monroe's official criticism to

Harcourt led Jenkinson to retort that the CID chief was making a mountain out of a molehill. If we were deceived, he said, then the fault had to lie with Mr Stanley (who may have been a Pinkerton agent). In conclusion Jenkinson regretted the line which had been chosen by Monroe, but it did show how very difficult it is 'with the best intentions in the world to get on with the local police'.[21]

The defection of Chamberlain and a Conservative deal with the Irish Party led to a defeat on the budget proposal to increase the duties on beer and spirits on 8 June 1885. The vote was 264 to 252 with as many as 76 Liberals not voting. Gladstone resigned the following day. Salisbury formed a minority Conservative government on 24 June 1885 which would survive almost seven months : a 'government of caretakers' Chamberlain labelled it. Yet how was the transition going to be effected with reference to the security establishment, especially with the open conflict raging within and the continued Irish-American threat without?

During this political crisis Jenkinson was in Dublin for one of his periodic official visits. Spencer recommended that he immediately return to London for discussions with Harcourt. Jenkinson had reason to be concerned about how future security work would be carried on. The crux of the matter lay in his supplying information to Scotland Yard; he was committed to supplying the intelligence but he strongly objected to Monroe making decisions on its use without reference to himself. Furthermore, 'in case of any divergence of opinion the question should be referred to the S[ecretary] of S[tate]'. Monroe was also making a bid to control the various activities of the RIC detectives operating in metropolitan London. Jenkinson argued that he must control their movements and be responsible for communicating relevant information to the Yard. They 'are not working *against* but *for* the London Police. . . . If the RIC men are to be watched and reported on and regarded with jealousy it is quite impossible that they can be of any use'.

Jenkinson's own position at the Home Office was 'anomalous' and his responsibility 'undefined'. Earl Spencer recommended that it was very important to have his role defined as soon as possible. This would encourage a smooth transition where the

incoming Conservative Home Secretary was concerned. Furthermore, Jenkinson should seek a decision by Harcourt on his
plea for consultation, and an agreement that the Home Secretary would take the decision in matters upon which he and
Monroe differed. Spencer was certain that Jenkinson could
remain in London and continue on Dublin's payroll as assistant
under secretary for crime. As an alternative arrangement it
would not, however, be advisable to make him, a civilian,
inspector-general of the RIC. The security situation in Ireland
had improved to the point that his 'temporary job', which was
what the under secretariat for crime amounted to, would be
discontinued if Jenkinson were to return to Dublin Castle. What
Jenkinson hoped for was, according to Spencer, a permanent
post in London 'where he could still work up secret information without any Executive and [*sic*] responsibility at all'. On
17 June Harcourt agreed upon a peace plan between Jenkinson
and the CID pending the issuance of fresh instructions from the
new Home Secretary, R. A. Cross. Writing to Cross five days
later, Harcourt offered such assistance as Cross might require.
Other than a briefing on Fenian matters, not much help should
have been required, Cross having been the Home Secretary in
the previous Conservative government.[22]

Harcourt had his private opinion on Jenkinson which he
shared with Spencer at the end of June. Friction with the CID
had been a problem for a long time and Harcourt believed that
it had been mainly due to Jenkinson's 'overbearing treatment'
of Scotland Yard. It had been pointed out to Jenkinson that
the Commissioners of Police were the only people constitutionally responsible for life and property. The Home Office would
not nor could not override their authority in London, nor could
there be an Imperial Police Force in England. The role of the
Secret Service was limited to collecting and evaluating information upon which the police were to act. Over the past months
Jenkinson had consistently refused to act on these instructions.
According to Harcourt he had withheld information from the
CID director, James Monroe, carried out the 'supervision of
supposed dangerous plots (which happily never existed) without
the knowledge of Scotland Yard' and had controlled the RIC
detectives independently of and recently in conflict with the
Metropolitan Police. Such high-handed behaviour justifiably

produced resentments. Making it perfectly clear they wished to co-operate with him on information he had gleaned, Scotland Yard remained, in Harcourt's view, 'perfectly reasonable'. When Harcourt had tried to 'cool' Jenkinson down, he had responded with a written demand *'which he informed me he had settled with you and that you advised him to insist upon them'*. (Harcourt's emphasis.) Harcourt reported that he replied that he found that impossible to accept, since he would no more dream of meddling in the affairs of Dublin Castle than Spencer in Whitehall.

A meeting on 17 June between Harcourt, Jenkinson, and Monroe took place at the Home Secretary's request to work out a settlement. Monroe accepted the arrangements offered by Harcourt but Jenkinson said 'I simply decline'. In retrospect Harcourt felt that he ought to have given him his *congé*. Jenkinson later accepted Harcourt's demands but then wrote a series of objectionable letters to Monroe. Finally he set aside Harcourt's instructions altogether and 'informed Monroe that he and Lord Spencer would settle the matter with the new Secretary of State!' Harcourt did not like this game at all and informed Spencer that he expected his support in advising Cross as to future policy, regardless of Jenkinson's personal views on the matter.

It was a bitter end to Harcourt's tenure at the Home Office for he had a genuine regard for the 'spymaster', who for many months had worked zealously and to the best of his ability. What became painfully obvious was that Jenkinson never possessed the tact of which he was so proud. Harcourt had stood by Jenkinson many times against the enemies he had made for himself elsewhere. Jenkinson's temper was, according to Harcourt, ungovernable and 'it is hopeless to attempt to get him to work with others whose co-operation is necessary'. Spencer confirmed that he had not in any way interfered and was extremely sorry, for he continued to believe that Jenkinson had done very efficient work and could continue to do so.[23]

As R. A. Cross came to the Home Office the question of costs became important, even if the Conservative Party was not so deeply committed to economy as were Gladstone's Liberals. Hicks Beach, the new Chancellor of the Exchequer, informed Cross on 27 June 1885 that so long as his Secret Service financial demands did not exceed the ordinary Home Office limit his signature was quite as good as A. Liddell's. 'But I am told', he continued, 'that of late years the HO has required, and been allowed SS money in excess of the ordinary limit, I suppose on account of Irish or dynamite affairs. If you wish these *extra* issues to be continued, you must write me a letter to say so. But perhaps we may not want so much of this kind of thing as our predecessors did : at least I hope we shall not'.[24] The cost of port protection continued to run at £10,000 per annum to which was added £1,300 in payments to locksmiths to open passengers' baggage. One finds it difficult to envisage that many lost keys and smashed locks. Rigorous searches by Customs officers continued. Jenkinson continued to work under R. A. Cross and it was he who recommended the gradual withdrawal of the Scotland Yard detectives (mostly probationers from the divisions) from the ports. Rewards continued to be offered to the Customs' Officers. Port protection was run down without publicity for fear that Irish-Americans might renew their campaign. Work at the ports was hard and conflicts between the Special Branch detectives from London and the local police were inevitable. The situation at Hull was amongst the most difficult since it was a transhipment point for the large numbers of emigrants from Europe to North America via Liverpool. Hull had three Special Branch and three local detectives working with the Customs Officers. Detective John Sweeney was one of these Special Branch officers and described those days in a fascinating autobiography :

> We seemed to spend night and day in boarding vessels and hunting keenly about for doubtful characters; we had to guard against an excess of zeal which might lead us into interfering with perfectly respectable and harmless travellers, or into making ourselves into a laughing-stock by over-eagerness in following up some false scent; we had to put up sometimes with all sorts of incivility from ship's Captains and Officers, knowing that we must keep on good terms with them. Above all we had to guard against being overprominent.[25]

The risk lay primarily in the shipments of dynamite disguised by bogus labels. Thus a large part of the quiet and security enjoyed in Great Britain from February on to the end of 1885 was the product of the difficulties dynamiters faced in getting explosives into England. William Mackey Lomasney had been across the Atlantic twice before he died underneath London Bridge in December 1884 and stockpiled the explosives which were used in late 1884 and early 1885; the dynamite having been brought in from France before the port protection scheme had gone into effect fully. Dynamite found in a deserted shop on the Harrow Road in early 1885 may have been the remains of that cache.

Whatever the risks were it is difficult to imagine that the Clan's executive and O'Donovan Rossa could not have found volunteers to carry on the dynamite attacks. Why then did the attacks come to such an abrupt and unexpected end? The answer has to be found in changes of tactics and strategy of the attacking organisations. A major factor in effecting this change was the continued opposition of the Irish Republican Brotherhood to the use of dynamite. The IRB position was reinforced by the success of the Irish Parliamentary Party which had played such an important part in the downfall of the Liberal government in June. It was feared that support for Irish-American dynamiting might well have lost the advantages already gained by constitutional, rather than revolutionary, tactics. That the IRB had preferred this policy during the period of 1880–85 to that of terrorist attacks had not in itself brought a change in American tactics; so why did it do so now?

Between 1882 and 1885 policy was directed by Alexander Sullivan, leader of the Clan, but he had been forced out of the National Land League presidency because he had offended the Democratic Clan members by using the organisation for Republican electioneering. Sullivan's influence increased in 1883 when the executive, in the interests of greater secrecy, was cut by two members to three men. The Triangle, as they were known, issued its first circular immediately after this September meeting. It alluded to some amendments in the Clan's constitution as well as to the fact that the 'active' policy adopted by the former executive, had been 'deliberately and unanimously adopted by the Convention as the rule of future operations'. The Triangle told the membership that security reasons prohibited disclosure of past operations for fear of jeopardising 'methods of future operations' against the enemy. Members were not to believe O'Donovan Rossa's false claims of responsibility for explosions in England. Nevertheless such claims were useful for they diverted attention from the real authors of the terror, the Clan. Secrecy was vital and few, if any, circulars on the 'active work' would be published; members who talked of the work would be expelled. The circular concluded:

> We ask that each and all make the next two years a period of the most active work in gathering the resources and extending the numbers and power of the organisation. The light of a great hope is breaking through the cloud of centuries. Work and organise with all the genius of the race.

E. G. Jenkinson said: 'exclusive of other balances in hand, and of the remains of the Skirmishing Fund' (the Trustees of which are under the control of the VC), amounting to about $37,000, the money received for these two funds (Special Fund and Percentage Fund) up to October 1884 was about $89,000. He estimated that the balance in hand at the close of 1884 was about $26,000. During 1884 Jenkinson said that the IRB received about $40,000 from American sources. American money was essential to the IRB for according to Jenkinson there was hardly enough money to pay the ordinary working expenses of the organisation. 'If the society is to be kept alive, if work is to be done, money must come from the richer organisation in America; and during the last two years the leaders of the IRB have been compelled to give their approval to the policy adopted by the VC in America, because, had they not done so, the supplies, as was threatened would have been stopped.' Yet he added that few IRB members were in favour of explosions and outrages, for such work could in the end only injure their cause and 'must do great harm to the Irish working population in Great Britain.'[26] A more active role by the IRB in support of the Clan attacks would have resulted in greater damage and loss of life. The IRB role was that of a reluctant partner of Clan na Gael at the very most. It was certainly prepared to help Lomasney track down and stop O'Donovan Rossa's amateurs and it may have entirely lost Clan financial support during 1883. What price did the IRB pay to have it restored?

The success of Parnell and his party in 1885 strengthened the IRB's position to the extent of its being able to resist more strongly the Clan demands for support in its terrorist tactics. It was then that Jenkinson believed that Irishmen were becoming convinced that they were going to win through with Parnell at the head of the victorious nation. Did not even the Clan leadership become finally convinced that tactics of terror were no longer needed, especially when the British security forces continued to exact large losses from the Clan's ranks of dynamiters? Or to what extent can the attitudes of the Democratic-controlled Congress and a new President, Grover Cleveland, be seen to contribute to the undeclared truce which came in to effect at the end of winter 1885? There may have been intimations that the American sanctuary was in danger of being lost as the French sanctuary had been withdrawn in mid-March 1885. Had American patience come to an end? O'Donovan Rossa was aware of this threat, which explains the emphasis of the following statement made in November 1885:

It is against the Constitution of the Fenian Brotherhood to strike at England's power on the continent of America. English intrigues had erected a monument to an English Spy [John André] on American soil. The monument was destroyed. I charge my accounts with a hundred dollars as a donation to the men who did their work. . . . I did not give the money to do the work or to have it done, but I gave it after it was done. . . . The whole amount collected from all sources during the years we have been working is fourteen or fifteen thousand dollars. When this skirmishing work commenced, some of the Irish societies that ought to be patriotic were opposed to it, but when some of the missioners whom we helped into the field succeeded in destroying the gas works in Glasgow and the Government House in Westminster, they changed their minds a little. The Fenian Brotherhood men have no alliance or understanding with men or with societies of men who endeavour to wrest Ireland's freedom from England by constitutional agitation, or agitation of any kind that has not fight of some kind in it.[27]

Despite promises like those of Brooklyn's Patrick Rellihan, editor of a new dynamite monthly called *Ireland's Liberation*, that, 'This dynamite work will go on till Ireland is free, or till London is laid in ashes', neither had in fact happened and an uneasy peace took hold. Money continued to be collected for dynamite work and the New York consulate informed Lord Salisbury on 31 December 1885 that $36,000 had been collected, including a donation of $250 from the Mayor of the City of New York.[28] By the end of 1886 port security was relaxed to the extent of recalling all Special Branch officers from the northern ports such as South Shields, Greenock and Hull. Only two of these probationer detectives, including John Sweeney, remained with Special Branch; the others returned to their divisions. The Royal Irish Constabulary force at the ports had been withdrawn in early 1886 and its London contingent returned to Ireland on 24 July leaving Special Branch to look after London's security. The mood had been well caught by Lewis Harcourt in his diary entry of 14 December 1885 :

> Hartington, Northbrook, W.V.H. and I had a long talk this evening on Irish affairs. They proved to their own satisfaction that the Irish Question must resolve itself into Civil War and their only difficulty was to decide whether Civil War could be best waged before and in consequence of the refusal of Home Rule or after it and in consequence of attempts of separation.[29]

Although the Irish-American dynamiters were gone, the main problem remained : what the English called the 'Irish Question'. It was a question which Gladstone's third and fourth governments following on Salisbury's interregnum, sought unsuccessfully to answer.

Epilogue: a Peace of Sorts

The House would thank me for saving it from the [attack] of
the most bloody-minded Fanatic [John Daly] since the days
of Guy Fawkes.

Major N. Gosselin to the Home Secretary,
28 January 1891

THE Dynamite War had begun at Salford Barracks on 14
January 1881; it would not finally end until the summer of
Queen Victoria's Jubilee in 1887. For over six years O'Donovan
Rossa's Skirmishers and Clan na Gael's Revolutionary Directory
had severely tested the defences of Britain's police forces and the
Home Office's Secret Service establishment. There was however
to be a time of truce between mid-January 1885, when the
Tower of London and the Houses of Parliament were attacked,
and the summer of 1887.

Major Henri Le Caron suggested that the pause in the
dynamite war was a direct by-product of Gladstone's conversion
to Home Rule for Ireland. He cited a secret circular of Clan
na Gael issued two days before Christmas of 1885 in support of
this opinion.

> The [dynamite] operations so far conducted have compelled
> the enemy to recognise the Constitutional party, and we are
> now in a fair way to reap the benefits and results of the
> heroic work of the members of the US [Sullivan's wing of the
> Clan na Gael]. . . . We expect to resume active operations
> after the present exigencies of the Constitutional party are
> passed. We have purposely and advisedly abstained from
> doing anything likely to embarrass them during the crisis of
> the elections.[1]

Clan na Gael was in serious trouble because the organisation
had broken into two wings as the result of charges by the

Cronin-Devoy faction that Sullivan and his Triangle Executive had embezzled over $250,000 of Clan funds. Cronin claimed that the Triangle destroyed the treasurer's records to conceal their crimes; also that they had knowingly sent men to England on dynamite attacks without adequate resources and then betrayed them.[2]

Circulars which precede the Sullivan wing's convention for 1886 asked the Clan's camps to raise money for a 'delusion' (dynamite) and to instruct their delegates to vote for either the 'silent secret warfare' or the 'planting of ploughs' (distribution of arms) and an open insurrectionary movement in Ireland. The latter policy would have been more difficult because Sullivan had broken off normal relationships with the IRB via the Revolutionary Directory two years before when the Supreme Council refused to support dynamite warfare. That August the convention agreed to continue to support Parnell's parliamentary movement in addition to renewing its own 'active service'.[3]

The parliamentary election referred to by the Clan's Christmas circular was a result of the Liberal government's collapse in the summer of 1885. Sir Richard Cross returned to the Home Office as the Home Secretary in the new Conservative government, inheriting E. G. Jenkinson and his Secret Service organisation. As Jenkinson had warned, a sense of false security did set in after the lull in attacks during 1885. He was kept at his post at the Home Office because, as one letter put it, he possessed valuable information and his services might become 'indispensable in a few months'. That was January of 1886 and not a bomb had been exploded for a year. Arguments continued unabated between the Irish government and the Home Office over who was to pay for the cost of the Secret Service establishment. The Conservative Home Secretary Cross took exactly the same position as his Liberal predecessor Harcourt; it was an Irish problem and the Irish government had to take financial responsibility for its solution at best, and its containment at worst. Jenkinson remained bitter about the frustrations which dogged his efforts; frustrations which Robert Anderson had suffered since 1867 while nonetheless remaining at the Home Office's Prison Board. Jenkinson's Dublin position of assistant under secretary of police and crime was abolished in April 1886. Lacking the patience of Anderson and, having private means, he made the break, resigning from the Home Office in January 1887. Major Nicholas Gosselin remained responsible for Secret Service work in the north of England. After what Robert Anderson, without further clarification, called a disastrous interval, James Monroe, Director of the CID, took charge of the Secret Service.[4]

Monroe had sent a confidential memorandum on 17 March 1886 to the Metropolitan Police's divisional superintendents (doubtless with the authority of the commissioner) indicating something of his approach to the subdued Fenian menace. He wanted the divisional superintendents to make it clear to their men that it was every policeman's duty, in the performance of his daily rounds, to acquire information at various meeting places and especially 'lodging houses where Irish-Americans, or men likely to be dangerous may go. . .'. Monroe said that there had been a tendency to think that such information came from 'special men' and that 'the other members of the force, whether CID or uniform, have little to do with this very important subject'. Greater emphasis was placed therefore upon the information-gathering function of the constable and considerably less upon the Secret Service's 'special men' and informants who had been so carefully nurtured by Edward Jenkinson. Prior to his departure from the Home Office Jenkinson destroyed all of the documents and information relating to counter-Fenian work in his possession in order to protect his informants and agents.[5]

At the end of 1886 Alexander Sullivan had commissioned General F. F. Millen to re-open negotiations with the IRB. Millen went to Paris, returning to the United States some weeks later full of enthusiasm for the success of his diplomacy. Luke Dillon was convinced that Millen had 'drawn upon his imagination for facts as usual'. Dillon was correct. The two organisations had not renewed their coalition, possibly because Millen could not offer the required assurances that dynamite warfare would not be restarted by Clan na Gael. Le Caron had left the United States for a visit to England that spring and had been sent on by Robert Anderson to meet Millen in Paris to see what he was up to. Le Caron reported that the 'General', although trying to patch up relations with the IRB, was not himself involved in any dynamite operation.[6]

Efforts to launch further attacks were however already in

the planning stages. As early as the beginning of February, Luke Dillon had been approached by a group he called the 'Fenian Council'. It wanted him to help them raise $2,000 to enable them to celebrate Queen Victoria's birthday celebrations set for that summer. The Fenian Council claimed that it had 150 men prepared to work with 'Greek fire'. Dillon excused his revealing any of this to John Devoy on the grounds that there was not the slightest possibility of the scheme coming to anything; 'men who are forced to proclaim their intentions in order to raise money to do anything more than get men into prison'. Certain that he would eventually be forced to talk to the 'council', Dillon regretted that they had 'learned in some way that I am not entirely ignorant of the manner those things are done. I regret this as it in a measure does away with my usefulness'. The secretive Dillon was one of the key Clan dynamiters. Born in Leeds in 1848, he was brought to the United States when his parents emigrated from Sligo. Dillon grew up in Trenton, New Jersey and later lived in Philadelphia. He reportedly ascribed his survival on 'active service' to the fact that he always worked alone while wearing a belt of explosives which he was prepared to detonate with his ever present cigar if he faced capture. Devoy believed that Dillon, along with Roger O'Neill, had been one of the bombers who had struck the Junior Carlton Club, Scotland Yard, and Nelson's Column at the end of May 1884. His final dynamite attack was to come during the Boer War when he was captured attempting to blow up Ontario's Welland Canal locks.

The next series of dynamite attacks were not however to come from this Fenian Council which, although prepared to talk to General Millen, had excluded O'Donovan Rossa.[7] Le Caron did not return to the United States until that autumn. Millen, Le Caron surmised, returned from France early in 1887 to find that the Revolutionary Directory, or at least the Triangle, had decided to mount another attack. He was asked to take charge of the arrangements. The dynamiters, however, were not to be supplied by the Clan but by O'Donovan Rossa who was now prepared to enter into a temporary alliance with Sullivan's Clan. In addition to Millen five other men were committed to the attacks, which were to take place during 'Mrs Brown's Jubilee celebrations'. According to Robert

Anderson they included a second attack on the Houses of Parliament and a major explosion during the Service of Thanksgiving at Westminster Abbey. Millen then returned to Europe. John J. Monroney (alias Joseph Melville), a personal friend of Sullivan, was in immediate charge of the attacks. He arrived in England on the *City of Chester* on 21 June with $1,200, accompanied by Thomas Callan, a forty-six year old labourer from Lowell, Mass. and a thirty-year old grocer from Philadelphia, Michael Harkins. The other two members of the team, including Joseph Cohen, were responsible for bringing the explosives into England. The Jubilee celebrations had already begun when the first three men arrived and although the festivities continued until 4 July no explosions were set off. As Le Caron quite rightly pointed out—'the whole undertaking was shrouded in mystery'.[8] Apparently Scotland Yard's Special Branch had been warned of the attack, given full descriptions, and had the men under surveillance from the time that they left the United States. Callan and Harkins were arrested but Cohen died in London before the police reached him. Monroney escaped the net. Millen, then in France, was not arrested because, according to contemporary newspaper accounts, he had been warned by a Scotland Yard detective at Boulogne that if he landed in England he would be arrested. Millen, who was on the Secret Service payroll at times, may well have 'shopped' the other bombers. This would explain the nature of the warning which he might well have received. Anderson gave the credit for the successful exposure of the plot to Assistant Commissioner Monroe of CID. John Mallon, chief inspector of Dublin's 'G' Division cryptically commented : 'Millen humbugged them'. Publicly the police reported that Rossa was not involved. Harkins and Callan were convicted at the Old Bailey of conspiring to cause explosions and were sentenced to comparatively light sentences of fifteen years imprisonment.[9] The affair was another Fenian fiasco which served to fan the fires of criticism which were already raging within Clan na Gael concerning Sullivan's leadership.

Monroe's success in upsetting the Clan's Jubilee Plot did not assure his own freedom of action as head of the CID. Sir Charles Warren, who succeeded Henderson as Commissioner of the Metropolitan Police in 1886, circumscribed the CID chief's traditional freedom of movement by applying the Metropolitan

Police Act of 1884, which made the CID director an assistant commissioner, thus depriving him of direct access to the Home Secretary. Monroe resigned in August; Warren resigned in December, because of what he considered unwarranted Home Office interference with Scotland Yard. He was replaced by Monroe! An even more extraordinary development was that Monroe's successor at the CID was Robert Anderson. Lord Spencer wrote to Harcourt (12 October 1888): 'What a queer appointment is that of Robert Anderson! He was utterly careless when employed by Brackenbury, and seemed to be a weak creature in every respect'.[10] Robert Anderson had finally received his reward in the most unexpected of ways; E. G. Jenkinson, who had received the CB in 1883, had to settle for a KCB in 1888. This may also have been something of a consolation for failing to receive the secretaryship at the India Office that year for which he was recommended by Lord Hartington. Nor was the Liberal party prepared to support Jenkinson's aspirations for a seat in the Commons.

Chief Inspector Adolphus 'Dolly' Williamson of the Special Irish Branch retired in the summer of 1889 and died that September without having written what would have proven to be amongst the most memorable of Victorian memoirs. Major Henri Le Caron (Thomas Beach) returned to England for good, tired of his undercover life and anxious to scuttle the pretensions of Gladstone's Home Rule policy and the Liberal–Irish Parnell coalition. Le Caron appeared before the Special Commission that sat in 1889 to hear evidence concerning Parnell's alleged complicity in the Phoenix Park murders. Stepping into the witness-box on 5 February he came out in his 'true colours as an Englishman, proud of his country, and in no sense ashamed of his record in her service'. Le Caron did not turn Gladstone from his Irish commitments, nor was he able to hammer the nail into Parnell's political coffin; that was a task which would remain for Captain O'Shea, the husband of Parnell's mistress. Le Caron's great achievement at end of life was his highly successful recounting of his twenty-five years in the Secret Service. Despite many Fenian threats against his life he died peacefully in his sleep.[11]

Such comfort was denied to the twenty-odd dynamiters residing in English prisons. The physical and mental conditions of the Fenian prisoners became of greater importance as the Liberal government and the Irish Home Rulers played out their political game of reconciliation. In January 1890 Thomas Gallagher contracted influenza and although he recovered it was feared by his friends that he was either insane or perilously close to it. A medical report to the Home Secretary on 4 February claimed that Gallagher had 'feigned religious mono-mania', and refused to work by claiming that he was God. It was also noted that he vomited a great deal which the medical officer was convinced was self-induced. His extremely poor health was blamed on his long period of 'feigned' insanity. Pressure continued to build in the United States for his release but American petitions to the British government were summarily rejected. Responsibility for the fate of the imprisoned dynamiters was inherited by John Redmond, leader of the Parnellite rump in the Irish Parliamentary Party. A year later (1891) Gallagher's health again excited concern and the governor of Portland Prison told the Home Secretary that the prisoner was 'perfectly sane and responsible'. The Irish Political Prisoners Amnesty Association, formed to carry on the battle, finally received Home Office permission to have an American doctor examine Gallagher. Dr T. St John Gaffney saw him that summer and reported to Asquith, the Home Secretary on 19 July 1893, that Gallagher was clearly insane. Asquith then paid £100 (plus 14/6 per mile) to have a Harley Street specialist, Dr Hack Tuke, go to Portland. He examined Gallagher and pronounced him sane. Three years later the government released Gallagher on 29 August 1896. He emerged insane. Gallagher died at Dr Coombs's Sanatorium, Flushing, New York in 1925. He was buried in the IRB Veterans' Plot in Calvary Cemetery, Long Island, not far from where he had taught himself the trade of a professional dynamiter. 'Alfred Whitehead' was released at the same time; he had also gone insane after thirteen years of British imprisonment.[12]

John Daly, who Major Gosselin described as the 'most bloody-minded Fanatic since the days of Guy Fawkes', was also released on 29 August 1896 after having been on a hunger strike. Apparently a New York doctor with a good practice before turning to dynamite warfare, Daly's case had stimulated controversy not because of his health but because of the circumstances of his arrest. Despite claims that the bombs had been planted on Daly at Birkenhead by Gosselin and his detectives, there is nothing remaining in the documents of the case to support this contention. Nor, might it be fairly added, would one expect there to be if the claims were true. The design and construction of bombs appear to be fully consistent with the developments of Clan na Gael technology. There is little doubt that Daly was betrayed by a Fenian in the pay of Jenkinson but the *agent provocateur* claim remains unproven; Daly, after his return to the United States, does not seem to have publicly elaborated on the circumstances of what he called at his trial 'a mystery'.[13]

Other dynamiters had been released prior to 1896. Michael Harkins, one of the Jubilee Plot men arrested in 1887 was released in August of 1891 and died of cancer a year later in Philadelphia. Eighteen months later, on 21 January 1893, his accomplice, Thomas Callan was released along with a very healthy James F. Egan. Egan, arrested with Daly, was a different matter because the evidence against him was circumstantial and depended upon the assumption that the nitroglycerine found buried in his back garden belonged to him. Daly had specifically taken responsibility for it claiming that Egan, who owned the house, knew nothing of it. Much was made of the fact that Egan was released on licence (ticket-of-leave) and was not pardoned. If he was innocent, he should have been pardoned and if his release was simply an act of amnesty, what about the other dynamite prisoners? The *St James's Gazette* of 23 January 1893 suggested :

> He must have been let out either because the Cabinet is of the opinion that the time has come to conciliate Ireland by enlarging the 'political prisoners', or because the ministers have convinced themselves that he was innocent.

Some like John Redmond MP, were prepared to interpret the move as an earnest of more, even if the nitroglycerine had been 'planted' in Egan's garden. Even more serious was the suggestion that this action of the government represented 'some sort of *prima facie* evidence' for the charge that Harcourt as the Home Secretary was in the plot of prostituting English justice. A letter to the *St James's Gazette* (24 January 1893) said that if, as

Henry Labouchere MP said, dynamiters must rot in prison, then Egan must be innocent and should have a lump sum compensation! If he was, however, a dynamiter then all the others have as much right to be set free. Although the various Home Secretaries privately reviewed the evidence surrounding the Egan–Daly trial, they maintained a studied silence. As soon as Egan was released he was appointed to the office of sword-bearer to Dublin Corporation. Daly on the other hand moved to Limerick where he was elected mayor of the corporation. Only the occasional leak disturbed the administrative tranquillity such as the press announcement that it was decided in 1887 that Callan's sentence was to be reviewed after five years. The marginal notation on this clipping from the *St James's Gazette* (24–25 January 1893) in a precise Home Office hand wondered how this had become known. The last man to be freed was Thomas Clarke of the Gallagher conspiracy in September 1898, and returning to the United States where he married John Daly's niece, he became John Devoy's secretary and worked at the *Gaelic American*. He returned to Ireland in 1907, signed the Republican Proclamation of 1916 becoming an Easter Martyr in the birth pangs of the new nation.[14]

The Secret Service continued to be housed deep in the confines of Whitehall. Robert Anderson may have temporarily inherited Monroe's oversight of the anti-Fenian work when he became assistant commissioner of the CID in 1888. Major Nicholas Gosselin was then appointed 'spymaster' to the Home Office in 1890. Totally unsatisfied with the work of the chief agent in the United States, New York's vice-consul Hoare, he personally reorganised the American operation after having Hoare recalled by the Foreign Office. Writing to Sir Matthew White-Ridley on 7 October 1896 in the wake of the Ivory Dynamite Plot he characterised his organisation in the following terms

I have in my employ a large number of faithful men who work like moles, who carry their lives in their hands. If I do not speak for them, nobody can or will. It is only in human nature that it should be galling to them that all public credit and praise should be showered by the press on Scotland Yard who in this and similar matters solely act, as the Secretary of State is well aware, as the instruments in the last instance for effecting the arrests of men whose plans have been laid bare and whose whereabouts discovered by my agents at the risk often of their lives, without thanks and with what, after all is not a high reward.[15]

The *Fenian Ram* which had excited the imagination of two nations did not make another public appearance until 1916 when the hull was the centrepiece of a bazaar at Madison Square Garden to raise money for the victims of the 1916 Irish uprising. The *Fenian Ram* was then donated to Fordham University/New York State Marine School at Clason Point. She remained there until purchased by Edward A. Brown of Paterson in 1927 who resited the boat in West Side Park, Paterson, New Jersey, within a few hundred yards of where Holland had first submerged in *Holland No. 1* beneath the Upper Passaic River. Although this Fenian secret weapon never was to attack a British ironclad or merchantman it was to be the prototype of a generation of submarines, which were launched in May 1897 with the *Holland VI* (*USS Holland/SS-1*) of the United States Navy. One might contemplate what the Fenian menace would have amounted to if the resources of the Skirmishing (National) Fund had not been diverted to what in the end, unexpectedly, had turned out to be peaceful purposes. So long as Holland could convince the trustees that he was on the very brink of the development of an invulnerable weapon which could be used against British seapower the Revolutionary Directory of Clan na Gael apparently approved this strategy and the bombing campaign was severely limited because of the shortage of funds. Although the submarine would wreak havoc on the high seas during World War I and eventually bring the United States in to the War, in the period 1877–1885 it made a small contribution towards the safety of London from Clan na Gael bombers.

The British Secret Service under Gosselin continued to probe the dark recesses of Clan na Gael's two organisations but the dynamite phase of the Irish struggle for independence was history. When the Boer War finally erupted there were young Irishmen and Irish-Americans prepared to fight against the British in South Africa and monuments in Irish churchyards testify to their sacrifice. When that war finally came, one for which Clan na Gael's military strategists had so long hoped, there was no fleet of Fenian rams to take to the high seas and destroy British commerce; nor were there Clan na Gael regiments to take the field against the British army. Leadership in the struggle for Irish freedom had however shifted, for the IRB prepared to raise the rebellion in Ireland itself. The Irish-American strategy had been founded upon the impossibility of an Irish revolution and had taken the initiative in the freedom movement during the 1880s. The Irish home organisation, encouraged by the political strides made constitutionally through the Irish Party at Westminster and then Liberal espousal of Home Rule, finally took up the gauntlet. And yet the American contribution must not be minimised for it was the men of the O'Donovan Rossa Skirmishers and Clan na Gael that kept alive the tradition of a military solution to the problem of a subjugated Ireland. When they failed to succeed through the dubious tactics of dynamite terrorism, Irish-Americans continued their financial and moral support of the IRB. From 1871 to 1916 Clan na Gael provided the financial life blood for Irish revolutionary hopes. During these years no man personified the Irish-American commitment to Irish freedom more than John Devoy. When the eighty-two year old revolutionary visited Ireland in 1924 he was able to do so as a guest of the new native Irish government of the Irish Free State.

In retrospect certain qualified judgements concerning the 'dynamite war' seem required. Were the Irish-American bombers inept and bungling? At least one knowledgeable historian believes that they were but I cannot share that opinion. A quick survey of their contemporary revolutionaries in Europe suggests that they did quite well, within their self-imposed limits. The leaders of Clan na Gael were extremely sensitive to world opinion concerning their dynamite terrorism and that is why Captain William Mackey Lomasney made such a great effort to run O'Donovan Rossa's Skirmishers—operating naively with gunpowder in the age of dynamite—out of Britain. The Clan thought the Skirmishers to be fools but John Mallon of Dublin's Detective Division thought *all* Fenians to be fools. One can almost hear the contemporary Irishman joke: 'Did you hear about the Irish bomber? He blew himself up!' The problem of hindsight is that it tends to minimise those very factors which at the time were the most frightening. The Home Secretary, William Vernon Harcourt, and his 'spymaster', E. G. Jenkinson, respected the Clan na Gael threat as only those responsible for the safety of the nation could. They were aware that the bombers could strike almost as they pleased beyond the ring of carefully guarded public buildings. They also undoubtedly had an unstated admiration for the refusal of the Clan to indulge in assassination or dynamite attacks in circumstances which would have led to a horrendous loss of life. The Clan adopted the principle of dynamite terror without loss of life and were able to adhere to it although the penetration of at least one Clan operation by O'Donovan Rossa, in the case of the Gallagher gang, did confuse the issue. The success of Scotland Yard's security operation forced the dynamiters to take chances such as dropping bombs into the underground tunnels from moving trains. Denied access to the tunnels by police vigilance, they came perilously close on two occasions to killing the passengers of an underground train. They chose not to try that again even though the parcels of every passenger could not be searched. Their potential targets were increasingly limited to meaningless buildings or the arches of London Bridge at night, or using continued public access to the House of Commons or the Tower of London to plant their charges. The bomb in the House of Commons went off in an empty chamber—it was not thrown from the Stranger's Gallery; the bomb in the crypt was intended to draw attention away from that in the chamber. The bomb in the Tower of London was placed behind a guncarriage; injuries were at a minimum as all the bombs were exploded before the large crowds of visitors arrived. These were the only gaps that could be found in the police security and only then because Scotland Yard had failed to anticipate that the bombers would strike in broad daylight.

The record is clear about the numbers of Clan bombers caught; of these almost a quarter came from the Gallagher arrests. These arrests need never have happened had not port security—which made the importation of explosives nearly impossible—necessitated their manufacture in Great Britain. From the point of view of the bombers, the arrests were no more than bad luck, since they had not been betrayed. The counter-

Fenian organisation begun by Brackenbury and developed by Jenkinson did have its important successes but at no time—and the documentary evidence shows this very clearly—did either Jenkinson or Harcourt feel that they had the opposition on the ropes. Right up to the moment when Clan na Gael pulled back, the British security establishment was trapped in its own despair over its inability to deal with the unseen enemy. It was evident that no amount of security was foolproof and that the dynamiters could operate at will if they chose. The number of men that escaped the attentions of Jenkinson and Scotland Yard may have numbered thirty or forty, although we have no way of being certain. The important point is not how many escaped but how many could have kept on coming had the Clan not changed its strategy. This change, in turn, was the result of many factors including the relative success of British security but perhaps most importantly the dissension within the Clan itself. What remains at this distance may be firstly an admiration for those Irish-Americans prepared to make the ultimate sacrifice to secure the freedom of Ireland, provided that it did not involve the loss of innocent life and secondly for the British security establishment of informers and agents, who were just as prepared to give their lives in the cause of the Empire.

The British public knew very little about the efforts to defend it from fire and blast except when the headlines of the popular press heralded the capture of bombers by members of the Special Irish Branch or detectives of the Glasgow or Liverpool forces. People might have imagined that there was a French-style secret service or a British equivalent to the Czar's infamous Third Section, but they did not have confirmation of the existence of their own secret service, or details of any of its activities until 1889, four years after the emergency had passed. The message of those harrowing years was impressively summed up by the *New York Tribune* of 18 April 1884 when its editorial acknowledged that the power of making war was no longer confined to governments: 'Dynamite, in fact, has put a tremendous power in the hands of individuals, and has reinforced all revolutionary and seditious tendencies enormously, making mere folly and fanaticism seriously dangerous, and increasing the natural bent of all lawless movements to gather strength as they go on. ... And though the use of dynamite for the furtherance of political or other ends may be shown to be futile, it is evident that pure reason will not control those who resort to it, but that in this as in many other cases, "the sight of means to do ill deeds, make ill deeds done".' The *Tribune* concluded: 'Indicators are that the new problem forced upon the world by the fertility of modern invention will give it serious trouble in the future'.[16] And so it has.

Notes

INTRODUCTION
(pp. 1–6)
1. N. Halasz, *Nobel, A Biography* (1960) *passim.*
2. A. Yarmolinsky, *Road to Revolution: A Century of Russian Radicalism*, New York 1962, pp. 223–83. On the subject of terrorism, see Walter Laquer, 'Interpretations of Terrorism: Fact, Fiction and Political Science', and Ze'ev Iviansky, 'Individual Terror: Concept and Typology', both in *Journal of Contemporary History*, xii (1977).

Chapter I
FENIANISM: AN IRISH ROOT AND AMERICAN BRANCHES
(pp. 7–34)
1. Report of Detective Inspector James J. Thomson, 18 December 1867 : S.Y./M.E.P.O. 3/1788. W. J. Lowe, in his article 'Lancashire Fenianism, 1864–71' (*Transactions of the Historic Society of Lancashire and Cheshire*, vol. 126, 1977) discusses the activity of the Irish Republican Brotherhood in that region as well as that of the Royal Irish Constabulary's detective force. He also documents the early role of John Joseph Corydon as an informer.
2. Copy of telegram(?) from Dublin Metropolitan Police, Superintendent 'G' Division, Daniel Ryan, 11 December 1867 : S.Y., M.E.P.O. 3/1788.
3. Littlechild, *The Reminiscences of Chief Inspector . . .*, 11.
4. Details on the explosion and its aftermath are based on reports in *The Times*, Hansard cxc (Third Series) 1005, 1215–18, and S.Y. series 3/1788. Sir Richard Mayne's memo on Clerkenwell security is in this last series dated 12 December 1868 [*sic*]. For the Home Secretary's handling of the affair see A. E. Gathorne Hardy, *Life of Gathorne Hardy*, i, 214ff. Robert Anderson in *The Lighter Side of my Official Life* (pp.19ff) provides some important insights to the secret service operation. According to

an account published in the *Irish Press* (13 December 1938), Jeremiah O'Sullivan claimed that he had fired the barrel and that it was Burke who had ordered 548 pounds of refined powder for the job. O'Sullivan said that all those concerned with the affair were horrified by the resulting catastrophe. Quoted in *Devoy's Post Bag*, i, 36.

5. P. O'Farrell, *England and Ireland Since 1800*, 29; F. S. L. Lyons, *Ireland Since the Famine* (rev.ed.), ch.2.
6. H. Le Caron, *Twenty-Five Years in the Secret Service*, passim. Charles Curran, 'The Spy Behind the Speaker's Chair', *History Today*, 1968.
7. *New York Herald* report quoted in *Devoy's Post Bag*, i, 4.
8. Quoted in W. D'Arcy, *The Fenian Movement in the United States*, 371.
9. ibid., 372f.
10. This can also be traced in *Devoy's Post Bag*, i, 1ff.
11. *Post Bag*, i, 217; Le Caron, 105ff, 117.
12. Le Caron, 128f; *Gaelic American,* 29 November 1924; E. G. Jenkinson, Memorandum on the Organisation of the United Brotherhood, or Clan na Gael in the United States. Printed for use of the Cabinet, 26 January 1885 (this is based almost entirely upon Le Caron information).
13. D'Arcy, 392f; *Devoy's Post Bag*, i, 81ff; 175ff; W. J. Laubenstein, *The Emerald Whaler.*

Chapter 2
SKIRMISHERS BY SEA AND BY LAND,
1876–1881
(pp. 35–70)

1. Quoted in R. K. Morris, *John P. Holland*, 20ff. Much of the information concerning the Holland boats is drawn from Mr Morris's research.
2. John Devoy to — White, 1 March, 1876, *Post Bag*, i, 143.
3. *Devoy's Post Bag*, i, 142.
4. William Carroll to Devoy, 1 February 1877, *Post Bag*, i, 230.
5. *Devoy's Post Bag*, i, 358ff; ii, 553ff (Appendix: The Skirmishing Fund Controversy).
6. Rossa to T. F. Bourke, undated, *Post Bag*, i, 322f; 330.
7. Michael Davitt, *The Fall of Feudalism in Ireland*, 125.
8. S(tate) P(aper) O(ffice), Dublin, A Series, A626, A630, A633.
9. Rossa to James —, 15 March 1880, *Post Bag*, i, 502f.
10. John Devoy, *Recollections of an Irish Rebel*, 210.
11. F. F. Millen to Devoy, Devoy dated as 27 March '78, *Post Bag*, i, 311.

12. ibid, ii, 27; also see Lomasney to Devoy, 16 December 1880, 25ff.
13. Lomasney to Devoy, 4 January 1881, ibid, ii, 31.
14. Le Caron, op. cit., 100ff. Lomasney had considered travelling openly for he had 'some very good and plausible excuses for being in Ireland . . .' (*Post Bag*, ii, 17f).
15. Jeyes and How, *Life of Sir Howard Vincent*, 106.
16. ibid, 105f; Vincent to Harcourt, 1 August 1881, : W. V. H. (Harcourt Papers) 100.
17. *The Times*, 27 June 1881.
18. John McEnnis, *The Clan na Gael and the Murder of Dr Cronin*, 71.
19. Special Expenses, 11 February 1881 : S.Y.,/M.E.P.O. R/b1832. Scotland Yard pressed the government to pay for these expenses since Davitt's arrest was its decision.
20. Lomasney to Devoy, 23 February 1881, *Post Bag*, ii, 44f.
21. F(oreign) O(ffice) 97/472/1932A/vol.1 : America : Press Incitements to Outrage (Confidential Print), week ending 23 April 1881 : W. V. H., Lewis Vernon Harcourt Diary, 18 March 1881 entry.
22. *Devoy's Post Bag*, ii, 33.
23. ibid, ii, 56ff.
24. ibid, ii, 44f, 51f. Lomasney mentions the need for secret correspondence. In a letter of James J. O'Kelly to Devoy (*Post Bag*, ii, 155, 24 October 1882) the process is described. One wrote with a weak solution of yellow prussiate of potash on rough unglazed paper in a small hand with a quill pen. The writing, which was apparently between the lines of a normal letter, was developed with a solution of copperas.
25. ibid, ii, 68.
26. S.P.O. A705.
27. S.P.O. A704
28. Morris, op. cit., ch. 4.
29. Drummond to Blaine, 28 July 1881 : Knaplund and Clewes, eds., *Private Letters from the British Embassy*, 144f; also P.R.O. 30/29 Granville Papers.
30. Drummond to Granville, 7 September 1881 : Knaplund, 147.
31. S.P.O. A635.
32. *Devoy's Post Bag*, ii, 41; S.P.O. A668
33. 'Explosion Town Hall, Liverpool', report 16 September 1881 : H.O. 144/81/A5836; also contemporary accounts in *The Times*.
34. *The Times*, 14 June 1881.

35. H.O. 144/81/A5836, dated 15, 23 June 1881.
36. H.O. 144/72/A19; A19/1 (telegrams dated 7, 9, 12 July 1881); S.P.O. A645 (24 January 1881).
37. Drummond to Granville, 2 August 1881 : Knaplund, op cit., 143f.
38. H.O. 144/84/A7266 (Foreign Office to Harcourt, 3 November 1881).
39. Drummond to Granville, 1 November 1881 : Knaplund, 151.
40. ibid, 96, Thornton to Granville, 18 May 1880.

Chapter 3
SPYMASTER-GENERAL
(pp. 71–101)

1. For a detailed discussion of these negotiations R. Hawkins, 'Gladstone, Forster and the Release of Parnell, 1882–8', *Irish Historical Studies*, v, 417–45.
2. 'Select Documents XXX, Lord Spencer on the Phoenix Park Murders', eds. A. G. Cooke and J. R. Vincent, *I.H.S.*, xviii; Tom Corfe, *The Phoenix Park Murders*.
3. Memorandum, Anderson to Harcourt, 6 May 1882 : W.V.H., 105.
4. *Illustrated London News*, 17 June 1882, 593. Hillier was the inspector-general of the RIC from 1876–82; Talbot was the chief commissioner of the DMP from 1877–82.
5. Spencer to Gladstone, 9 May 1882 : B(ritish) M(useum) Add. mss. 44308/234. Lt. J. F. G. Ross of Bladensburg had been seriously considered, upon Forster's recommendation, as Burke's replacement. He was an extra ADC to the viceroy serving as the military expert in the use of the army in support of the civil power. He had not endeared himself to Spencer for having apparently led the Queen to believe, in a recent interview, that the whole Irish population was either members or tools of secret societies.
6. Sir Henry Brackenbury, *Some Memories of My Spare Time*, 311f. Harcourt at one time characterised Childers as 'generally cold as ice and as impassive as dough'.
7. Spencer to Gladstone, 10 May 1882 : B.M.Add.mss. 44308/238. Edward Hamilton, one of Gladstone's two secretaries, noted in his diary, Tuesday 9 May 1882 : 'He [Spencer] has replaced Hillier by Colonel Brackenbury as Head of the Constabulary (I have always believed Hillier was a weak vessel); and has secured an Indian officer, Colonel Bradford, to assist in the secret police work and to supply a want which has, I know, been felt for long, but to which Forster always turned a deaf

ear' : *The Diary of Sir Edward Walter Hamilton, 1880–1885,*
D. W. R. Bahlman, i, 268.

8. Spencer to Gladstone, 17 May 1882 : B.M. Add.mss. 44308/
   253, 261; 11 June 1882 : 44309/1. On Friday, 9 June Brackenbury and Hamilton discussed the former's report on the Irish
   secret societies 'which are clearly in a terribly rampant state'.
   Money was seen as the only effective tool (in Hamilton, op. cit.,
   i, 286). Brackenbury's report is in the Spencer Papers and is
   discussed in R. Hawkins, 'Government versus Secret Societies :
   The Parnell Era' in T. D. Williams (ed.) *Secret Societies in
   Ireland,* 100–112.

9. Spencer to Harcourt, 30 May 1882 : W.V.H., 39.

10. Harcourt to Spencer, 12 June 1882 : W.V.H., 39. The British
    minister to Washington, Thornton, had asked Archibald to
    raise the problem of Fenianism with Allan Pinkerton. Born
    in Glasgow in 1819, he had taken part in the Chartist demon-
    strations of 1842 and fled to the United States to avoid arrest.
    In 1850 he set up a private detective agency in Chicago and
    gradually acquired the most complete set of records on
    criminals in the USA. Archibald reported to Thornton who in
    turn wrote to Granville on 25 January 1881 (P.R.O.30/29/
    154) with Pinkerton's reply that 'even he does not feel himself
    capable of getting at their inmost secrets'.

11. Hamilton, op. cit., 290.

12. S.P.O. B1/5.

13. For Archibald see Edith Archibald, *Life and Letters of Sir
    Edward Mortimer Archibald.*

14. S.P.O. B1/65.

15. Brackenbury, op. cit., 311. For a later conversation with Glad-
    stone (c.1890) see p. 348. Brackenbury was by then Head of the
    Army Intelligence Department. Alfred E. Turner, in *Sixty
    Years of a Soldier's Life* (London 1912, p. 55f.) provides a
    detailed description of the contents of Brackenbury's letter in
    which he asked the viceroy 'whether, in the event of Lord
    Wolseley finding a place for him on his staff, he would allow
    him to resign his appointment in Ireland'. Turner, who was
    Brackenbury's assistant, remembered that Brackenbury recom-
    mended that Mr Clifford Lloyd and E. G. Jenkinson be con-
    sidered as his successors. While recording the events that
    accompanied the resignation, Turner also makes it quite
    clear that Spencer continued to hold Brackenbury in high
    regard.

16. Spencer to Gladstone, 2 July 1882 : B.M. Add.mss. 44309/74.

17. Harcourt to Spencer, 19 July 1882 : W.V.H.39.

18. Spencer to Harcourt, 20 July 1882 : W.V.H.39.
19. Harcourt to Spencer, 31 July 1882 : W.V.H.39.
20. Spencer to Harcourt, 2 August 1882 : W.V.H.40.
21. Spencer to Gladstone, 3 August 1882 : B.M. Add.mss. 44309/78; Spencer to Harcourt, 2 August 1882 : W.V.H.40.
22. *Hansard* cclxxiii (Third Series), 3 August 1882, 683–99.
23. Draft memo Spencer to Jenkinson on Limerick Police, no date, c. 9 August 1882 : H.O. 144/72/A19; Spencer to Harcourt, 27 August 1882 : W.V.H.40. On 1 September Spencer had dismissed 234 Dublin policemen for staging a meeting on their conditions which he had forbidden. Almost all of the remaining members of the force then resigned.
24. Vincent to Harcourt, 11 May 1882 : W.V.H.100.
25. Sackville West to Granville, 16 May 1882 : P.R.O.30/29/154.
26. Vincent to Harcourt, 11, 25, 30 May 1882 : W.V.H.100.
27. Press cuttings for week ending 25 February 1882 : P.R.O./F.O.97/472/1932A.
28. Vincent to Harcourt, 13 May 1882 : W.V.H.100 : Vincent to Harcourt, 14 May 1882 : W.V.H.39. Harcourt to Spencer, 14 May 1882 : W.V.H.39.
29. Diary entry, 15 May 1882, Lewis Harcourt : Harcourt Papers.
30. Vincent to Harcourt, 16, 17, 21 June 1882 : W.V.H.100.
31. Lewis Harcourt to Harcourt, 17 June 1882 : W.V.H.100.
32. Vincent to Harcourt, 19 June 1882 : W.V.H.100. Vincent also had an anonymous letter warning that Gladstone would 'fall by the hands of the Fenians' within three months as a direct consequence of the arms haul. Vincent reported to Harcourt that the prime minister had 'consented to submit to all the precautions and so co-operate in them as far as he can; also Trevelyan satisfied with protection'. (13 June 1882 : W.V.H. 100) Edward Hamilton (i, 288) recorded in his diary how both Harcourt and Vincent had asked him to persuade Gladstone of the necessity of his protection. He was to confine his walks to principal thoroughfares and to have someone in plain clothes following him : he proved to be 'good natured and submissive' and consented without demurring. Vincent noted that there had been no further incidents involving Gladstone's embarrassing and widely misunderstood 'night walks' (during which he attempted to 'rescue' London's prostitutes from their 'wicked ways') since early May.
33. Anderson to Harcourt, 14 October 1882 : W.V.H.105.
34. Harcourt to Spencer, 17 October, 17, 24 November 1882 : W.V.H.40.
35. Anderson, *Lighter Side of My Official Life*, 18f, 89.

36. S.P.O. B1/B118.
37. S.P.O. B1/65.
38. Anderson to Harcourt, 21 August 1882 : W.V.H.105.
39. S.P.O. A739, 740. For a diagram of the improved model see page 120.

Chapter 4
A STATE OF EMERGENCY: GLASGOW,
LONDON AND LIVERPOOL
(pp.102–124)

1. Spencer to Harcourt, 30 January 1883; W.V.H.42; Harcourt to Spencer, 1 February 1883 : W.V.H.41.
2. *Devoy's Post Bag*, ii, 140ff (dated 21 September 1882); Le Caron, op. cit., 254f.
3. P.R.O./F.O. 97/472/1932A (24 February 1883).
4. C. T. Couper, *Report of the Trial of the Dynamitards, passim*.
5. ibid., p. 101f.
6. The event as described is conjecture.
7. Henderson to Harcourt, 16, 17 March 1883 : W.V.H.101
8. M.E.P.O. Report, 17 March 1883 : W.V.H.101.
9. S.Y./M.E.P.O.3, diagram dated 17 March 1883; Draft letter (17 March 1883)—'Protection of Public Buildings'; Henderson to Liddell, 17 March 1883 : H.O.144/115/A25928.
10. H.O. 144/114/A25908 (letters dated 16, 19 March 1883).
11. Harcourt to Spencer, 16 March 1883 : W.V.H.42.
12. S.P.O. A768. This document also suggests that the damage to the building amounted to some £4,000.
13. *New York Times*, 17 March 1883.
14. Jenkinson to Harcourt, 16 March 1883 : W.V.H.103.
15. Vincent memo(?), 17 March 1883 : W.V.H.101.
16. Anderson memorandum, 17 March 1883 : W.V.H.105.
17. Harcourt to Spencer, 15 April 1883 : W.V.H.42.
18. E. G. Jenkinson memorandum, 22 March 1883 : W.V.H.103.
19. Henderson to Harcourt, 26 March 1883 : W.V.H.101.
20. *The Times*, 11 April 1883.
21. ibid., 1 May 1883.
22. Majendie to Harcourt, 19 March 1883 : H.O.144/114/A25908; Vincent to Harcourt, 23 March 1883 : W.V.H.101.
23. P.R.O./F.O. 97/472/1932A, week ending 24 March 1883.
24. H.O. 151, ii, Liddell to Commissioners of Customs, 5 February 1883.
25. S.P.O. B1/B43,B194 : W. Nott-Bower, *Fifty-Two Years a Policeman*, 78ff.
26. Jenkinson to Harcourt, 29 March, 4 April 1883 : W.V.H.103.

I

27. H.O. 144/115/A26302 : Chief Constable Liverpool to Harcourt, 29 March, 30 April 1883.
28. Diagram from W.V.H.102.
29. H.O. 144/115/26302 : Report dated 30 March 1883.
30. Harcourt (Anderson) then telegraphed Jenkinson for clarification, 30 March 1883 : W.V.H. 105.
31. Harcourt to Spencer, 31 March 1883 : W.V.H.42
32. Jenkinson to Harcourt, 1 April 1883 : W.V.H.103.

Chapter 5
THE GALLAGHER TEAM
(pp. 125–153)

1. For Gallagher see H.O. 144/116/A26493/53 (M.E.P.O./C.I.D. 17 May 1887). *Hansard*, cclxxiv (Third Series), 1533f. Letters of admission for these two dates were found on Gallagher when arrested. See also H. Le Caron, *Twenty-Five Years in the Secret Service*, 239f.
2. Pritchard Depositions : H.O. 144/116/A26493G/2,G/5,E; *The Times*, 30 April 1883. The identification of 'Whitehead' as John J. Murphy of Massachusetts is based upon a memorandum of 24 January 1884 found in S.P.O. Police and Crime Reports (1882–4), 1883, Carton 2, 492W/2832. The source of the information was Detective Superintendent Black of Birmingham who based the assumption on a piece of paper found in the Ledsam St shop which contained the name of James Murphy. 'Whitehead' refused to confirm this but apparently gave the name of his uncle as T. J. Murphy, 269 Essex St, Lawrence, Massachusetts.
3. *The Times*, 11, 30 April 1883.
4. Trial Proceedings in *The Times*, 12 June 1883 (evidence of 11 June).
5. Report by Detective Inspector Littlechild; H.O. 144/116/ A26493/59 (M.E.P.O./C.I.D., 17 May 1887).
6. L. N. Le Roux, *Tom Clarke and the Irish Freedom Movement*, 21ff.
7. The plot reconstruction is based in large part upon the evidence given during the trial : Trial Proceedings, *The Times*, 12, 13, 14, 15 June 1883.
   Before his release in July, Lynch (Norman) said that one day Gallagher had sent him to Birmingham, after a telegram had been received from Whitehead, to tell him that if he was being watched it would be better to let the stuff run off. Whitehead replied : 'I will stick by it by God and die, now we have gone so far' (H.O. 144/116/A26493F).

8. Quoted in A. G. Gardiner, *Life of Harcourt,* 479.
9. R. Anderson, *Lighter Side,* 109.
10. Hansard, cclxxvii (3rd Series), 1802–11 (Commons), 1842–63 (Lords); Gardiner, op. cit., 480.
11. Jenkinson to Harcourt, 19 April, 7 May 1883 : W.V.H.103. Colonel Charles Warren, later to become chief commissioner of the Metropolitan Police, was seriously considered for the head of the new Crime Department but was considered to be far too expensive.
12. Jenkinson Memorandum, 8 May 1883 : W.V.H.103.
13. Jenkinson to Harcourt, 18 May 1883 : W.V.H.103.
14. Anderson to Harcourt, 21 May 1883 : W.V.H.105.
15. Jenkinson to Harcourt, 24, 31 May 1883 : W.V.H.103.
16. Gosselin to Harcourt, 1 June (?) 1883 : W.V.H.105.
17. L. O'Broin, *Revolutionary Underground,* 9. Although Leon O'Broin in his excellent study of the IRB does not mention this period of possible co-operation, it would appear that the general policy of the Supreme Council was firmly against dynamiting. This particular message concerning the 'travellers' is probably authentic for it uses the vocabulary and form characteristic of the disguised correspondence of 'the organisation'—often referred to as the *firm* or *business.* The members of the Supreme Council were *directors* or *heads of the firm,* while *stock* and *cargo* were arms and ammunition. The President was, inelegantly, the *Boss.* There were *meetings of shareholders, picnics, foremen of divisions* and the area/province, of which there were four in Ireland, plus the North and South of England, and Scotland were called the *agencies.* Clan na Gael was called *Logan,* and Patrick Egan was the *Broker.*
18. Spencer to Harcourt, 2 June, 22 November, 19 December 1883. Harcourt to Spencer, 5 June, 21 November, 23 December 1883 : W.V.H.42.
19. Originally three and later at least two judges sat together to try cases in the Judges' List at the Old Bailey. The practice fell into disuse until revived by Chief Justice John Duke Coleridge for the Gallagher trial. It then promptly fell into disuse again. The Gallagher conspirators had been charged under the Treason Felony Act 1848. This act had been passed, said Poland, because of the 'troublesome technicalities connected with a trial for Treason, or as it is called, unnecessarily, because there is no longer such an offence as Petty Treason, High Treason—and furthermore, in the majority of cases the passing of obligatory sentence of death on a convicted Traitor had become farcical'. Gallagher and his accomplices had been

252 Notes to pages 149-160

tried at the Old Bailey under only the second application of the 1848 Act, to allow for the application of less severe penalties if convicted. Coleridge had decided that the three judges (which included himself, Sir Baliol Brett, the Master of the Rolls and the senior Puisne Judge Mr Justice Grove) should sit as Commissioners in order to lay down the law as regards to Treason Felony and 'clear up some certain points on it'. (E.B. Bowen-Rowlands, *Seventy-Two Years at the Bar*, 190.)

20. N.Y. Consulate to Granville, 24 April 1883 : H.O. 144/116/26493, 139 (Treasury Solicitor/Report of Trial).
21. Town Clerk, Birmingham to Harcourt, 15 August 1883 : H.O. 144/116/A26493E.
22. Gosselin Memorandum to Harcourt, 12 July 1883 : W.V.H.103.
23. Chief Constable, Bristol to Harcourt, 9 August 1883 : W.V.H. 102; Jenkinson to Harcourt, 11 August 1883 : W.V.H.103.
24. Chief Constable, Liverpool to Harcourt, 4 July 1883, A. Liddell to Harcourt, 5 July 1883 : H.O. 144/115/A26302.
25. W. Nott-Bower, *Fifty-Two Years a Policeman*, 84f. The evidence used in the reconstruction of the Liverpool 'operation' is derived from the trial of the Glasgow bombers in C. T. Couper, *Report of the Trial of the Dynamitards....*
26. Mayor, Manchester to Home Office, 29 October 1883; Inland Revenue to A. Liddell, Home Office, 16 November 1883 : H.O. 144/166/A26730; Telegram, Liverpool Police to Home Office, 11 September 1883 : H.O. 144/166/A26493G/7; Williams to Howard Vincent, 9 August 1883 : W.V.H.101.

Chapter 6
TO LEVY WAR UPON THE QUEEN
(pp. 154-172)
1. Clan na Gael memorandum, September 1883; Anderson memorandum, 3 November 1883 : W.V.H.105.
2. M. Davitt, *Fall of Feudalism*, 429ff.
3. Jenkinson to Harcourt, 17 June 1883 : W.V.H.103.
4. Davitt, op. cit., 431.
5. Jenkinson to Harcourt, 18, 20, 21 June, 17 September, 1883 : W.V.H.103.
6. Jenkinson to Harcourt, 2 August, 24 September 1883 : W.V.H. 103.
7. Gosselin to Harcourt, 1 August 1883 : W.V.H.105.
8. Williamson to Harcourt, 3 September 1883 : W.V.H.101.
9. C. T. Couper, *Report of the Trial of the Dynamitards*.
10. M.E.P.O. Report 30 October 1883 : H.O. 45/9638/A32915/1; ('A' Div. Report by Gernon).

11. M.E.P.O. 'D' Div. Report by William Smith-Guard : H.O. 45/9638; also depositions by other witnesses in same series, including Chief Inspector Gosden.
12. W. V. Harcourt to Lewis Harcourt, 1 November 1883 : W.V.H.14.
13. W. Gardiner, *Harcourt*, i, 490.
14. Vincent, C.I.D., 30 October 1883 : H.O. 45/9638/A32915/39; H.O. 45/9638/A32915/4.
15. Jenkinson to Harcourt, 31 October 1883 : W.V.H.103; S.Y. 'A' Div. Report 6 Nov. 188(3).
16. Granville to West, 12 May 1883 : P.R.O.30/29/154.
17. Granville to Frelinghuysen, 12 May 1883 : P.R.O.30/29/154.
18. E. H. Coleridge, *Life and Correspondence of John Duke Lord Coleridge*, ii, 332.
19. *loc. cit.*
20. P.R.O.30/29/154, 17 January 1884.
21. P.R.O.30/29/154, p. 289
22. Harcourt to Spencer, 14 June 1883 : Gardiner, *Life of Sir William Vernon Harcourt*, i, 481f.
23. Harcourt to Spencer, 10, 31 January 1884 : W.V.H.43; B.M. Add.mss. (R. A. Cross Papers) 51274, Spencer to Cross, 3 August 1884
24. Morris, *Holland*, 45.
25. Breslin to Devoy, 14 April 1883 : *Devoy's Post Bag*, ii, 189.
26. Reynolds to Breslin, 8 October 1883 : *Devoy's Post Bag*, ii, 213.
27. Morris, op. cit., 46f.
28. *Devoy's Post Bag*, ii, 213f.
29. *Irish World*, 25 December 1883.
30. Harcourt to Spencer, 10 September 1883 : W.V.H.42.

Chapter 7
THE AMERICAN CONNECTION, 1884
(pp. 173–199)
1. Farndale to Harcourt, 24 December 1883 : W.V.H.102.
2. Detective Supt Black Report attached to Farndale-Harcourt, 24 December 1883 : W.V.H.102.
3. Jenkinson to Harcourt, 14, 16, 18 January 1884 : W.V.H.104; Harcourt to Spencer, 19 January 1884; Spencer to Harcourt, 20 January 1884 : W.V.H.43.
4. Details established during trial of Burton and Cunningham : reported by *The Times* 12–18 May 1885.
5. Telegram—Queen Victoria to Harcourt, 26 February 1884 : H.O. 144/133/A34707/1. The mechanisms of the unexploded

devices are now part of the Black Museum collection at New Scotland Yard.

6. A. G. Gardiner, *Life of Sir William Harcourt*, i, 503.

7. Jenkinson to Harcourt, 2 March 1884 : W.V.H.104.

8. Jenkinson Memorandum, n.d., : W.V.H.103.

9. Henderson to 'Port Police', 7 March 1884 : H.O. 144/133/A34848 B/1a; Jenkinson Memorandum, 11 March 1884 : H.O. 144/133/A34848 B/1.

10. Harcourt to Spencer, Spencer to Harcourt, 5–9 March 1884 : W.V.H.43.

11. Farndale to Home Secretary, 22 October 1884 : H.O. 144/133/A46664 B/13 : Jenkinson to Harcourt, 12 April 1884 : W.V.H. 104; Diary entries 11, 27 April 1884, L. V. Harcourt : Harcourt Papers.

12. Daly to Devoy, n.d., *Devoy's Post Bag*, ii, 242.

13. *The Times*, 2 August 1884.

14. Report of 8 May 1884 : H.O. 144/133/A34848 B/17.

15. Davitt, *Fall of Feudalism*, 437f.

16. Jenkinson to Harcourt, 14 June 1884 : W.V.H.104.

17. M.E.P.O. Special Report, 'C' Div, 31 May 1884; Henderson to Jenkinson, 31 May 1884; Jenkinson to Harcourt, 31 May 1884 : W.V.H.104; S.Y./M.E.P.O. 3, Jenkinson Memorandum to Henderson, 31 May 1884; Jenkinson to Harcourt, 2 June 1884 : WV.H.104.

18. Jenkinson to Harcourt, 31 May, 30 June 1884 : W.V.H.104.

19. 'Policing Arrangements 1883–4 : memorandum of 14 September 1883 : H.O. 144/115/A25928; Jenkinson to Harcourt 18, 26 August 1884 : W.V.H.104.

20. Jenkinson to Harcourt, 19 September 1884 : W.V.H.104.

21. *loc cit.*

22. Jenkinson to Harcourt, 3 October 1884 : W.V.H.104.

23. Harcourt to Spencer 23 November 1884 : W.V.H. Richard Hawkins suggests that Hamilton and Jenkinson had strong disagreements on several occasions over matters of policy and division of responsibility between them. At the same time if Hamilton were to become 'monarch of all he surveys' (Harcourt's words), it would only have been a return to the traditional position of the under secretary, not a usurpation; the trouble was that in 1881–2 it had been recognised that even the best under secretary could not run the whole show in a continuing crisis.

24. Davitt, op. cit., 438; Bussy, *Irish Conspiracies*, 205; *Hansard* ccxcl (Third Series), 495.

25. The official correspondence on the issue of the bombings

between the Foreign Office and the State Department is found
in P.R.O./F.O. 97/472(1881–3); 473(1882–3); 474(1884); 475
(1885).
26. Quoted in Gibson, *Attitudes of the New York Irish*, 368.
27. West to Granville, 10 June 1884 : P.R.O. 30/29/154.
28. West to Granville, 6 July 1884 : P.R.O. 30/29/154.
29. Frelinghuysen to Lowell, 24 November 1884 : P.R.O./F.O.
97/474/1932C.
30. Jenkinson to Harcourt, 1 January 1885 (Moore letter attached):
W.V.H.104.

Chapter 8
LONDON BRIDGE IS FALLING DOWN,
FALLING DOWN . . .
(pp. 200–228)
1. J. Devoy, *Recollections*, 212; *Post Bag*, ii, 8.
2. Jenkinson to Harcourt, 25 January 1885 : W.V.H.104; Jenkinson to Monroe, 26 December 1884 : S.Y./M.E.P.O. 3.
3. City of London to Harcourt, 19 December 1884; Harcourt to
City, 20 December 1884 : H.O. 144/145/A38008/1.
4. Jenkinson to Harcourt, 18 December 1884, 28 January 1885 :
W.V.H.104; Harcourt to Gosselin, 11 December 1884 : W.V.H.
105.
5. Jenkinson to Monroe, 28 January 1885 : S.Y./M.E.P.O. 3;
Jenkinson to Harcourt, 25 January 1885 : W.V.H.104; Spencer
to Harcourt, 4 January 1885; Harcourt to Spencer, 6 January
1885 : W.V.H.44.
6. Jenkinson to Harcourt, 10, 13 January 1885 : W.V.H.104.
7. Jenkinson to Harcourt, 25 January 1885 : W.V.H.104. This is
an unexplained gap in the official records and the foregoing is
reconstructed from the evidence given at the trial of Cunningham and Burton as reported in *The Times* (12–18 May 1885).
8. R. L. O. Pearson was the senior official who had not anticipated an attack in 'broad day light'. He was responsible for the
protection of the buildings (27 January 1885 : S.Y./M.E.P.O.3).
9. Jenkinson to Harcourt, 27 January 1885 : W.V.H.104.
10. Monroe to Jenkinson, 30 January 1885 : W.V.H.104; Harcourt
to Henderson(?), copy, 28 January 1885 : W.V.H.101.
11. Harcourt to Spencer, 18 January 1885 : W.V.H.44.
12. Diary entry, 4 January 1885; L. V. Harcourt, Harcourt Papers.
13. E. G. Jenkinson, Memorandum on the Organization of the
United Brotherhood or Clan na Gael in the United States
(Printed for use of Cabinet, 26 January 1885) p. 2 : W.V.H.
106.

14. Spencer to Harcourt, 10 February 1885 : W.V.H.44.
15. Jenkinson to Harcourt, 21 February 1885 : W.V.H.104.
16. F.O. to Harcourt, 17 March 1885; Granville to Lyons (Copy No. 232) : W.V.H.44.
17. Devoy, *Recollections*, 277.
18. West to Granville, 1 January 1885; P.R.O./F.O. 97/475/1932D; Harcourt to Pauncefote [9 March 1885], Harcourt to F.O., 2 February 1885; final despatch of 21 February 1885 in F.O. 97/475; with Harcourt emendations : W.V.H. 106.
19. Harcourt to Spencer, 19, 31 May 1885 : W.V.H.44.
20. S.P.O. A753, A775.
21. Jenkinson to Harcourt, 3, 4, 5, 11 June 1885 : W.V.H.104.
22. Jenkinson to Harcourt, 16 June 1885 : W.V.H.104; Spencer to Harcourt, 17 June 1885 : W.V.H.44; Harcourt to Cross, 22 June 1885 : B.M. Add.mss.(R.A.C.)51274.
23. Harcourt to Spencer, 23 June 1885; Spencer to Harcourt, 23 June 1885 : W.V.H.44.
24. Hicks Beach to Cross, 27 June 1885 : B.M.Add.mss.(R.A.C.) 51274.
25. Jenkinson to Cross, 9 December 1885; Customs House to Treasury, 26 November 1885 : H.O. 144/133/A34848 B/56; J. Sweeney, *At Scotland Yard*, 51ff.
26. Jenkinson, Memorandum. . . . Clan na Gael (26 January 1885) : W.V.H.106.
27. Quoted in D'Arcy, op. cit., 407.
28. N.Y. Consulate to Salisbury, 31 December 1885 : P.R.O./F.O. 97/475/132D.
29. Diary entry, 14 December 1885, L. V. Harcourt : Harcourt Papers.

EPILOGUE—A PEACE OF SORTS
(pp. 229–242)

1. Le Caron, *Twenty-Five Years*, 246f.
2. M. Funchion in *Chicago's Irish Nationalists* (ch. v, vi) has a very competent discussion of the Clan's problems including the murder of Dr Cronin and its aftermath; also Le Caron, op, cit., Appendix 2.
3. Le Caron, op. cit., 247ff.
4. R. Anderson, *The Lighter Side of My Official Life*, 117–20.
5. J. Monroe, Minute from Central Office to all Divisions, 17 March 1886, Confidential : S.Y./M.E.P.O. 3.
6. *Devoy's Post Bag*, ii, 299 (Dillon to Devoy, 7 February 1887); Le Caron, op. cit., 255ff.

7. *Devoy's Post Bag*, ii, 299 (Dillon to Devoy, 7 February 1887); ii, 302 (M. Breslin to Devoy, 14 March 1887).

8. Le Caron, op. cit., 255.

9. Official documentation for the 'Jubilee Plot' is unavailable : the details have therefore been taken from contemporary press accounts especially *The Times*; Le Caron, op. cit., Appendix 1.

10. Spencer to Harcourt, 12 October 1888 : W.V.H.45.

11. For Le Caron's testimony and a great deal of documentation on Clan na Gael activity (originally sent to R. Anderson) see *Special Commission of 1888, Report of Proceedings*. For details concerning the closing months of Le Caron's life see the account provided by John Sweeney in his memoirs—*At Scotland Yard*.

12. H.O. 144/116/26493/60/78; H.O. 144/255/A55190.

13. The *agent provocateur* claim appears in F. M. Bussy (ed) *Irish Conspiracies* where John Mallon reported a conversation with a journalist who, along with another newspaperman, was told by a detective that he had 'planted the apples' on an alleged dynamiter at the time of his arrest. This had been done, he claimed, with the instructions of a superior officer. Although this book does not appear until 1910, Earl Spencer and Harcourt were well aware of these rumours as early as November 1887 (Spencer to Harcourt, 2 November 1887 : W.V.H.45). Spencer had been given the details by Wickham Stead of the *Pall Mall Gazette* who said the rumour came from an old member of the Birmingham Watch Committee (this was probably Alderman Henry Manton, J.P., *Turning the Last Stone*, Birmingham, Private Circulation, 1895/6). The possibility of Daly's being 'framed' was considered subsequently by Jenkinson, Gosselin, Monroe, and a series of Home Secretaries, who were convinced that he had been justly convicted (H.O. A46664B/24c,e; H.O. A46664B/15).

14. Egan and Clarke went to great lengths to maintain both their humour and sanity. Clarke secretly published a newspaper and worked a 'telegraph' in prison. The following poem was written by Egan and sent to Clarke while they were in Chatham Prison.

    . . . . .

    And I again
    Unearth the pen [blacklead pencil bits]
    To try what I can do
    At stringing rhyme
    This Christmas time
    For comrades staunch and true.

Another year
For Ireland dear,
We've spent in these drear cells
　　where England strives
　　To blast our lives
with torments fierce as hell's.

But their worst we scorn,
For we're Fenians born,
And, by heaven, the same we'll die;
　　No slaves are we,
　　we bend the knee
To none but God on high.

Ah! no, old man,
They never can
Our Fenian souls subdue,
　　For our love is bound
　　Too firmly round
Our cause to prove untrue.

Here's to our land
May she withstand
The might of England vile;
　　May the future bring
　　On swifter wing
True freedom to our Isle.

(T. Clarke, *Glimpses of an Irish Felon's Prison Life*, 23.) This memoir also contains a vivid description of the conditions the dynamiters suffered and is similar in tone to O'Donovan Rossa's earlier (1882) *Irish Rebels in English Prisons*.

15. K. Young, *Arthur James Balfour*, 175. This letter was written at the time of the Ivory Dynamite Plot of 1896; see *Devoy's Post Bag*, ii, 342ff.

16. Press cutting in H.O. 144/133/A34707/6.

Great Britain	Ireland	United States
1858	Irish Revolutionary Brotherhood founded	Fenian Brotherhood founded
1867 Clerkenwell explosion	Abortive Fenian Rising	Clan na Gael founded
1866-70		Attacks on Canada by Fenian Brotherhood
1871 Amnesty and exile for Fenian political prisoners		
1876		Skirmishing Fund begun, *Catalpa* rescue
1877 Criminal Investigation Division, Scotland Yard organised	Land League agitation	
1878		Holland's first submarine launched
1880 Gladstone's second ministry	Adoption of 'New Departure' policy	Rossa split in Irish-American ranks
1881 Rossa attack on Salford Barracks (January) Clan na Gael prepares for attacks (W. Mackey Lomasney) Rossa attack: Mansion House, London (March) Rossa attack: Liverpool (May/June)	Coercion Policy of Dublin Castle continues; Arrest of Parnell, Dillon, J. J. O'Kelly—Kilmainham Jail	Holland's 'Fenian Ram' launched (May) Reorganisation of Clan (Alexander Sullivan, President)
1882 Gladstone moves towards reconciliation, appoints Earl Spencer to Dublin; Rossa: Second attempt on Mansion House (May); Secret Service operation mounted Discovery of IRB arms ring (June); Egyptian intervention (Summer) Dr T. Gallagher reconnaissance in London (November)	Kilmainham Treaty (May); Phoenix Park Murders (6 May); Secret Service operation established; Col. H. Brackenbury, Dublin; E. G. Jenkinson replaces Brackenbury	Dr T. Gallagher-Rossa secret agreement
1883 Rossa: three dynamite attacks in Glasgow (January); Rossa: attacks in London—	Arrest of 'Featherstone'[x] in Cork (Rossa bomber, 30 March)	Major Le Caron continues spying on Clan na Gael

Year			
	Whitehall and *The Times* (March) CID Special Irish Branch organised (April)	E. G. Jenkinson co-ordinates counter-terrorist work with Robert Anderson in London	Continued tests and development of 'Fenian Ram'; third boat constructed
	Arrest of Deasy and Flanagan in Liverpool (Rossa bombers, 28 March)		British Foreign Office repeats appeal for help to United States government
	Bomb factory (Gallagher/Rossa) in Birmingham (2 April)		Last public convention of Clan na Gael Alexander Sullivan's 'Triangle' takes control of Clan na Gael (September)
	Arrest of Gallagher Team (4–5 April)		
	Passage of Explosives Act, 1883		Holland severs connection with Clan na Gael; boats 'grounded' (December)
	Gallagher and associates sentenced to life imprisonment (June)		
	'Featherstone', Deasy *et al* life imprisonment (August)		Ford and *Irish World* organise Emergency Fund (December)
	Clan attacks on London underground (October)		
	Glasgow Ribbonmen tried and convicted (December)		
1884	Bombs planted in four of London's railway stations, (Clan na Gael, February)	E. G. Jenkinson moved from Dublin to London to direct anti-Fenian effort (March)	US Government continues in refusal to take action against Irish-American press and organisations (May)
	Port security tightened		
	Daly arrested at Birkenhead (April)	IRB continues policy of non-co-operation with Irish-American dynamiters	
	Bomb attacks (Clan) London including Scotland Yard (May) Lomasney (Clan) attack on London Bridge (December)		
1885	Second bomb attack on underground; Clan attacks on Tower of London and House of Commons (January)	Period of continued constitutional development towards Irish Home Rule	
	Gladstone's government falls; Salisbury prime minister (summer)		
1886	Unofficial truce continues	Royal Irish Constabulary units withdrawn from Britain	Clan breaks into two wings: 'Triangle' accused of malpractice
1887	Jenkinson resigns Secret Service post, succeeded by CID chief		

Biographical Notes

Fuller notes on several of the following can be found in William O'Brien and Desmond Ryan, *Devoy's Post Bag 1871–1928* (2 vols 1948–53) *et al.*

ANDERSON, SIR ROBERT (1841–1918)
Barrister, educated Trinity College, Dublin, B.A. and Middle Temple 1862, LL.D. 1875. Law Officer, Dublin Castle; transferred to London, Irish Office at time of Clerkenwell explosion 1868. Later Secretary to Prison Board, Home Office while continuing to co-ordinate anti-Fenian work with Dublin Castle. Assistant Commissioner at Scotland Yard, CID, 1888–1901; KCB 1901. Prolific writer on religious subjects in addition to crime and Ireland.

ARCHIBALD, SIR EDWARD MORTIMER (1810–1884)
British consul-general at New York 1857–1883; directed the collection of intelligence on Fenian activity.

BRESLIN, JOHN J. (*c.* 1836–1888)
Born Drogheda, he was a leading figure in engineering the escape of James Stephens from Richmond Prison on 24 November 1865. He soon emigrated to the United States, joined Clan na Gael and led the *Catalpa* rescue operation. Intimately involved with the Holland submarine project, he joined Devoy as Business Manager of the *Irish Nation.*

BURKE, COL. RICARD O'SULLIVAN (1838–1922)
Began military career in Cork Militia at age of fifteen. Emigrated to United States, joined Union Army during Civil War emerging from conflict as a Colonel in the Corps of Engineers. A member of the Fenian Brotherhood, he became the chief agent for the purchase of arms for the IRB. He planned and led the Manchester rescue and was arrested in London in late 1867. Incarcerated in the Clerkenwell House of Detention he planned the explosion which took a great many lives and caused unprecedented destruction. Sentenced

to fifteen years penal servitude, he was released in 1872, returning to the United States two years later when he took a leading role in Clan na Gael while holding successive positions as an engineer both for the government and a Mexican railway.

CARROLL, DR WILLIAM (1835–1926)
Born in Rathmullen, Co. Donegal of an Ulster Presbyterian family he was raised in the United States. Qualified as a physician he acted as surgeon-major in the Union Army during the Civil War. A member of the Fenian Brotherhood he joined Clan na Gael soon after setting up a medical practice in Philadelphia. From 1875 to 1880 he was the Chairman of the Clan executive, resigning in protest over its acceptance of the 'New Departure' policy. He was also a trustee of the Skirmishing Fund and a confidant of John Devoy.

DALY, JOHN (1845–1916)
Limerick Fenian, joined IRB in 1863; arrested at Birkenhead with bombs in his possession in 1884, sentenced to life imprisonment. Released in August of 1896 he was elected mayor of Limerick in 1899, 1900 and 1901.

DEVOY, JOHN (1842–1928)
Born at Kill near Naas, Co. Kildare. A Fenian (IRB) organiser in British Army until his arrest in 1866. Sentenced to fifteen years penal servitude, he was released in the amnesty of 1871. A leading figure in the *Catalpa* rescue, he later played a key role in the development of the American Clan na Gael as a member of the Revolutionary Directory. Supported the 'New Departure' in 1879; edited *The Irish Nation* (1881–1885) and later the *Gaelic American*. He died on 30 September 1928 and was buried in Glasnevin Cemetery, Dublin the next year.

EGAN, PATRICK (1841–1919)
Fenian and Treasurer of Supreme Council of the IRB until 1877. Later Treasurer of the Land League and closely associated after 1883 with the Sullivan wing of Clan na Gael. Becoming a successful mid-western miller he later became US Minister to Chile.

FORD, PATRICK (1834–1913)
Born in Galway he learned the printing trade in Garrison's *Liberator* offices in Boston. Founding the *Irish World* in 1870, he became the leading opinion-maker for Irish-Americans. Remaining aloof from both the Clan and FB he supported various nationalist

causes including the Skirmishing Fund, which he for a time controlled, as well as his later Emergency Fund.

HARCOURT, SIR WILLIAM VERNON (1827–1904)
Youngest son of William Vernon, Earl Harcourt. He was educated at Trinity College, Cambridge, and the Inner Temple and became Professor of International Law, Cambridge in 1869; solicitor-general, 1873–4; Home Secretary, 1880–5; Chancellor of the Exchequer, 1886 and 1892–5; Liberal leader, 1896–8. For full biographical note see *DNB* (1901–11).

HOLLAND, JOHN PHILIP (1840–1914)
Member of Christian Brothers, he emigrated to the United States in 1873 where he was employed by Skirmishing Fund of Clan na Gael to construct three submarines. The culmination of his work came with the launching of the *Holland* in 1898 which was purchased by the United States Navy in 1900.

JENKINSON, SIR EDWARD GEORGE (1835–1919)
Educated at Harrow and Haileybury College. Member of Indian Civil Service, 1856–80, then Private Secretary to Lord Spencer 1882. Assistant under secretary for police and crime in Ireland, 1882–86, where his duties included directing the Secret Service. KCB 1888.

LE CARON, MAJOR/DOCTOR HENRI or Thomas Billis Beach (1841–1894)
Born at Colchester, he emigrated to Paris in 1857 and then to the United States in 1861. He fought in the Civil War under a French alias which he retained while working as a spy for the British government from 1866. An important source of information first on the Fenian Brotherhood and later Clan na Gael he returned to England in late 1887 to appear before the Special Commission of 1888.

LOMASNEY, WILLIAM MACKEY (1841–1884)
Born in Cincinnati, Ohio of Irish parents, he went to Ireland in the 1860s where he became famous for arms raids. Captured and imprisoned in 1867 he was amnestied in 1871. Returning to the United States he was active in Clan na Gael and during the 1880s was in charge of its dynamite operations, dying in an explosion under London Bridge in December 1884.

MILLEN, GENERAL F.F.
After military experience in the Mexican Army in the early 1860s,

he became active in the military affairs of the IRB, FB, and later Clan na Gael. Characterised as 'an adventurer' by John Devoy, Millen was involved with the Jubilee Plot of 1887. Apparently he was also on the British Secret Service payroll at times.

MULCAHY, DENIS DOWLING

As a member of the *Irish People* staff he was arrested in 1865 and sentenced to ten years' imprisonment. He was released in 1871 and practised medicine in the United States. Accompanying O'Mahony's remains to Ireland he was later involved in a lengthy lawsuit against the Trustees of the National (Skirmishing) Fund to recover his expenses.

O'CONNOR, JAMES (1836–1910)

Born in Wicklow he had been a member of the staff of the *Irish People*, arrested in 1865 and released four years later. Apparently a member of the Clan na Gael–IRB Revolutionary Directory he was closely associated with William Mackey Lomasney's dynamite reconnaissance in 1880. Arrested in 1881 he later became an anti-Parnellite MP for West Wicklow, 1892–1910.

O'DONOVAN ROSSA, JEREMIAH (1831–1915)

Born Roscarbery, Co. Cork. First arrested for nationalist activity in December 1858 he spent four years in the United States before returning to Ireland in 1863. Believed by John Devoy to have sworn in more members of the IRB than any other ten men in the land, he was arrested and sentenced to life imprisonment in 1865. Reputed to have been inhumanely treated in prison he was released in 1871 after having been elected MP for Tipperary in 1869 while still in prison. Became Head Centre of the American Fenian Brotherhood, inaugurated The Skirmishing Fund and was an early advocate of Clan na Gael. He was to break with the Clan in 1880 over dynamite tactics and founded his own organisation and newspaper, the *United Irishman*. The majority of dynamite attackers were launched by Rossa's organisation. He died on 29 June 1915 at Staten Island, New York.

O'MAHONY, JOHN (1819–1877)

Born at Clonkilla, Co. Cork, he was the founder and leader of the American Fenian Brotherhood (1858). Unable to provide revolutionary leadership to the badly divided movement he died in poverty in 1877. O'Mahony was buried in Glasnevin Cemetery later that year at Clan na Gael expense, which produced a great deal of later controversy (q.v. Denis Dowling Mulcahy).

O'REILLY, JOHN BOYLE (1844–1890)
As a Fenian in the British Army, O'Reilly, born in Dowth Castle, Co. Meath, was sentenced to death in 1866, commuted to twenty years imprisonment and transported to Australia; he escaped in 1869. Involved in the second Fenian raid on Canada while a correspondent for the Boston *Pilot* in June 1870, he became editor and proprietor of the paper in 1876. A trusted Irish-American, he was consulted on most issues although never a member of Clan na Gael.

REYNOLDS, JAMES
Brass foundry owner in New Haven, Conn. Succeeded Dr Carroll as Chairman of Clan na Gael executive committee in 1880 and was a leading trustee of the Skirmishing Fund.

SPENCER, JOHN POYNTZ, fifth earl (1835–1910)
Educated at Harrow and Trinity College, Cambridge, he was lord lieutenant of Ireland in 1868–74 and 1882–5; in 1880–2 and 1886, lord president of the council; in 1892–5, first lord of admiralty. Spencer was one of the few whig aristocrats who supported Gladstone over home rule for Ireland in 1886. (*DNB*, 1901 –11).

SULLIVAN, ALEXANDER (*c.* 1847–1913)
Born in either Canada or Maine of Co. Cork parentage. Grew up in Amherstburg, Ontario where his father was a sergeant in the British Army. Moved to Detroit, then to New Mexico, Washington D.C., arriving in Chicago in 1872. Became a lawyer and a power in local politics (Republican) and in Clan na Gael, of which he was National Chairman from 1881–5. He was the President of the Irish National League 1883–4. Accused of the murder of Dr P. H. Cronin in 1889 he remained influential in Irish-American affairs until his death.

VINCENT, SIR HOWARD (1849–1908)
Educated Westminster School, well versed in foreign languages. 1868 Sandhurst, commissioned in Royal Welsh Fusiliers. Called to bar (Inner Temple) 1876; faculté de droit, University of Paris 1877 and first Director of Criminal Investigation Division, Scotland Yard 1878. Resigned in 1884 and elected as Conservative MP for Central Sheffield in November 1885. Leading advocate of imperialism and protectionism (*DNB* 1901–11).

WILLIAMSON, ADOLPHUS ('DOLLY') (*c.* 1834–1889)
Joined Scotland Yard in 1852, becoming the first Superintendent of
Detective Branch and later Chief Superintendent, Criminal Investi-
gation Division.

A note on Sources

The collected papers of Sir William Vernon Harcourt, Home
Secretary of the Liberal government of 1880–1885, provided the
most important of the unpublished sources upon which this book
is based. These papers, now on deposit in the Bodleian Library,
Oxford, were used by A. G. Gardiner in *The Life of Sir William
Harcourt* (2 vols., 1923) but little reference is made in this biography
to his stewardship of the nation's security agencies during the 'dynamite years'. Home Office and Scotland Yard papers, not scheduled
to be opened until the 1980s, form another valuable source, but are
limited in their usefulness because all of most important documents
were in the possession of Mr E. G. Jenkinson. Jenkinson, who
directed the Secret Service operation, destroyed this material sometime in 1886 or early 1887, when he resigned his position, probably
in protest over the government's running down of Secret Service
organisation because of a prolonged lull in Irish-American activity.
What was burned at that time doubtless included any significant
material which had not been previously destroyed when the Special
Irish Branch Office in Scotland Yard was bombed on 30 May 1884,
leaving virtually nothing of importance relating to the Special
Branch's activity in this period. Such papers as are now to be found
in the possession of the Home Office are of a less sensitive nature
than those destroyed by Jenkinson. They occasionally contain information which might well have been duplicated in the Secret
Service files as well as information which, correlated with other
materials (especially those derived from Foreign Office papers)
allows for a partial reconstruction of both intelligence and operations.

Foreign Office papers preserve cuttings from the Irish-American
press, which had been collected by the librarian of the chief secretary's office at Dublin Castle, as well as the lengthy correspondence
between Lord Granville and his counterparts in Washington. Diplo-

matic pressure was actively applied to the State Department in an attempt to force the United States' government to take action against the 'dynamite press' which both raised money for and encouraged the dynamite attacks on Great Britain. This effort failed, despite the fact that the American minister at the Court of St James, James Russell Lowell, was a zealous anglophile. There are moments in his relationships with Granville in which he clearly transgressed the bounds of propriety in keeping the Foreign Office notified of what was going on in the Washington 'mind'.

Among the published sources listed in the bibliography the most useful as well as the most frustrating are those by Sir Robert Anderson—*Sidelights on the Home Rule Movement* (1906, also published in a 6d. edition as *A Great Conspiracy*) and *The Lighter Side of my Official Life* (1910) which first appeared in serial form in *Blackwood's Magazine* that year. These two volumes present something of a history of the Secret Service and Special Branch in this period but are written, as Winston Churchill described them in 1910, in a 'spirit of gross boastfulness in the style of "How Bill Adams won the Battle of Waterloo" '. Of equal importance for an understanding of the Irish-American operations in the United States is the memoir of the 'prince of spies', Major Henri Le Caron, entitled *Twenty-Five Years in the Secret Service: the Recollections of a Spy* (1892). Much of the information contained in this memoir had already been disclosed publicly during the Special Inquiry in 1889. Le Caron had become an agent of the British government in 1867 and began his long relationship with Robert Anderson, who was to remain his contact until he dropped his 'cover' for the Parnell inquiry. Le Caron's communications were to remain his own property subject to later collection. The correspondence was carried out with Anderson directly and the letters remained at Anderson's home at No. 39 Linden Gardens, Bayswater.

Le Caron, on the basis of a meeting with Parnell in May of 1881, was convinced that Parnell was guilty at the very least of condoning the murder of Cavendish and Burke, and wrote to Anderson in late 1888 offering to testify at the Special Inquiry because only a full disclosure of the 'foul conspiracy' existing in the United States would alert the nation and the world of the dangers. Although Anderson apparently discouraged this offer, a second appeal met with a more encouraging reply, which, coupled with the failing health of Le Caron's father at Colchester, brought the spy back to England in December 1888. As he had no desire to return to the United States, Le Caron's family followed him to England. He then applied to Anderson for the letters of the past twenty-odd years which would provide him with the documentation upon which to base his evidence for the inquiry. Anderson returned the correspondence, excluding those 'which he had made official by passing them on at the time of their receipt'. On Tuesday 5 February 1889 the British people were introduced to their secret agent. Within a month, Anderson, by then the Assistant Commissioner of the Criminal Investigation Division of the Metropolitan Police, was facing severe criticism by Sir William Vernon Harcourt, leader of the opposition in the Commons, for having provided Le Caron with the documents, which Harcourt considered government property, and thus confidential. Anderson weathered the storm, but not without registering a public protest of innocence in a letter to *The Times* on 21 March. It was against this background that the first Official Secrets Act (Royal assent, 26 August 1889) had been debated and passed. The storm was to grow up again with even greater intensity, when beginning in October 1909, Anderson's serialised memoirs began to appear in *Blackwood's Magazine*. In *The Lighter Side* he admitted to writing the second series on 'Parnellism and Crime' in *The Times* of 1887, justifying his violation of the Treasury Rule of 1875, (republished in 1884) which forbade publication without official sanction, by claiming that he had implicit permission from his superior, the Commissioner of the Metropolitan Police, James Monroe. Monroe denied this allegation. Harcourt was by now dead but his place was ably taken in the Commons debate which followed between April 11 and April 21, by the Irish nationalist members led by John Redmond, outraged about this obvious collusion between the Home Secretary of Lord Salisbury's second cabinet, Henry Matthews, and *The Times*.* Although Matthews denied having given any such permission, the government's aid to the newspaper in its unsuccessful bid to destroy Parnell was in fact wholehearted and very secret. The story of this aid was recorded in an unpublished manuscript (a clear allusion to Anderson's first book) 'Sidelights on British Conspiracies' by W. H. Joyce. In the summer of 1888 Joyce, whose story is told by Leon O'Broin in *The Prime Informer, A Suppressed Scandal* (1971), had the task of leading a team in collating some two tons of material in an unsuccessful attempt to build an air-tight case against Parnell for the newspaper. Winston Churchill, Home Secretary in the Asquith government, had to answer the questions in the Commons about Anderson's revelations, and he made it quite clear that if such a thing were to happen then, Anderson would be dismissed; Asquith having been equally critical at an earlier stage in the debates. The Irish members, seeking a limited revenge for

---

* See Hansard, Parliamentary Debates, 5th Series, vol. XVI (1910). See index under 'Parnell case'.

Anderson's contributions to *The Times* scandalmongering, in addition to embarrassing Asquith's government if possible, put forward a motion reducing the civil services supply vote by £900, the amount of Anderson's pension. The motion was lost, 164 to 94, but Anderson had admitted to Churchill that he still had some of the papers from his Secret Service period. The Home Secretary demanded and received what were described as papers 'equally miscellaneous and uninteresting', but Anderson, probably through oversight, had at least protected them from Jenkinson's 'fires'.

There is an interesting analogy between Anderson's retention of a few papers and the files of his most trenchant critic, William Vernon Harcourt. The former Home Secretary might well have been accused of an even more serious breach of conduct, for when he left the Home Office in 1885 he took with him as personal papers what appears in retrospect to be virtually all of his secret and confidential correspondence relating to the security agencies under his supervision. Although his correspondence with the Irish viceroy, Lord Spencer, was always a mixture of the personal and the official, no such distinction is admissible with either E. G. Jenkinson, Robert Anderson or the Metropolitan Police. Thus when Gladstone's second government finally stumbled out of office that July, R. A. Cross, who had been Home Secretary in Disraeli's government of 1874–80, found, as it were, nothing in the Secret Service larder. A search of Cross's personal papers reveals little except a letter of 2 January 1886, a month before the fall of that government, concerning Jenkinson's future now that the Irish menace had abated. The reason for the absence of analogous documents may be because Cross allowed Jenkinson almost total responsibility for national security, whereas Harcourt took an intense personal interest in every move and countermove in the war. Thus the material from the Cross period was amongst that destroyed by Jenkinson. It does seem however, that Cross, Childers and Matthews used a very different set of criteria for deciding which papers to leave within the Home Office when they left office. Harcourt must be open to criticism of the same sort that he levelled at Anderson when it was discovered that he had returned Le Caron's correspondence, yet if it had not been for Harcourt's retention of the wide-ranging documentation on the security forces it would not have been possible to recreate this story in any detail, or provide the necessary correctives to how Sir Robert Anderson 'won the war'.

One of the major reasons given by Anderson for writing his book, *The Lighter Side of My Official Life*, was to provide a corrective on what Harcourt's biographer would say about him, although he never did find out since he died 15 November 1918, and the biography did not appear until 1923. Regretfully two of the men who knew the most about what had happened in those years, the 'spymaster-general', E. G. Jenkinson, and the chief superintendent of the Special Irish Branch, Adolphus Williamson never wrote their memoirs, and Inspector Littlechild of Special Branch never produced the promised sequel to the book on his initial years at Scotland Yard.

One might justifiably expect to gain access to the carefully guarded files of the Secret Service or the Special Branch at the end of one hundred years. Such expectations with reference to the Irish-American revolutionary organisations such as O'Donovan Rossa's Skirmishers or Clan na Gael are seldom realised. This study is based primarily upon the security organisations' documents, in addition to such information which became public knowledge during the trials of bombers. There is one important exception to what must be understood as severely flawed evidence and that is the correspondence retained within *John Devoy's Postbag* (2 vols., Dublin, 1948, 1953). Correspondence between this leading Clan na Gael journalist, and particularly William Mackey Lomasney, a leading dynamiter of the Clan, has filled some tantalising gaps.

Bibliography

PRINCIPAL MANUSCRIPT SOURCES

Public Record Office, London : Cabinet Office; Granville Papers; Foreign Office Papers; Home Office Papers; Metropolitan Police Reports.

Home Office, London : Closed class HO 144, including H. L. Jephson Papers; HO 151 Confidential Letter Books.

Metropolitan Police, New Scotland Yard, London : Closed class MEPO 3.

British Library, London : Gladstone Papers; R. A. Cross Papers.

Bodleian Library, Oxford : Harcourt Papers, including a journal of Lewis Vernon Harcourt.

State Paper Office, Dublin : Chief Secretary's Office Registered Papers; Fenian Papers; Crime Branch Special Papers, A & B files.

National Library, Dublin: Devoy Papers.

NEWSPAPERS AND PERIODICALS

The Times; Gaelic American (New York); *Pall Mall Gazette; Police Gazette* (London); *United Irishman* (New York, cuttings in Public Record Office); *Irish World* (New York, cuttings in Public Record Office); *Hansard's Parliamentary Debates,* Fifth Series.

BOOKS AND ARTICLES

Anderson, Sir R., *The Lighter Side of my Official Life,* London 1910; also in *Blackwood's Magazine* (9 parts, 1909–10).

Anderson, Sir R., *Sidelights on the Home Rule Movement,* London 1906.

Archibald, Edith, *Life and Letters of Sir Edward Mortimer Archibald. A Memoir of Fifty Years Service,* Toronto 1924.

Beckett, J. C., *The Making of Modern Ireland,* 1603–1923, London 1966.

Bourke, Marcus, *John O'Leary,* Tralee 1967.

Brackenbury, Sir Henry, *Some Memories of My Spare Time, 1856–1885,* Edinburgh 1909.

Brown, Thomas N., *Irish-American Nationalism*, Philadelphia and New York 1966.

Browne, Douglas G., *The Rise of Scotland Yard: A History of the Metropolitan Police*, London 1956.

Bowen-Rowlands, E. B., *Seventy-Two Years at the Bar*, London 1924.

Bussy, F. M. ed., *Irish Conspiracies. Recollections of John Mallon, The Great Irish Detective*, London 1910.

Clarke, T. J., *Glimpses of an Irish Felon's Prison Life . . .*, Dublin and London 1922.

Coleridge, E. H., *Life and Correspondence of John Duke Lord Coleridge, Lord Chief Justice of England*, 2 vols, London 1904.

Cooke, A. B. and Vincent, J. R., eds., 'Herbert Gladstone, Forster, and Ireland 1881-2', *Irish Historical Studies*, vols xvii, xviii.

Corfe, T. H., *The Phoenix Park Murders*, London 1968.

Couper, Charles Tennant, *Report of the Trial of the Dynamitards . . .*, Edinburgh 1884.

Curran, Charles, 'The Spy behind the Speaker's Chair', *History Today*, xviii, (1968).

Curtis, L. P., *Coercion and Conciliation in Ireland, 1880–92 : A Study in Conservative Unionism*, Princeton and London 1963.

D'Arcy, William, *The Fenian Movement in the United States*, Washington D.C. 1947.

Davitt, Michael, *The Fall of Feudalism in Ireland*, London and New York 1904.

Devoy, John, *Recollections of an Irish Rebel*, New York 1929.

Edwards, R. Dudley, 'Parnell and the American Challenge to Irish Nationalism', *University Review* II, 2 (1958).

Gardiner, A. G., *The Life of Sir William Harcourt*, 2 vols, London 1923.

Gathorne Hardy, A. E., *Life of Gathorne Hardy, 1st Earl of Cranbrook*, 2 vols, London 1910.

Grant, Douglas, *The Thin Blue Line: The Story of the City of Glasgow Police*, London 1973.

Gibson, Florence E., *The Attitudes of the New York Irish Toward State And National Affairs, 1848–1892*, New York 1951.

Green, E. R. R., 'The Fenians', *History Today*, viii (1958).

Halasz, N., *Nobel, A Biography*, London 1960.

Hamilton, Edward, *The Diary of Sir Edward Walter Hamilton, 1880–1885*, ed. D. W. R. Bahlman, 2 vols, Oxford 1972.

Hawkins, Richard, 'Gladstone, Forster and the Release of Parnell, 1882–8', *Irish Historical Studies*, v (1969).

(Anon.), *Incipient Irish Revolution, an Exposé of Fenianism of Today in the United Kingdom and America . . . containing a map showing spheres of Fenian Influence in the United Kingdom in 1889*, London 1889.

Jenkins, Brian, *Fenians and Anglo-American Relations during Reconstruction*, Ithaca 1969.

Jeyes, S. H. and How, F. D., *The Life of Sir Howard Vincent*, London and Plymouth 1912.

Jones, M. A., *Destination America*, London 1976.

Kee, Robert, *The Green Flag: A History of Irish Nationalism*, London 1972.

Laubenstein, W. J., *The Emerald Whaler*, London 1961.

Le Caron, Major Henri, *Twenty-Five Years in the Secret Service; the Recollections of a Spy*, 6th ed., London 1892.

Le Roux, L. N., *Tom Clarke and the Irish Freedom Movement*, Dublin 1936.

Littlechild, *The Reminiscences of Chief Inspector. . . .*, 2nd ed., London 1894.

Lyons, F. S. L., *Ireland since the Famine*, 2nd ed., London 1973.

McEnnis, John T., *The Clan-Na-Gael and the Murder of Dr Cronin*, Chicago 1889.

MacSwiney, T. J., *Rossa*, n.p. 1915.

Moody, T. W., ed., *The Fenian Movement*, Cork 1968.

Moody, T. W., 'The New Departure in Irish Politics, 1878–79' in *Essays in Honour of James Eadie Todd*, ed. H. A. Cronne, T. W. Moody and D. B. Quinn, London 1949.

Moody, T. W., and Leon O'Broin, 'The IRB Supreme Council, 1868–78', *Irish Historical Studies* xix (March 1975).

Morris, Richard K., *John P. Holland*, Annapolis, Maryland 1966.

Nott-Bower, William, *Fifty-two Years a Policeman*, London 1926.

Neidhardt, W. S., *Fenianism in North America*, State College, Pa. 1975.

O'Brien, William and Desmond Ryan, ed., *Devoy's Post Bag, 1871–1928*, 2 vols, Dublin 1948–53.

O'Broin, Leon, *Fenian Fever: An Anglo-American Dilemma*, London 1971.

O'Broin, Leon, *The Prime Informer*, London 1971.

O'Broin, Leon, *Revolutionary Underground*, Dublin 1976.

O'Hegarty, P. S., *A History of Ireland under the Union, 1801–1922*, London 1952.

O'Leary, John, *Recollections of Fenians and Fenianism*, 2 vols, London 1896.

Ó Lúing, Sean, *John Devoy*, Dublin 1961.

Pletcher, David M., *The Awkward Years: American Foreign Relations under Garfield and Arthur*, Columbia, Mo. 1962.

Pollard, H. B. C., *The Secret Societies of Ireland: Their Rise and Progress*, London 1922.

Ramm, Agatha, *Political Correspondence of Mr Gladstone and Lord Granville, 1876–1886*, 2 vols, Oxford 1962.

Rossa, Jeremiah O'Donovan, *Rossa's Recollections, 1838–1898*, Mariner's Harbor, New York 1898.

Rossa, Jeremiah O'Donovan, *Irish Rebels in English Prisons*, New York 1882.

Rutherford, John, *Secret History of the Fenian Conspiracy*, London 1887.

Ryan, Desmond, *The Fenian Chief: A Biography of James Stephens*, Dublin 1967.

Ryan, Desmond, *The Phoenix Flame: A Study of Fenianism and John Devoy*, London 1937.

Schrier, Arnold, *Ireland and the American Emigration, 1850–1900*, Minneapolis 1958.

Shannon, William V., *The American Irish*, New York 1963.

Special Commission of 1888, *Report of the Proceedings*, London 1890.

Sweeney, Detective Inspector John, *At Scotland Yard, experiences during twenty-seven years' service*, ed. F. Richards, new ed., London 1905.

Tansill, C. C., *America and the Fight for Irish Freedom, 1866–1922*, New York 1957.

Turner, Alfred E., *Sixty Years of a Soldier's Life*, London 1912.

Williams, T. D., ed., *Secret Societies in Ireland*, Dublin 1973.

Wittke, Carl, *The Irish in America*, Baton Rouge, La. 1956.

Young, Kenneth, *Arthur James Balfour*, London 1963.

Unfortunately I was not aware until too late of two books which touch on the subject of this study. They are Joseph Patrick O'Grady's *Irish-Americans and Anglo-American Relations, 1880–1888* and Michael Francis Funchion's *Chicago's Irish Nationalists, 1881–1890* both of which were published in New York in 1976.

Index